W0037168

Citizens at the Gates

Stephen R. Barnard

Citizens at the Gates

Twitter, Networked Publics, and the
Transformation of American Journalism

Stephen R. Barnard
Department of Sociology
St. Lawrence University
Canton, NY, USA

ISBN 978-3-030-08017-4   ISBN 978-3-319-90446-7   (Ebook)
https://doi.org/10.1007/978-3-319-90446-7

Cover photo © d3sign

Printed on acid-free paper

This Palgrave Macmillan imprint is published by the registered company Springer International Publishing AG part of Springer Nature.
The registered company address is: Gewerbestrasse 11, 6330 Cham, Switzerland

For Anna, Ryan, and Everett

ACKNOWLEDGMENTS

It may be cliché to say it takes a village to produce a book, but it is most certainly true. This book is the product of nearly a decade's worth of research, writing, and even more revising. Over the course of that time my work was made better and more gratifying thanks to the support of three institutions as well as many more friends and colleagues.

First and foremost, I am forever grateful to the Department of Sociology at the University of Missouri for supporting me and this project. I am especially thankful for my long-time mentor Victoria Johnson, whose wisdom and guidance throughout the dissertation process helped create the foundation on which this book now rests. What began as a seedling for a dissertation proposal during her graduate seminar on Power and Media in Comparative Perspective, slowly evolved into this project, due in no small part to our long conversations in her office or over a glass of wine. Thanks also to my seminar colleagues—especially Joshua Olsberg, Seth Ashley, and Mark Poepsel—for their thoughtful feedback on the earliest project proposals. I am also indebted to Clarence Lo and Wayne Brekhus for their comments on early drafts, and to Amit Prasad for introducing me to the theorizing of Pierre Bourdieu. Special thanks to my dear friend and writing group partner, David Criger, who read and offered thoughtful comments on numerous chapters as they neared completion.

The bulk of Chaps. 4 and 5 were written during two successive post-doctoral fellowships. First, many thanks to my colleagues in the Missouri School of Journalism, for being such gracious hosts and inviting me into your bustling community of scholarship and practice. While much of my time was spent in the bowels of the Reynolds Journalism Institute, I am also grateful to the Department of Journalism Studies for welcoming me into their midst. My year in the Mizzou J-school was made possible in large part by Charles Davis and Stephanie Craft, who generously shared their time and wisdom with me. The kindness they showed me as a stranger, and later, a friend and colleague, still inspires me today. Thanks also to Alecia Swasy, Tim Vos, and many others in Journalism Studies for the comradery and conversations we shared. I can only hope that this book contributes to the ongoing scholarship on the "media of the future," which my fellowship was named to support.

After leaving Mizzou, I was fortunate to spend a year as a lecturer and postdoctoral fellow in the Department of Media, Film, and Journalism Studies at the University of Denver. While there, I met Adrienne Russell, whose friendship and guidance has proven to be invaluable, especially as I began to discover my place in our interdisciplinary field. Her thoughtful comments on early drafts of numerous chapters were immeasurably helpful in framing the book and honing its arguments. Thanks also to Derigan Silver, Renee Botta, Lynn Schofield Clark, Erika Polson, Andrew Matranga, and the rest of the department for their mentorship as I explored life and work in that magnificent place they call home.

The bulk of this book was completed during my initial years as an Assistant Professor of Sociology at St. Lawrence University. It is difficult to overstate how integral SLU has been to the completion of this project. Over the years, I have been fortunate to receive numerous institutional grants and awards that funded my research, as well as a semester sabbatical that provided the time and space to complete this manuscript. I am especially thankful for the support I received from Alison Del Rossi, Judith DeGroat, Eric Williams-Bergen, and SLU's Crossing Boundaries initiative, which provided financial and technical support for digital research projects like this one. The data collection and analysis for various chapters was made possible, thanks in large part to these awards, which among other things, funded access to the social media research tools DiscoverText and Pulsar. I am also grateful for the three semesters' worth of seminar participants who helped conduct pilot studies for Chaps. 6 and 8, and who inspire me to continue to explore the ways digital sociology can help make sense of our ever-changing world. My colleagues in the Sociology department, especially Leah Rohlfsen and Abye Assefa, have provided the encouragement and comradery necessary to survive this endeavor, as well as the long, cold North Country winters. Thanks also to John Collins for the enriching conversations on the state of journalism today, for providing feedback on early drafts, and for leading Weave News, which is a citizen journalism and media literacy organization based at SLU that inspires me to think, teach, and live in ways that better this world. Both Jeff Macharyas my dad, Robert Barnard, helped format the images used in Chaps. 6 and 7.

I am pleased to be part of a community of scholars in the growing fields of media sociology and digital sociology, fostered in large part by the American Sociological Association's section on Communication, Information Technology, and Media Sociology (CITAMS), and the Eastern Sociological Association's recurring Digital Sociology mini-conference. Though our meetings only happen once a year, the conversations and connections that transpire there have had a lasting effect on me and my work. I am especially thankful to Rodney Benson for his thoughtful comments on the initial conference paper that inspired this work, and to Jessie Daniels for helping to establish a new frontier for sociology in the digital age. At one of these meetings I met my friend and collaborator, Andrew Lindner, who over the years has generously offered his astute advice on various aspects of this project. I am also grateful to Nick Couldry for his insightful comments on the book's theoretical underpinnings (especially Chap. 3), and to Ian Sheinheit for his valuable feedback on Chap. 8.

Thanks especially to my wife, parents, grandparents, sister, aunts, uncles, and the rest of my family for encouraging my journey of discovery and listening to me prattle on about what I have learned along the way. If there was an award for time served in this capacity, my wife and life partner, Anna, would be most deserving. The patience she has shown as I have struggled over the difficulties of researching and writing my first solo-authored book is incomparable. She shows me how to be a better person and parent every day.

This book has also benefitted from an extraordinary wealth of editorial expertise. I am especially grateful to my commissioning editor, Alexis Nelson, who saw the value in this project and offered her support. The manuscript was completed under the editorial guidance of Mary Al-Sayed, who was a supportive and thoughtful sounding board in its later stages. My heartfelt thanks to Alexis, Mary, Kyra Saniewski, and the rest of the Palgrave Macmillan team for their support along the way. My outside editor, Jared Gassen, also contributed immeasurably to this project by copyediting and providing substantive advice on every chapter. Jared is as good an editor as he is a friend, which considering the quality of his work, says a lot.

Finally, I am thankful to SAGE Publishing for permitting the use of material from two previous articles. Much of Chap. 4 was previously published as: Barnard, S. R. (2016). 'Tweet or be sacked': Twitter and the new elements of journalistic practice. *Journalism*, 17(2), 190–207, https://doi.org/10.1177/1464884914553079. Chapter 6 previously appeared as: Barnard, S. R. (2017). Tweeting #Ferguson: Mediatized fields and the new activist journalist. *New Media & Society*, Advanced online publication, https://doi.org/10.1177/1461444817712723. The editors and anonymous reviewers for these journals, like those commissioned by Palgrave, have also helped improve this work immensely. Of course, any remaining errors are my own.

CONTENTS

LIST OF FIGURES

LIST OF TABLES

CHAPTER 1

Introduction

A lot was changing in the world of media and journalism when I first joined Twitter in early 2009. Due in part to the surge of media stories on the topic, a large portion of the American public and the entire journalism profession were growing increasingly worried about the lasting effects of a press system that appeared to be dying. The 2008 financial crisis hit the news industry hard, as did the radical drop in advertising revenue, which was almost universally recognized as a necessary condition for running a successful newspaper. At the same time, a revolution in new media technologies was also starting to shake the profession to its core. This era of journalistic transformation can be explained from at least two distinct perspectives.

The first perspective focuses largely on economic factors. The 2008 financial crisis spread throughout most sectors of the economy, leaving newspapers and other media companies with fewer resources. Print advertising revenues declined steadily during the 2000s (Barthel 2017). This problem was exacerbated by the media industry's shift toward online publication, where advertising revenues typically yielded pennies on the dollar compared to traditional newspaper advertising (Edmonds et al. 2013). The combined results shocked the journalism world. The value of newspaper companies across the United States began a steady decline (Mitchell and Matsa 2015). Newspaper closures were so numerous by 2007 that a long-time journalist created a "Newspaper Death Watch" to document the death and rebirth of the news industry. The website lists 15 major metropolitan

© The Author(s) 2018
S. R. Barnard, *Citizens at the Gates*,
https://doi.org/10.1007/978-3-319-90446-7_1

dailies having closed since it went online, while another dozen are "in progress," meaning they have "cut frequency or adopted hybrid … or online-only models" (Newspaper Death Watch 2017). Meanwhile, the "people formerly known as the audience," as Jay Rosen (2006) famously named them, grew less trusting of mainstream media sources and more likely to contribute to the stream of news and information (Alterman 2003). While much debate remains about the value and originality of user-generated content and the future of professional journalism, these broad changes illustrate a key shift in the structure and practices of journalism in America.

Another way to view these changes requires a somewhat different focus. At roughly the same time as the economic crisis was hitting American journalism, another important shift was occurring within the political, cultural, and technological corners of the field. Enabled by the growth of digital tools and social networks—namely, "smart" mobile phones equipped with Twitter, Facebook, and YouTube—citizen and professional journalists alike were increasingly likely to engage with one another and share real-time information of civic importance. This shift was not simply journalistic in nature, but it inevitably took on cultural and political characteristics as producing and sharing cultural artifacts with political and/or journalistic significance reemerged as a valuable and increasingly normalized practice for citizen engagement. Thus, given the hybridity of the political and journalistic fields, the shaping of journalism's history must also be attributed to institutional norms and structures, actors' decisions and dispositions, as well as the technological affordances that manifest across the field.

While these changes may seem like a relatively routine evolution in what it means to be part of "the public" in the digital age, a close and historically conscious examination suggests that a more remarkable shift is underway. Whereas previous generations of American citizens had a limited number of opportunities to engage with media-makers—let alone to contribute to the conversation around news products and processes—the press–public relationship is steadily changing in the new media environment. What began with expanding access to computers with internet connectivity in the 1990s has evolved over the last decade into the proliferation of mobile phones with cameras, video, and high-speed internet. Access to these technologies, along with the explosion of social media on these devices, has contributed to profound shifts in culture and communication. Of all the platforms that facilitate journalistic discourses, Twitter plays a central role, both for citizens as well as media professionals. While the implications of these shifts can be felt across American society, the fields of journalism and politics have been among the hardest hit.

As the gatekeeping tradition suggests, journalistic actors and institutions have historically controlled the processes of newsmaking (Shoemaker and Vos 2009). This communicative privilege has proved quite powerful in defining reality and shaping public opinion (Bourdieu 1999; McCombs and Shaw 1972). But in recent years, the metaphorical *gates* that legacy institutions have been poised to *keep* have attracted the attention of networked publics, who are increasingly prone to *watching* what flows through the mainstream media's gates. Furthermore, some have utilized social networks like Twitter to *crash* (i.e., bypass) the legacy media's gates entirely. Such efforts are not simply self-serving; they aim to shape public opinion and influence professional gatekeeping processes.

Nevertheless, the power of new media tools is hardly relegated to citizens alone. As will be demonstrated, growing numbers of journalism professionals have embraced new communication technologies, especially Twitter, with remarkable enthusiasm. While this trend is interesting in its own right, the broader array of transformations spanning the field of American journalism are central to this project, and to the field more broadly. Although "acts of journalism" by citizens on social media have been somewhat mythologized in recent years, their significance remains considerable. By assessing this significance empirically, and in concert with accordant shifts in professional journalism, this book examines the ongoing hybridization of journalism and political activism as these fields adopt Twitter, and therefore adapt to the new norms and practices that have followed.

The book considers the converging influences of technological affordances, professional practices, and networked cultures amid overarching norms and power structures that shape action in social fields. It seeks to answer questions, both pressing and enduring, about journalistic practices, networked publics, and the dynamics of social change. In doing so, it provides a vivid account of hybridity at the margins of two converging fields—networked journalism and political activism. I have chosen to focus on the margins of the journalistic field, emphasizing cultural and technological influences over traditional economic and political ones for a number of reasons. As a researcher, I marvel at the combined disruptive power of technological and cultural innovations and seek to understand and explain them. As a citizen, I am amazed and enriched, though admittedly overwhelmed at times, by the converging, communicative potential of new media and communication technologies. Like all instances of disruptive innovation, this one did not occur in a vacuum. Rather, a near-perfect storm of factors combined to make the current environment of American journalism such a revolutionary one.

The major crisis that hit American newspapers, spurred greatly by the economic recession of 2008, played a crucial role in overhauling the media ecosystem. The digital revolution and the increased adoption by greater portions of journalism and media professions brought new actors, practices, and challenges into the mix. The growing cultural and political trends surrounding social media gave rise to a new kind of civic participation and collective intelligence. Each of these is a powerful factor of social change. Altogether, they constitute a disruptive set of innovations that may be utterly transformative, which appears to be occurring, of all places, on Twitter.

TWITTER, SOCIAL MEDIA, AND THE NETWORKED REVOLUTION

In today's networked society, everyday life is increasingly augmented by digitally mediated forms of communication, which lead to transformations in social relations (Couldry and Hepp 2016; Jurgenson 2012). Lee Rainie and Barry Wellman (2012) contend that American society is in the midst of a "triple revolution" due to the proliferation of the internet, mobile phones, and social networking services. When considered in concert, this revolution has led to a reboot of many sociological dynamics; the result is the emergence of a "new social operating system" brought about by the convergence of these technological and cultural innovations. Approximately 95% of American adults own a cell phone of some kind, and 77% own a smartphone, which are frequently used to access the internet ("Social media" 2017). Specifically, much of this mobile internet usage is social, meaning that users frequently interact with others often through social networks.

Since its emergence in 2006, Twitter has steadily gained popularity. As of April 2016, Twitter was used by 24% of American adult internet users, which amounts to more than one-fifth (21%) of all American adults (Greenwood et al. 2016). However, Twitter users are not fully representative of the American population, as a study by the Pew Research Center recently found that the social network "is particularly popular among those under 50 and the college-educated" (Duggan et al. 2015, para. 4). By comparison, a growing majority of Americans (68%, or 79% of online adults) use Facebook (Greenwood et al. 2016).

While Twitter is not the most used social media platform, what it lacks in popularity, it makes up with its open, fast-paced communicative structure comprised of a dedicated community of highly networked individuals. Thus, it serves as a clear illustration of digital media's expanding role in the social construction of reality (Couldry and Hepp 2016). In all, the networked environment is defined by the intersection of the technological innovations discussed above—the triple revolution—as well as the various affordances, structures, practices, and communities that emerge from them. In other words, no matter how significant Twitter may be to this discussion, it is impossible to address the significance of the platform without first considering its place within the broader context of the increasingly networked society. Accordingly, although this book places particular emphasis on Twitter, the discussion extends into other parts of the networked world on numerous occasions.

With this in mind, the goal of this book is to explore and explain the vast array of implications that Twitter's growing acceptance holds for the field of American journalism. In doing so, it argues that the structural transformation of the journalistic field is both a cause and consequence of the various changes in the field's relations with nonprofessionals. Among these changes are shifts in field boundaries, practices, and power relations—enabled, in part, by access to new forms of capital. Not only is this capital available to professional journalists, but also increasingly to members of networked publics, as they leverage new media and enter the field with growing ease. Twitter has played a central role in this shift, largely because of its speedy, accessible, and interactive format, convergence with other parts of the web, and growing acceptance in the fields of journalism and politics.

As norms and practices change, and journalists' interactions with nonprofessionals span beyond the borders of the journalistic field, this results in noteworthy changes to its structure. The field was once made up of journalists, editors, and profit-driven corporations who dominated the journalistic field through economic, social, cultural, and symbolic capital. While this more traditional field occasionally published letters to the editor by a small group of engaged citizens, the journalistic field—both on Twitter and beyond—now increasingly includes contributions by nonprofessionals (Reich 2011). This shift has opened up the boundaries of the journalistic field, making room for entry by actors situated primarily in other fields of cultural production. Such a transformation is not only structural, but has also influenced the kinds of practices employed by journalistic actors as nontraditional reporting increasingly gains traction in the field.

As the journalistic field becomes increasingly normalized to Twitter and the participatory web, the values and dispositions of a growing portion of the journalistic field become an increasingly hybrid integration of traditional and new media forms. Most notably, this book considers how new articulations of journalistic norms, values, practices, and dispositions have evolved out of the profession's orthodox traditions and their growing overlap with competing values of the participatory web. In doing so, it demonstrates how the combination of cultural, political, and technological shifts has opened up the boundaries of the journalistic field, making room for actors and practices that have historically been located at or beyond the margins of the field.

This Book

Citizens at the Gates provides a revealing analysis of how the institution of journalism, which is simultaneously a public practice and professional field, is undergoing a drastic change facilitated by a variety of social forces. The analysis is framed around the combination of two prominent theoretical perspectives: field theory from sociology, and mediatization from communication and media studies. While field theory offers a powerful conceptual framework to examine (inter)action and change within and across spaces of social relations, mediatization provides cutting-edge insights about the transformative realities of social life in a world shaped by new media logics. Despite profound potential and compatibility, few empirical studies have combined these two perspectives.

Whereas most studies of the journalistic field emphasize structural dynamics influenced by traditional political and economic factors, this work broadens the discussion to emphasize the role of micro- and mezzo-level factors that make up what are referred to throughout this book as the field's "elements of practice." Insights from mediatization help elucidate the transformations occurring within and across the structure of fields, which amounts to what are termed a "mediatized superstructure." In placing a particular emphasis on case studies that illustrate the role Twitter plays in journalistic practice, *Citizens at the Gates* aims to strike a healthy balance between the extremes of techno-optimism and pessimism. Thus, it resists determinism and avoids fetishizing either digital or face-to-face phenomena, instead acknowledging their mutual role in the shaping and reflection of structure, culture, and practice.

With this orientation, *Citizens at the Gates* employs a mixed-methods approach that combines the use of digital data with historical and contextual analysis made possible by prolonged participant-observation of Twitter's journalistic and activist subfields. The research presented in this book incorporates a diverse array of methodological approaches, including digital ethnography, content analysis, network analysis, and link analysis.[1] This book is the synthesis of more than eight years of collecting data and conducting online participant-observations of the ever-growing community of journalists on Twitter. It will provide a thick description and revealing in-depth analysis of the realities of journalism and activism in the world of Twitter and beyond. Accordingly, the case studies have been selected to offer diverse and revealing accounts of Twitter's role in the journalistic field over the last eight years of observation.

The book is comprised of nine chapters. Chapter 2 provides a comprehensive review of Twitter and a brief reflection on its contemporary significance for journalism, politics, and culture. In addition to summarizing the nuts and bolts of Twitter as a social network—what it is, its basic technical functions, who uses it, and how—Chap. 2 also offers a concise history of Twitter as a media company. This includes a consideration of the enduring question, "What is Twitter for?"—a double entendre intended to emphasize both the significance of the company's operating principles as well as the platform's technological affordances. These issues are further examined through the lens of recent controversies that Twitter has faced, including uses of the platform to market products, spark activist campaigns, engage in bullying, as well as to spread hatred and "fake news." After laying this important groundwork, the chapter concludes with a brief discussion of Twitter's significance within the field of American journalism.

Chapter 3 offers an informative yet accessible introduction to the conceptual framework that guides the book. It begins with an introduction to Pierre Bourdieu's (1993) field theory to explain how and why this lens is applied throughout the book. After a brief overview, the discussion of field theory is applied directly to the case of American journalism, and is broken into two main sections. The first section focuses on the level of *practice* within the journalistic field. Particular attention is paid to what is termed the "elements of practice," or what Bourdieu referred to as capital, habitus, and doxa. These concepts—and the dynamic manner in which they interact—play a central role in the book's analysis of micro- and mezzo-level dynamics demonstrated by journalists' and activists' use of Twitter. The second section on the *structure* of fields provides a succinct summation of how the journalistic field functions, with subsections on field formation and professionalization, inter-field relations, and field transformation. After introducing field theory and demonstrating its utility for the case of study, the focus of the chapter shifts to the issue of mediatization. In addition to providing an overview of this theoretical perspective, this section introduces the key concepts of "networked habitus," "media meta-capital," and "mediatized superstructure," which are further developed and applied later in the book. The chapter concludes with a brief discussion of emergent field dynamics like gatewatching and gatecrashing, which are driven by networked publics' collaborative efforts to fulfill the function of a "fifth estate." The consideration of how these innovations affect the gatekeeping process provides an ideal bridge to the examination of Twitter-based practices by professional journalists, which is the focus of the next chapter.

Chapter 4 marks the book's first empirical analysis of Twitter's place in the journalistic field. Based on a combination of digital ethnography and content analysis of journalists' tweets about Twitter (i.e., journalistic meta-discourse), the chapter analyzes journalistic practices and perspectives to help explain their significance for the profession. Findings suggest that each of the "elements of practice" is undergoing notable change as the journalistic field adapts to the networked era. Furthermore, this chapter constructs a typology of Twitter-journalism practices and demonstrates Twitter's role in the transformation of journalistic norms, values, and means of distinction by drawing on numerous examples from Twitter-journalists. Most importantly, the chapter argues that these changes have contributed to new opportunities for capital exchange as well as to the emergence of a hybrid, networked habitus that integrates values and practices from the traditional journalistic field with those from digital and non-professional origins.

The first of four case studies is presented in Chap. 5, which considers the successes and failures of professional and citizen journalists in the aftermath of the 2013 Boston Marathon Bombing. What were the success and failures of the journalistic response to the bombings? What role did

Twitter and other prominent platforms play in this response? What can this case tell us about the state of the American journalistic field? To address these questions, this chapter examines a wide variety of media responses following the bombing, with an emphasis placed on key actors' use of Twitter and other social media. After providing some context about the media response to the bombing and reviewing Twitter's role in the evolving process of reporting on breaking news, this chapter compares and contrasts competing accounts published in legacy media outlets with examples of collaborative, pro-am reporting. Accordingly, the chapter considers the case of Andrew Kitzenberg, a witness who became a source and correspondent for multiple legacy news organizations after live-tweeting about the manhunt, in order to demonstrate the networked public's growing influence in the changing field. It argues that such collaborative approaches to networked news reflect shifts in the mediatization of networked society, and thus, are of central importance to the future of American journalism. The chapter concludes by considering how the trend of convergence contributes to changes in journalistic practice, including sourcing, gatekeeping, and boundary maintenance.

Chapter 6 examines a targeted sample of tweets during four months of unrest in and around Ferguson, Missouri. As a hybrid, journo-activist space, tweeting #Ferguson quickly emerged as a way for activists and journalists to network and spread information. Using a mixed-methods approach combining digital ethnography and content analysis with social network analysis and link analysis, this chapter examines uses of Twitter by a small cohort of journalists and activists to identify changes in field structure and practices. After providing context about the case and reviewing literature on networked journalism and activism, the chapter compares tweets from each cohort. Expectedly, this chapter finds both similarities and differences in the themes, frames, format, and discourse of journalist and activist tweets. While the traditions of objective journalism and affective activism are found to persist, notable exceptions occurred, particularly following acts of police suppression. The networked communities of professional and activist Twitter users were overlapping and interactive, suggesting hybridity at the margins of the journalistic field. Given the hybridizing of journalistic and journo-activist practices, this case study examines the role of social media in efforts to report on and bolster social change.

Continuing the line of inquiry started in the previous chapter, Chap. 7 focuses on the potential for networked publics on Twitter to affect the flows and frames of news on legacy and digital news sites. Mainstream news organizations have long held the power to control what information gets into the news cycle, and according to what frames. Nevertheless, the growth of online publishing platforms like blogs and social media has altered traditional gatekeeping processes, permitting networked publics with greater access to the journalistic field. But to what extent does this access translate to power within the journalistic field? To address this question, the chapter considers a case study of a controversy in cable news: the spectacle surrounding MSNBC's cancellation of the Melissa Harris-Perry show. Accordingly, this study compares and contrasts information flows and trends in citizen (i.e., Twitter and citizen blogs) and professional media (i.e., legacy, online, and wire services). By tracing the hashtag #Nerdland—named for the program hosted by professor/pundit Melissa Harris-Perry—and contextualizing it within the broader ecosystem of news discourse on the subject, this chapter examines the agenda-setting function of networked publics. Through an examination of the themes, frames, discourses, and formats of networked communication around a specific issue, this chapter assesses similarities and differences between social media and digital news discourses as well as the relationships between them. This comparative approach offers a unique view of the structure of the journalistic field and its ongoing transformation by empirically demonstrating citizens' growing influence as "gatewatchers" and "gatecrashers." Findings suggest a two-way process of networked gatekeeping and agenda-setting—both top-down and bottom-up—that operates at the intersection of the political and journalistic fields.

Chapter 8 picks up where the previous chapter left off, examining the disparate means of influence exhibited by various media actors in response to the 2016 presidential election. Donald Trump's infamous use of Twitter affords him immense symbolic power through acts of gatewatching and gatecrashing. That is, he can criticize legacy media in the first instance, circumvent it in the second, while at the same time, drawing huge attention from legacy media. Drawing data from four sources, including tweets by prominent political journalists, journo-activists' reflections on #TrumpsAmerica, @realDonaldTrump himself, as well as digital news stories referencing Trump's tweets, this chapter examines the workings of symbolic power on Twitter, and how this bears on the practices of the journalistic field. Thus, this chapter asks: what happens to Twitter's journalistic field in the age of Trump? And what role are citizens playing in this process? After considering Trump's use of Twitter as a form of gatecrashing, spectacle, and symbolic power, the chapter examines the realities of a mediatized field context. Next, the chapter includes a brief assessment of the framing and symbolic power of Trump's tweets, which is then compared and contrasted with those posted by journalists and activists. This includes a brief examination of trends in online news coverage. Finally, the chapter compares and contrasts each group's potential for influence before drawing some conclusions about the hybridizing of journalism and politics in a time of mediatization.

In considering the breadth of implications posed by opening up the journalistic field to increasing influence from networked publics, the final chapter summarizes and assesses the significance of changes to gatekeeping, gatewatching, and gatecrashing processes. This includes a discussion of professional and citizen journalists' use of Twitter to gather and share the news, critique it, as well to hold media institutions accountable for violations of the public trust. It also considers how related changes in journalistic capital, norms, and values in the age of Twitter demonstrate hybridity across fields and bolster change within them. After reviewing these changing dynamics at each level, the final chapter contends with the larger shifts that are underway. It argues that a "mediatized superstructure" that alters the dynamics of media power is emerging. This includes a brief reflection on how the field's structures, as well as the accordant "elements of practice," are being adapted to suit an increasingly hybrid, interactive field. Finally, the chapter considers key challenges American journalism will face going forward. While the ongoing mediatization of society affords significant power to networked publics, the hegemony of legacy and digital news institutions remains considerable. Through hidden algorithms that determine what news and views users are exposed to, which are often guided by political and economic goals, social media platforms are acting more and more like traditional gatekeepers. This marks the enduring paradox of American journalism in the twenty-first century: what networked power giveth, institutional power can taketh away, and vice versa.

NOTE

1. See the appendix for additional details about the methodology applied throughout the book.

REFERENCES

Alterman, E. (2003). *What liberal media?: The truth about bias and the news.* New York: Basic Books.

Barthel, M. (2017, June 1). *Despite subscription surges for largest U.S. newspapers, circulation and revenue fall for industry overall.* Pew Research Center.

Retrieved October 4, 2017, from http://www.pewresearch.org/fact-tank/2017/06/01/circulation-and-revenue-fall-for-newspaper-industry/.

Bourdieu, P. (1993). *The field of cultural production*. New York: Columbia University Press.

Bourdieu, P. (1999). *On television*. New York: New Press.

Couldry, N., & Hepp, A. (2016). *The mediated construction of reality*. Malden, MA: Polity.

Duggan, M., Ellison, N. B., Lampe, C., Lenhart, A., & Madden, M. (2015). *Demographics of key social networking platforms*. Pew Research Center. Retrieved November 13, 2017, from http://www.pewinternet.org/2015/01/09/demographics-of-key-social-networking-platforms-2/.

Edmonds, R., Guskin, E., Mitchell, A., & Jurkowitz, M. (2013). Newspapers: Stabilizing, but still threatened. *The State of the News Media 2013*. Retrieved November 13, 2017, from http://www.pewresearch.org/topics/state-of-the-news-media/2013/.

Greenwood, S., Perrin, A., & Duggan, M. (2016, November 11). *Social media update 2016*. Pew Research Center. Retrieved November 13, 2017, from http://www.pewinternet.org/2016/11/11/social-media-update-2016/.

Jurgenson, N. (2012). When atoms meet bits: Social media, the mobile web and augmented revolution. *Future Internet, 4*(1), 83–91.

McCombs, M. E., & Shaw, D. L. (1972). The agenda-setting function of mass media. *Public Opinion Quarterly, 36*(2), 176–187.

Mitchell, A., & Matsa, K. E. (2015, May 22). *The declining value of U.S. newspapers*. Pew Research Center. Retrieved May 5, 2018, from http://www.pewresearch.org/fact-tank/2015/05/22/the-declining-value-of-u-s-newspapers/.

Newspaper Death Watch. (2017). Retrieved October 3, 2017, from http://newspaperdeathwatch.com/.

Rainie, L., & Wellman, B. (2012). *Networked: The new social operating system*. Cambridge, MA: MIT Press.

Reich, Z. (2011). User comments: The transformation of participatory space. In J. B. Singer, A. Hermida, D. Domingo, A. Heinonen, S. Paulussen, T. Quandt, Z. Reich, & M. Vujnovic (Eds.), *Participatory Journalism: Guarding open gates at online newspapers* (pp. 96–117). Malden, MA: Wiley-Blackwell.

Rosen, J. (2006). PressThink: The people formerly known as the audience. *PressThink*. Retrieved November 13, 2017, from http://archive.pressthink.org/2006/06/27/ppl_frmr.html.

Shoemaker, P. J., & Vos, T. (2009). *Gatekeeping theory*. Hoboken, NJ: Taylor & Francis.

Social media fact sheet. (2017, January 12). Pew Research Center. Retrieved November 13, 2017, from http://www.pewinternet.org/fact-sheet/social-media/.

CHAPTER 2

Twitter: More than 140 Characters

Twitter has as many uses as it has users. Since its launch on March 21, 2006, Twitter has risen to prominence in communities across the networked world. As a streamlined, short-form communication platform embedded within the larger context of the networked web, Twitter affords countless opportunities for those wanting to read, write, or interact. Whether tracking breaking news events in real time or catching up on the latest updates, the platform provides a variety of social and informational experiences, especially since users do not have to be "friends" with those they "follow." Twitter's famous 140-character limit, which was expanded to 280 characters in November 2017, requires brevity while still allowing users to share, interact, sequence, tag, and embed links, photos, and videos.

I heard a metaphorical description of Twitter years ago that I have come to adopt, which goes something like this: Twitter is best thought of as a *cocktail party* (Fritz 2014). Not a cocktail party with a dozen close friends who get together regularly, but one with millions of people, both similar and different to yourself. And just like any other party, you have some agency in choosing your interactions, although the outcome will likely depend on your social networks and personal interests. More importantly, the view from the balcony of the party reveals fairly distinct boundaries between different conversational communities. Relatively separate spaces exist for "celebrity Twitter," "sports Twitter," "political Twitter," "weird Twitter," "Black Twitter," "academic Twitter," and of course, "news Twitter." Like other discursive communities, each of these spaces is

© The Author(s) 2018
S. R. Barnard, *Citizens at the Gates*,
https://doi.org/10.1007/978-3-319-90446-7_2

comprised of accounts and hashtag conversations fitting their namesake. For example, political Twitter is made up of politicians, pundits, automated "bots," and members of the public engaging in political commentary. Weird Twitter is full of obscure jokes. Black Twitter, as it has come to be known, is marked by expressive commentary pertaining to African-American culture—a group that is demographically overrepresented on Twitter (Duggan 2015; Smith 2014).[1] News Twitter is made up of information about news events as well as commentary about news-related issues, which this book describes as journalistic meta-discourse.

Keeping with the cocktail party metaphor, you can choose to listen, engage, or dominate the conversation, whether it is with people complaining about (or praising) their meal, or discussing the intricacies of Marxist philosophy, and everything in between. The space for politics on Twitter is rather amorphous, given the liquidity of modern political discourse. Many users frequently float between conversations about news and politics to cultural commentary with relative ease, often changing behavior (i.e., language) to fit the intended context and audience. Such code switching is common, and is often done with little or no warning. At the same time, these conversations are frequently homophilous—the aphorism, "birds of a feather flock together," is especially true on Twitter—since interactions on the platform are more likely to be defined by similarity, rather than difference (cf. Adamic and Glance 2005; Himelboim et al. 2016).

However, one major difference between Twitter and a face-to-face cocktail party, besides getting to taste the food and drink, is the ease at which users can follow many conversations at once. With a little help from Twitter "lists," users can even keep each conversation separate, thus minimizing the white noise. Therefore, Twitter may be less of a cocktail party and more of an "unconference," where users can listen in and (un)follow as they please, depending on their interests. Twitter, like any other technology, is far from homogeneous or deterministic.

Although organizational structures and technological affordances do matter, Twitter is no better suited to publish tweets about users' breakfasts than about breaking news experiences. These are just a few of the many capabilities or "affordances" built into the platform, which users can "leverage" as they choose (Davis and Chouinard 2017; Earl and Kimport 2011). Furthermore, when considered among the broader journalistic, political, cultural, and economic factors, it becomes clear that purely technological analyses do not sufficiently address the complexity of networked reality (Alexander 2015). Rather, this would require perspectives that are appropriately attuned to technological factors without fetishizing or downplaying them (Barnard 2016). As the "leveraged affordances" and "mutual shaping" perspectives remind us, "[I]t is people's usage of technology—not technology itself—that can change social processes" (Earl and Kimport 2011, p. 14; cf. Trottier 2013). Indeed, just as technologies are *constructed* by people, they are also *used* by people in ways that fit their disposition and social location. While some will choose to tweet photos and descriptions of their breakfast—a most elementary form of reporting (Gans 2007)—many more will choose to share information that is likely to be of interest to their community of "followers." This is one example of how Twitter is implicated in the practice of journalism, however mundane.

In the years since I began studying Twitter, I have observed countless expressions of journalistic (inter)action shared on the platform. Most visibly, I have witnessed one major news event after another break on Twitter. Indeed, this trend is so common that it seems one Twitter record simply begets another ("Celebrating a new" 2011; "#numbers" 2011; Dewey 2014; Sweney 2014; Reisinger 2015; Kottasova 2016). While much of the records surround cultural events—like the Academy Awards, the NFL Super Bowl, or the celebration of a new year—others were broken during natural disasters or on election nights. In this sense, Twitter is a predominantly cultural space. As of this writing, four of the top five most popular Twitter accounts (and six of the top ten) are registered to famous musicians. The other four accounts are registered to the former president of the United States (@BarackObama, #3), comedic celebrity Ellen Degeneres (@TheEllenShow, #6), and for social media sites (@YouTube, #7 and @twitter, #10) ("Twitter: Most-followed" 2017). Yet, while "celebrity Twitter" may be receiving the most buzz at the metaphorical party, it is far from the only conversation taking place. Each discursive community may be more or less vocal or populated, and some will have a better seat at the table, but each has their place in the room.

According to the Pew Research Center, 24% of adults who use the internet (21% of all American adults) use Twitter (Greenwood et al. 2016). As the third most popular social media platform behind Facebook (79%) and Instagram (32%), Twitter has approximately 328 million active monthly users from across the world (Greenwood et al. 2016; "About" 2017). In the United States alone, these users are fairly well distributed across all demographic groups, though they are slightly more likely to be non-White (Duggan 2015), female, young, urban, and college-educated ("Social media" 2017). While uses of the platform vary widely, a growing majority (74%) of these users get news from Twitter (Shearer and Gottfried 2017). This is hardly surprising, given the steps Twitter has taken to attract members of the media and tech industries, starting with its soft launch at an industry party in Silicon Valley (Bilton 2013, p. 72). Yet, how (and of course, *if*) people use Twitter varies greatly, depending on their skillset (capital), disposition (habitus), and field location, as well as the structural makeup of the platform.

The #Evolution of @Twitter

Current users are familiar with a Twitter that is a far cry from the one launched in 2006. What started as an idea for "Stat.us," a site focused on users sharing their status with friends, became a more open and interactive platform where networked publics can form and spread information of all kinds (see Fig. 2.1). Like the culture of Twitter, many of the site's technical functions—including the famous hashtag (#), retweet (RT), and "at reply" (@)—were also a product of user experimentation and innovation (Bilton 2013; Bruns and Moe 2014; Messina 2017). While it is true that these technical functions were somewhat user-driven, they have also been used to advance Twitter's own self-crafted "creation myth" (Halavais 2014, p. 37)—which, like most modern tech companies, aims to paint a picture of the company as uniquely open and inclusive. In reality, technologies are always socially constructed, which means implementing suggestions from users in order to meet market demands.

Despite the hype, the history of Twitter's technical functions is less mythical than it is wrapped in the logical evolution of communicative platforms in the digital age. While the @reply was an adaptation from the popular Internet Relay Chat (IRC), the #hashtag, like the retweet, slowly evolved as technical functions following suggestions and "hacks" from the user community (Halavais 2014). Indeed, Twitter's decision to leave the source code and application programming interface (API) open for developers led to countless innovations, such as the mobile app, social media dashboards (i.e., HootSuite and TweetDeck), and many other prominent applications. While this adaptability is largely attributable to Twitter's culture of relative openness and experimentation in its early days, recent developments suggest that changes to the platform are driven more by industry pressures than by user innovation.

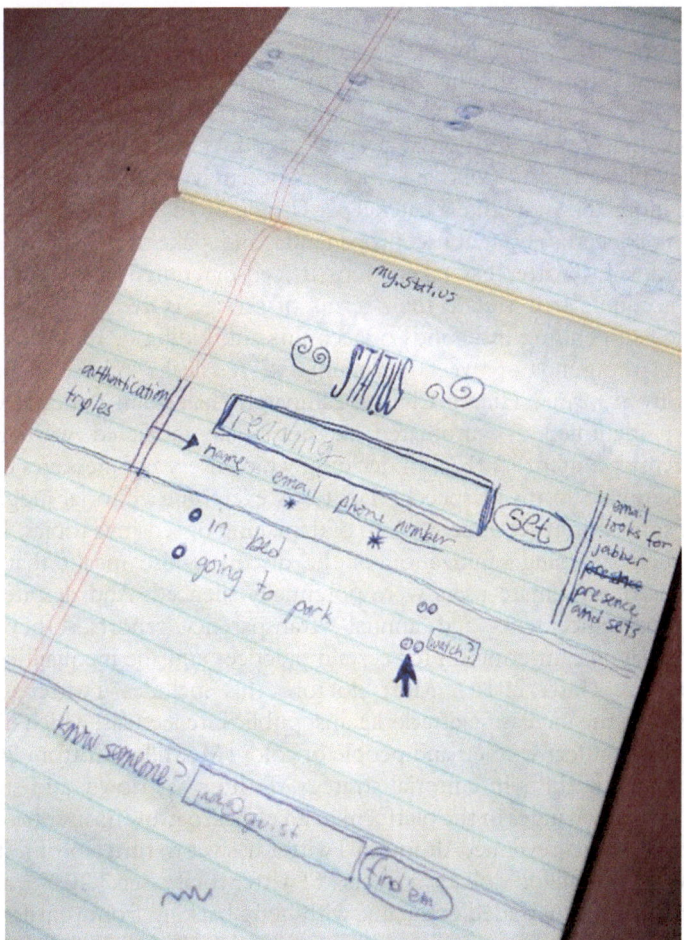

Fig. 2.1 Jack Dorsey's (2006) "twttr sketch" posted on Flickr days after Twitter's launch

Much like its competitors, Facebook and Snapchat, in recent years, Twitter has implemented algorithms on their platform, which serve as content filters that prioritize advertising, breaking news, and other popular trends. As such, social media companies like Twitter have begun the shift from a (not-so) neutral *platform* that relies on users to post and circulate content, to also acting as a *publisher* that makes editorial decisions to promote (or restrict) portions of this content. Whether through the use of algorithms that highlight "recommended" content, "trends," and "moments"—a function that highlights tweets and topics curated by Twitter, Inc.—or its decision to "verify" accounts that are "determined to be of public interest" (who are disproportionately male), the company is acting more and more like a gatekeeper (Bogle 2016). Furthermore, amid growing concerns about abuse, propaganda, and "fake news" spreading on the platform, Twitter has taken steps to censor content and shut down some accounts that violate their terms of service (Oremus 2017). This included suspending thousands of accounts and hiding or removing hundreds of thousands of tweets pertaining to Wikileaks' release of hacked emails from former Hillary Clinton campaign chair John Podesta, which Twitter identified as automated or potentially affiliated with Russia ("Extremist content" 2017). In deciding which users and messages constitute legitimate forms of speech, Twitter is exercising editorial judgment, which some might see as censorship of damaging or sensitive topics. In this case, such sweeping sanitization of the discourse also meant that large numbers of legitimate users were potentially silenced. And despite their policy announcements and annual "transparency reports," they have received significant criticism for certain practices and the inequalities they (re)produce (Jaffa 2016). Most notably, this includes Twitter's tepid response to the increasing attacks against public intellectuals, which disproportionately affect women and people of color (McMillan Cottom 2015).

Beyond the shifts in editorial strategy, Twitter has slowly and steadily implemented changes in the platform in an effort to grow its user base, and consequently, its revenue. Although Twitter has yet to turn a profit, it now has over seven billion dollars in assets ("Twitter total assets" 2017), and its status as a publicly traded company, with hefty backing from venture capitalists, has resulted in numerous changes to the platform's functionality. For example, in an effort to make sharing and conversing on the platform easier—which, the developers reasoned, would increase user engagement—Twitter expanded their renowned 140-character limit to 280 characters. Such changes have been driven in large part by a need to increase revenues while striving to maintain a balance between its competing interests. As José van Dijck (2013, p. 83) argued, "Twitter-the-ambient-utility promoting user connectedness finds itself at odds with Twitter-the-information-network exploiting connectivity to help businesses promote their brands among users." This paradox begs the question: what is Twitter *for*?

This question has been at the heart of the company's decision-making since it was only an idea. From the outset, two of Twitter's creators, Jack Dorsey and Evan Williams, had competing but ultimately complementary visions for the service. Former *New York Times* reporter and Twitter biographer Nick Bilton (2013, p. 260) described the result as "the perfect equilibrium of two ways of looking at the world: the need to talk about yourself, compared with the need to let people talk about what was happening around them." The combination of the two creators' ideal uses shaped Twitter's vision into a ubiquitous backchannel, something like a public utility that powers all kinds of interpersonal relations (Dijck 2013). Meanwhile, the service is also wrapped in a multiyear struggle to discover and disentangle its mission as an information system and a marketing and promotion network (Dijck 2013). This includes struggles over what to do about the spread of fake news, hate speech, propaganda and violent extremism, as well as the automated bots that are frequently used to aid these causes. This book promises no resolutions to these challenges. Instead, it seeks to review and contextualize them in order to provide the background necessary to understand what role Twitter has played in the journalistic field, and how that role may evolve in the future.

On the Promise of "Free Speech"

Another related concern is the extent to which Twitter, the media company, opts to protect the First Amendment rights of its users, and when it is compelled to remove content, restrict accounts, or provide user information to governing bodies. Twitter receives such requests from corporations and governments across the world, ranging from authoritarian regimes seeking to quell dissent (i.e., Turkey), to democratic countries seeking to uphold standards for online speech (i.e., France and Germany). In their biannual "transparency report," the company explained that between July and December, 2016 they

> Received 88 legal requests from around the world directing us to remove content posted by verified journalists or news outlet accounts. We did not take any action on the majority of these requests, with limited exceptions in Germany and Turkey, the latter of which accounted for 88% of all requests of this nature. For example, we were compelled to withhold Tweets sharing graphic imagery following terror attacks in Turkey in response to a court order. ("Removal requests" 2017)

While Twitter reported receiving 102 removal requests from the United States during this period, it reportedly did not comply. On the other hand, during the same time period, Twitter complied with 82% of the 2304 requests for user information submitted by the US government alone ("Removal requests" 2017).

Despite their apparent cooperation with many governments today, Twitter has generally operated with a default premise of protecting users' rights. For example, when the FBI and other law-enforcement agencies first came knocking with requests for users' data, Twitter executives reportedly refused (Bilton 2013, p. 134). Similarly, after being asked by law enforcement to hand over data from one of its users involved in the Occupy Wall Street protests in 2011, the company fought the matter in court. While they eventually complied following a court ruling, the legal battle helped determine what social media platforms are required to do when faced with such requests without a warrant, and have vowed to inform users of these requests (Kravets 2012; Sengupta 2012). This commitment to transparency and users' rights should be considered alongside its support of press freedom (Crowell 2017a) and net neutrality (Culbertson 2017). While these efforts have earned the company a reputation as a supporter of free expression in the United States as well as abroad, their recent crackdown on accounts deemed "abusive" has drawn the ire of free speech advocates from across the political spectrum (Ho 2017; Leetaru 2017).

Crafting a public image as a supporter and arbiter of free expression has been an important component of Twitter's marketing strategy. As a result, Twitter has typically tried to appear politically neutral, but the company has occasionally come out in support of particular causes. Examples of the company's support for progressive causes include, among many others, Twitter's display of the messages "#Ferguson" (Tiku 2014) and "#BlackLivesMatter" (Blackbirds 2014) in their company headquarters, co-founder and CEO Jack Dorsey's public friendship with activists like DeRay McKesson, and their collaboration with citizen journalism groups in Turkey (Onder 2017; Tufekci 2017). The company was also accused of harboring bias for progressive causes due in part to high-profile cases where members of the political Right, including "alt-Right" poster children Richard Spencer and Milo Yiannopoulos, were banned from the platform for harassment and hate speech. Twitter said these accounts were banned because they violated its terms of service (Andrews 2016).

In November 2017, the company made headlines when a (now former) Twitter employee allegedly deleted Donald Trump's personal account, @ realDonaldTrump. Although the account was reinstated 11 minutes later, the incident brought added scrutiny to the company, whose general counsel had testified before a Senate judiciary committee investigating Russia's alleged meddling in the 2016 election earlier that week (Isaac and Wakabayashi 2017). Despite these accusations, Twitter continues to play host to user communities from across the political spectrum, including many on the far-right. Indeed, publishing and publicizing such spectacular rhetoric appears to be part of Twitter's business plan, as evidenced by the company's international advertising campaign centered on Trump's infamous use of the platform (Deathvies 2017).

Considering these contradictions, it should not be surprising that Twitter, like the majority of today's prominent (tech) companies, has also been accused of discrimination (Hennelly 2015). Indeed, the company is known to lack gender, racial, and ethnic diversity in its ranks, especially in executive positions (Kidd 2017; Luckie 2015; Ramsey 2016). This lack of representation may help explain why Twitter has not done more to curb harassment targeting journalists, scholars, and people of color, among many others, who use the platform to share their work (Angwin 2017; Kidd 2017). However ironically, countless users, some of them famous in their own right, have also taken to Twitter to tell their stories of sexual harassment, using the hashtag #metoo, following a slew of accusations against high-profile celebrities in late 2017 (Ong 2017).

Perhaps a less obvious (and arguably more consequential) site for bias can be found in the platform's algorithms, which help determine topics that are trending, the placement of tweets in users' timelines, suggestions for accounts to follow, and even what accounts will be suspended (Ho 2017). Each of these platform functions provide an opportunity for the promotion or demotion of particular kinds of content, whether to advance or stifle the flow of information by users supporting political causes. And while critics decry many of these interventions as disrupting the flow of free speech, the reality is that there are no legally protected public forums on the web. All digital spaces are privately owned, and thus, are subject to the structures and policies implemented by their hosts. Although Twitter's policy and public statements express the company's desire to host a diverse debate on a wide range of social issues, such principles are difficult to realize in absolute.

Another potential site for bias are the challenges imposed by automated bots, which some researchers estimate make up between 9% and 15% of user accounts (Varol et al. 2017). A "bot," which is short for "robot," is an automated account that is programmed to follow and tweet automatically. They are often designed to game Twitter's algorithms to amplify certain users, posts, or perspectives, including "fake news" (Crowell 2017b). Although bots can be created by anyone who knows how to code, the most prominent bots are created by information technology professionals. The uses for bots are even more diverse, ranging from chat-bots designed to automate customer service or create absurd poetry to those designed to troll ideological opponents or manipulate public opinion (Earle 2017). Twitter bots have even been used to add context to the informational diets of the President and White House staffers (Bump 2017; Peiser 2017). Though many of these uses appear valuable, the fact that bots are often difficult to (algorithmically) distinguish from human users poses a challenge to the principles of free speech when hundreds of thousands are used to distort public opinion. Despite the political havoc that bots have wreaked in the United States and abroad, it seems to be Twitter's desire to cultivate corporate favor that guides their continued allowance of automated accounts on the platform (Wang 2017a, b; Woodruff and Ackerman 2017). While these challenges are significant and ongoing, they did not arise until recent years, and thus, are not reflected in the bulk of the empirical analyses presented in this book. Nevertheless, we will return to them again in Chap. 9.

As is common with many First Amendment issues and regardless of legal precedent, Twitter still struggles to strike a balance that enables free speech without helping to amplify hate or incite violence. It also must grapple with the inherent tensions between Twitter's competing aspirations to foster social ties, on the one hand, and to help other companies market products, on the other (Dijck 2013). Given that increased user engagement on the platform results in an increased value to advertisers, it is clear that the relationship with these advertisers poses challenges for free speech, as it long has for traditional media.

These concerns regarding free speech have only increased in recent years for Twitter and across social media at large. This is likely to continue to be the case as long as these platforms continue to gain more capital. These same forces also bear notably on the field of journalism as it exists through these platforms, since its health and legitimacy relies on, among other things, civil discourse, a belief in facts, and the free exchange of ideas.

Twitter and American Journalism

It may come as no surprise that Twitter is the leading source for news among social media sites (Barthel et al. 2015). Twitter's place at the center of the journalistic field is solidified by the sheer number of media professionals (and amateurs) who use it as part of their reporting routines (Hedman 2015; Santana and Hopp 2016; Willnat and Weaver 2014). This is no accident. Indeed, the company has taken steps to help ensure its status as an arbiter of news, including attempts to increase the visibility of breaking news, as well as of reporters themselves. Research found that a quarter of Twitter's "verified" users were journalists—a status marker that adds legitimacy and publicity for these elite users, despite the fact that Twitter has long been criticized for the lack of diversity in the accounts they choose to "verify" (Moses 2015). Altogether, these factors contribute to the self-fulfilling prophecy that Twitter is the go-to place for the production, dissemination, and reception of news for many connected to the journalistic field.

As discussed above, gatekeeping procedures have undergone a rapid transformation as the growth of new media tools affords large swaths of the networked citizenry with increased influence in the news environment. Many reporting practices have also changed significantly as these tools evolve, connecting journalists, sources, and audiences in ways the profession has never seen. Along with these changes comes the transformation of many longstanding norms and values, as well as the field's boundaries (Carlson and Lewis 2015). Indeed, despite the relative persistence of American journalism's traditional structure and practices, the field has steadily taken to Twitter, to the point of normalization (Lasorsa et al. 2012).

Evidence of this normalization is reinforced by accounts from working journalists. As *Denver Post* journalist Daniel Petty remarked in 2013, "We in mainstream media have a bias toward Twitter ... it's where we're spending most of our time" ("Hashtag #Journalism" 2013). Indeed, Twitter has become such a norm for journalists that, as CBS Denver News Director Tim Wieland confessed, "There are times when I'm on Twitter and it feels like a bunch of reporters talking to each other." This experience may be due, in part, to the heavy saturation of reporters on the network, as well as the way they engage on the platform. As digital media manager Phil Tenser, formerly of Denver's KMGH-TV admitted, he has TweetDeck, a Twitter dashboard, "Open as long as [he's] breathing." KUSA's Kyle

Clark concurred, explaining that he is on Twitter from the moment he wakes up until he falls asleep ("Hashtag #Journalism" 2013). While much of the excitement may have subsided over the years, the trend of heavy use by journalists has been well documented (Lawlor 2017).

Twitter's significance in journalists' routines is considerable and growing, whether journalists use it to stay aware of breaking news (Hermida 2010; Vis 2013), identify sources (Willnat and Weaver 2014), query their followers (Santana and Hopp 2016), work on branding and self-promotion (Hanusch 2017; Molyneux et al. 2017), connect with fellow professionals or members of the public (Willnat and Weaver 2014) or otherwise. Similarly, networked activists have found social media platforms like Twitter to be useful tools for communication and dissemination of information, including to members of the journalism establishment (Hermida et al. 2014; Poell and Rajagopalan 2015). Such "alternative media" have long been used to spread less conventional perspectives as well as to monitor more traditional media (Poepsel and Painter 2016), further blurring boundaries between journalism and activism. This should come as no surprise to those versed in the history of journalism's relationship to technology. As Monica Krause (2011, pp. 100–101) made clear:

> Technological change has played an important yet also limited role in the history of journalism. Innovation has become an integral aspect of maintaining field autonomy vis-a-vis outside forces, by limiting concentration and creating venues and audiences for new forms of journalistic practices—a role first played by radio, then TV and now the internet. In each case, the new entrant was not initially a journalistic medium but became partially incorporated into the field. This incorporation at the same time limited the role the new medium could play. Under what conditions are new technologies and media incorporated into fields? Under what conditions might they have a more transformative impact?

This book seeks to address these two questions, with an emphasis on Twitter's role in the process of transformation, as well as its contribution to journalism's hybridity as it intersects with citizen journalism and political activism.

Not only have the changes brought about by mediatization greatly impacted journalistic practices, they have also had a marked influence on the structure of the journalistic field itself and power relations within it. As will become clear, this is due, in large part, to the (deeply interrelated) technological and politico-cultural changes happening across field con-texts. Given the increasingly normative role that Twitter is taking on in journalism and political activism, it is an exemplary case through which to investigate the structural and practical transformation occurring in the field. Accordingly, the following chapter will further examine how profes-sional journalists use Twitter, within what structural contexts, and to what practical ends.

NOTE

1. See Chaps. 6 and 7 for a more detailed discussion of Black Twitter.

REFERENCES

About. (2017). Twitter. Retrieved November 13, 2017, from https://about. twitter.com/company.

Adamic, L. A., & Glance, N. (2005). *The political blogosphere and the 2004 U.S. election: Divided they blog.* Presented at the Proceedings of the 3rd international workshop on Link discovery, ACM. https://doi.org/10.1145/1134271. 1134277.

Alexander, J. C. (2015). The crisis of journalism reconsidered: Cultural power. *Fudan Journal of the Humanities and Social Sciences, 8*(1), 9–31. https://doi. org/10.1007/s40647-014-0056-5.

Andrews, T. M. (2016, November 16). "A great purge?": Twitter suspends Richard Spencer, other prominent alt-right accounts. *Washington Post.* Retrieved November 13, 2017, from https://www.washingtonpost.com/ news/morning-mix/wp/2016/11/16/a-great-purge-twitter-suspends-richard-spencer-other-prominent-alt-right-accounts/.

Angwin, J. (2017, November 9). Cheap tricks: The low cost of internet harass-ment. *ProPublica.* Retrieved November 15, 2017, from https://www. propublica.org/article/cheap-tricks-the-low-cost-of-internet-harassment.

Barnard, S. (2016). Digital sociology's vocational promise. In J. Daniels, K. Gregory, & T. McMillan Cottom (Eds.), *Digital sociologies* (pp. 195–210). Bristol: Policy Press.

Barthel, M., Shearer, E., Gottfried, J., & Mitchell, A. (2015, July 14). *The evolving role of news on Twitter and Facebook.* Pew Research Center. Retrieved November 15, 2017, from http://www.journalism.org/2015/07/14/the-evolving-role-of-news-on-twitter-and-facebook/.

Bilton, N. (2013). *Hatching Twitter: A true story of money, power, friendship, and betrayal.* New York, NY: Portfolio.

Blackbirds, T. (2014, December 9). #BlackLivesMatterpic.twitter.com/lgWjqt-fkUe [Tweet]. Twitter. Retrieved November 13, 2017, from https://twitter.com/blackbirds/status/540700339192598528.

Bogle, A. (2016, November 15). Guess which gender is more likely to be verified on Twitter? We'll wait. *Mashable*. Retrieved November 13, 2017, from http://mashable.com/2016/11/15/twitter-verification-women-men/.

Bruns, A., & Moe, H. (2014). Structural layers of communication on Twitter. In K. Weller, A. Bruns, J. Burgess, M. Mahrt, & C. Puschmann (Eds.), *Twitter and society* (pp. 15–28). New York: Peter Lang.

Bump, P. (2017, August 17). Analysis: Now you can see what Donald Trump sees every time he opens Twitter. *Washington Post*. Retrieved November 13, 2017, from https://www.washingtonpost.com/news/politics/wp/2017/08/17/now-you-can-see-what-donald-trump-sees-every-time-he-opens-twitter/.

Carlson, M., & Lewis, S. C. (Eds.). (2015). *Boundaries of journalism: Professionalism, practices and participation*. New York: Routledge.

Celebrating a new year with a new tweet record. (2011, January 6). Twitter. Retrieved November 13, 2017, from https://blog.twitter.com/official/en_us/a/2011/celebrating-a-new-year-with-a-new-tweet-record.html.

Crowell, C. (2017a, May 3). #PressFreedom 2017. Twitter. Retrieved November 13, 2017, from https://blog.twitter.com/official/en_us/topics/events/2017/-pressfreedom-2017.html.

Crowell, C. (2017b, June 14). Our approach to bots & misinformation. Twitter. Retrieved November 13, 2017, from https://blog.twitter.com/official/en_us/topics/company/2017/Our-Approach-Bots-Misinformation.html.

Culbertson, L. (2017, July 11). Join the fight for #NetNeutrality. Twitter. Retrieved November 13, 2017, from https://blog.twitter.com/official/en_us/topics/company/2017/Join-the-Fight-for-NetNeutrality.html.

Davis, J. L., & Chouinard, J. B. (2017). Theorizing affordances: From request to refuse. *Bulletin of Science, Technology & Society, 36*(4), 241–248. https://doi.org/10.1177/0270467617714944.

Deathvies, A. (2017). 'The things you don't know, now'—@Twitter is actively marketing itself off fear of what Trump is tweeting. Twitter. Retrieved November 13, 2017, from https://twitter.com/outstandy/status/914639977102938113.

Dewey, C. (2014, March 3). Ellen DeGeneres' Oscar selfie broke Twitter, and world records. *Washington Post*. Retrieved November 13, 2017, from https://www.washingtonpost.com/news/arts-and-entertainment/wp/2014/03/03/ellen-degeneres-oscar-selfie-broke-twitter-and-world-records/.

Dijck, J. v. (2013). *The culture of connectivity: A critical history of social media*. Oxford: New York.

Dorsey, J. (2006). *twttr sketch* [Photo]. Flickr. Retrieved November 13, 2017, from https://www.flickr.com/photos/jackdorsey/182613360/.

Duggan, M. (2015). *The demographics of social media users.* Pew Research Center's Internet & American Life Project. Retrieved November 13, 2017, from http://www.pewinternet.org/2015/08/19/the-demographics-of-social-media-users/.

Earl, J., & Kimport, K. (2011). *Digitally enabled social change: Activism in the Internet age.* Cambridge, MA: MIT Press.

Earle, S. (2017, October 14). How social media is being used by governments to settle scores and silence critics. *Newsweek.* Retrieved November 13, 2017, from http://www.newsweek.com/trolls-bots-and-fake-news-dark-and-mysterious-world-social-media-manipulation-682155.

Extremist Content and Russian Disinformation Online: Working with Tech to Find Solutions. (2017). Senate, 115th Congress, Testimony of Sean Edgett. Retrieved October 16, 2017, from https://www.judiciary.senate.gov/meetings/extremist-content-and-russian-disinformation-online-working-with-tech-to-find-solutions.

Fritz, J. (2014). How nonprofits use LinkedIn. *About.com Money.* Retrieved July 30, 2015, from http://nonprofit.about.com/od/socialmedia/a/Tips-For-Using-Linkedin-For-Nonprofits.htm.

Gans, H. J. (2007). Everyday news, newsworkers, and professional Journalism. *Political Communication, 24*(2), 161–166. https://doi.org/10.1080/10584600701312878.

Greenwood, S., Perrin, A., & Duggan, M. (2016, November 11). *Social media update 2016.* Pew Research Center. Retrieved November 13, 2017, from http://www.pewinternet.org/2016/11/11/social-media-update-2016/.

Halavais, A. (2014). Structure of Twitter: Social and technical. In K. Weller, A. Bruns, J. Burgess, N. Mahrt, & C. Puschmann (Eds.), *Twitter and society* (pp. 29–41). New York: Peter Lang.

Hanusch, F. (2017). Political journalists' corporate and personal identities on Twitter profile pages: A comparative analysis in four Westminster democracies. *New Media & Society.* Advance online publication. https://doi.org/10.1177/1461444817698479.

Hashtag: #Journalism redefined [Session 1] [VideoCast]. (2013, September 20). *University of Denver Videocast.* Retrieved November 19, 2017, from http://videocast.du.edu/video/hashtag-journalism-redefined---session-1.

Hedman, U. (2015). J-Tweeters. *Digital Journalism, 3*(2), 279–297. https://doi.org/10.1080/21670811.2014.897833.

Hennelly, R. (2015, September 1). Does Twitter's reset on race and gender go far enough? *CBS News.* Retrieved November 13, 2017, from https://www.cbsnews.com/news/does-twitters-reset-on-race-and-gender-go-far-enough/.

Hermida, A. (2010). Twittering the news. *Journalism Practice, 4*(3), 297–308. https://doi.org/10.1080/17512781003640703.

Hermida, A., Lewis, S. C., & Zamith, R. (2014). Sourcing the Arab Spring: A case study of Andy Carvin's sources on Twitter during the Tunisian and Egyptian revolutions. *Journal of Computer-Mediated Communication, 19*(3), 479–499. https://doi.org/10.1111/jcc4.12074.

Himelboim, I., Sweetser, K. D., Tinkham, S. F., Cameron, K., Danelo, M., & West, K. (2016). Valence-based homophily on Twitter: Network analysis of emotions and political talk in the 2012 presidential election. *New Media & Society, 18*(7), 1382–1400. https://doi.org/10.1177/1461444814555096.

Ho, E. (2017, March 1). Our latest update on safety. Twitter. Retrieved October 11, 2017, from https://blog.twitter.com/official/en_us/topics/product/2017/our-latest-update-on-safety.html.

Isaac, M., & Wakabayashi, D. (2017, November 3). Twitter's panic after Trump's account is deleted caps a rough week. *The New York Times*. Retrieved November 13, 2017, from https://www.nytimes.com/2017/11/03/technology/trump-twitter-deleted.html.

Jaffa, V. (2016, August 15). Twitter's new verification process is a game rigged against its marginalized users. *Model View Culture*. Retrieved November 13, 2017, from https://modelviewculture.com/pieces/twitters-new-verification-process-is-a-game-rigged-against-its-marginalized-users.

Kidd, D. (2017). *Social media freaks*. Boulder, CO: Westview Press.

Kottasova, I. (2016, December 6). Twitter reveals the top tweeted events of 2016. *CNN Money*. Retrieved October 18, 2017, from http://money.cnn.com/2016/12/06/technology/twitter-top-events-hashtags-2016/index.html.

Krause, M. (2011). Reporting and the transformations of the journalistic field: US news media, 1890–2000. *Media, Culture & Society, 33*(1), 89–104. https://doi.org/10.1177/0163443710385502.

Kravets, D. (2012). Twitter reluctantly coughs up occupy protester's data. *Wired*. Retrieved November 13, 2017, from https://www.wired.com/2012/09/twitter-occupy-data/.

Lasorsa, D. L., Lewis, S. C., & Holton, A. E. (2012). Normalizing Twitter. *Journalism Studies, 13*(1), 19–36. https://doi.org/10.1080/1461670X.2011.571825.

Lawlor, J. (2017, May 31). New muck rack survey: 72% of journalists say they are optimistic about the future. *Muck Rack*. Retrieved November 13, 2017, from https://muckrack.com/daily/2017/05/31/annual-journalist-survey-2017/.

Leetaru, K. (2017, February 17). How Twitter's new censorship tools are the Pandora's box moving us towards the end of free speech. *Forbes*. Retrieved from http://www.forbes.com/sites/kalevleetaru/2017/02/17/how-twitters-new-censorship-tools-are-the-pandoras-box-moving-us-towards-the-end-of-free-speech/.

Luckie, M. S. (2015, December 30). Twitter still has a major problem with employee diversity. *The Verge*. Retrieved November 13, 2017, from https://www.theverge.com/2015/12/30/10688126/twitter-diversity-jeffrey-siminoff.

McMillan Cottom, T. (2015). Who do you think you are?: When marginality meets academic microcelebrity. *Ada: A Journal of Gender, New Media, and Technology*, (7). Retrieved from http://adanewmedia.org/2015/04/issue7-mcmillancottom/.

Messina, C. (2017, August 23). The hashtag is 10: What the hashtag means to me ten years after its invention. *Medium*. Retrieved November 13, 2017, from https://medium.com/chris-messina/hashtag10-8e114c382b06.

Molyneux, L., Holton, A., & Lewis, S. C. (2017). How journalists engage in branding on Twitter: Individual, organizational, and institutional levels. *Information, Communication & Society*, *0*(0), 1–16. https://doi.org/10.1080/1369118X.2017.1314532.

Moses, L. (2015, July 6). Internet mysteries: How does Twitter's verification system work? *Digiday*. Retrieved November 13, 2017, from https://digiday.com/media/internet-mysteries-whats-twitters-verification-system/.

Onder, E. (2017, March 9). 140journos partners with Twitter to promote online safety & citizen jour. *Twitter*. Retrieved November 13, 2017, from https://blog.twitter.com/official/en_us/topics/company/2017/140journos-partners-with-twitter.html.

Ong, T. (2017, October 16). Thousands of women share experiences of sexual assault on Twitter through #MeToo. *The Verge*. Retrieved November 15, 2017, from https://www.theverge.com/2017/10/16/16481658/twitter-metoo-hashtag-wome-sexual-assault-share-experiences-harassment.

Oremus, W. (2017, March 5). Twitter's new order. *Slate*. Retrieved November 13, 2017, from http://www.slate.com/articles/technology/cover_story/2017/03/twitter_s_timeline_algorithm_and_its_effect_on_us_explained.html.

Peiser, J. (2017, October 15). A bot that makes Trump's tweets presidential. *The New York Times*. Retrieved November 13, 2017, from https://www.nytimes.com/2017/10/15/business/media/trump-twitter-bots.html.

Poell, T., & Rajagopalan, S. (2015). Connecting activists and journalists. *Journalism Studies*, *16*(5), 719–733. https://doi.org/10.1080/1461670X.2015.1054182.

Poepsel, M., & Painter, C. (2016). Alternative media and normative theory: A case of Ferguson, Missouri. *CM: Communication and Media*, *11*(36.) Retrieved from http://ecommons.udayton.edu/cmm_fac_pub/34.

Ramsey, D. X. (2016, January 6). Twitter's white-people problem. *The Nation*. Retrieved November 13, 2017, from https://www.thenation.com/article/twitters-white-people-problem/.

Reisinger, D. (2015, February 2). Facebook, Twitter report records for Super Bowl posts. *CNet*. Retrieved November 13, 2017, from https://www.cnet.com/news/facebook-twitter-report-records-for-super-bowl-posts/.

Removal requests. (2017). Twitter. Retrieved November 13, 2017, from https://transparency.twitter.com/en/removal-requests.html.

Santana, A. D., & Hopp, T. (2016). Tapping into a new stream of (personal) data: Assessing journalists' different use of social media. *Journalism & Mass Communication Quarterly, 93*(2), 383–408. https://doi.org/10.1177/1077699016637105.

Sengupta, S. (2012, July 16). Twitter releases statistics on government requests. *New York Times*. Retrieved November 13, 2017, from https://bits.blogs.nytimes.com/2012/07/02/twitter-releases-statistics-on-government-requests/.

Shearer, E., & Gottfried, J. (2017, September 7). *News use across social media platforms 2017*. Pew Research Center. Retrieved November 13, 2017, from http://www.journalism.org/2017/09/07/news-use-across-social-media-platforms-2017/.

Smith, A. (2014). *African Americans and technology use*. Pew Research Center. Retrieved November 13, 2017, from http://www.pewinternet.org/2014/01/06/african-americans-and-technology-use/.

Social media fact sheet. (2017, January 12). Pew Research Center. Retrieved November 13, 2017, from http://www.pewinternet.org/fact-sheet/social-media/.

Sweney, M. (2014, July 14). World Cup final breaks Facebook and Twitter records. *The Guardian*. Retrieved November 13, 2017, from http://www.theguardian.com/media/2014/jul/14/world-cup-final-breaks-facebook-and-twitter-records.

Tiku, N. (2014, August 21). Twitter headquarters has painted #Ferguson on its office wall. *Gawker*. Retrieved November 13, 2017, from http://valleywag.gawker.com/twitter-headquarters-has-painted-ferguson-on-its-offic-1625162041.

Trottier, D. (2013). *Identity problems in the Facebook era*. New York, NY: Routledge.

Tufekci, Z. (2017). *Twitter and tear gas: The power and fragility of networked protest*. New Haven, CT: Yale University Press.

Twitter total assets (quarterly). (2017). *YCharts*. Retrieved November 14, 2017, from https://ycharts.com/companies/TWTR/assets.

Twitter: Most-followed accounts worldwide as of November 2017. (2017). *Statista*. Retrieved November 13, 2017, from https://www.statista.com/statistics/273172/twitter-accounts-with-the-most-followers-worldwide/.

Varol, O., Ferrara, E., Davis, C. A., Menczer, F., & Flammini, A. (2017, May). *Online human-bot interactions: Detection, estimation, and characterization*.

International AAAI Conference on Web and Social Media. Retrieved May 17, 2018, from https://aaai.org/ocs/index.php/ICWSM/ICWSM17/paper/view/15587/14817.

Vis, F. (2013). Twitter as a reporting tool for breaking news. *Digital Journalism, 1*(1), 27–47. https://doi.org/10.1080/21670811.2012.741316.

Wang, S. (2017a, October 13). Twitter is crawling with bots and lacks incentive to expel them. *Bloomberg.* Retrieved November 13, 2017, from https://www.bloomberg.com/news/articles/2017-10-13/twitter-is-crawling-with-bots-and-lacks-incentive-to-expel-them.

Wang, S. (2017b, November 3). Twitter sidestepped Russian account warnings, former worker says. *Bloomberg.* Retrieved November 13, 2017, from https://www.bloomberg.com/news/articles/2017-11-03/former-twitter-employee-says-fake-russian-accounts-were-not-taken-seriously.

Willnat, L., & Weaver, D. H. (2014, May). *The American journalist in a digital age: A first look.* Paper presented at the International Communication Association Annual Conference, Seattle, WA. Retrieved November 13, 2017, from http://news.indiana.edu/releases/iu/2014/05/2013-american-journalist-key-findings.pdf.

Woodruff, B., & Ackerman, S. (2017, October 19). Twitter gives just a sliver of data to Senate Russia probe. *The Daily Beast.* Retrieved November 13, 2017, from https://www.thedailybeast.com/twitter-gives-just-a-sliver-of-data-to-senate-russia-probe.

#numbers. (2011, March 14). Twitter. Retrieved November 13, 2017, from https://blog.twitter.com/official/en_us/a/2011/numbers.html.

CHAPTER 3

Understanding the Gates: The Journalistic Field in a Time of Mediatization

The profession of American journalism is bound by its adherence to the norm of objectivity. Objectivity is part of the taken-for-granted norms of the field—or the field's doxa, in Bourdieu's terms. Despite this fact, no journalist, or piece of journalism for that matter, is ever truly objective. News stories are shaped by one's orientation to the world, the questions we ask (or do not), the people we talk to (or do not), the topics we cover, the frames we apply, and so on. Much of the same can be said about this book. It is not without perspective. In fact, the questions asked, the frames applied, and the sources consulted, each have a consequential bearing on the tone and tenor of the book. As such, it is worth explaining what is being asked and from what perspectives. In particular, what are the lenses are being applied and how do they frame and shape our view of the past, present, and future of American journalism? This chapter is devoted to answering these very questions by providing a contextualized examination of the theoretical frameworks that structure this book. If the introduction is the atlas, then this chapter is the legend, providing the tools necessary to more fully interpret the claims made throughout.

A central challenge of the book is to make better sense of the apparent transformations occurring at the intersections of journalism and activism in an age of Twitter. To meet that challenge requires a cogent examination of the theoretical and conceptual foundation on which the analysis will rest. Two main theoretical perspectives drive this project: field theory and mediatization. This chapter provides an overview of each perspective, with

© The Author(s) 2018
S. R. Barnard, *Citizens at the Gates*,
https://doi.org/10.1007/978-3-319-90446-7_3

a particular focus on the practice and profession of journalism, and then considers what they can render visible about the state of the journalistic field in a time of mediatization.

FIELD THEORY

Developed and popularized by French sociologist Pierre Bourdieu, field theory views social dynamics as occurring within the context of separate but interconnected fields of strategic action (Bourdieu 1993). In recent years, Bourdieu's field theory has been adapted for a variety of analytical applications, particularly in the contexts of media and journalism (Benson and Neveu 2005). Rodney Benson and Erik Neveu (2005, p. 4) explained, "Fields are arenas of struggle in which individuals and organizations compete, unconsciously and consciously, to valorize those forms of capital which they possess." Thus, as competitive, relational, and primarily institutional spaces, fields are made up of agents whose positions and dispositions are shaped by the dynamics of power and practice that structure action in any given context (Thompson 1991). While there are many elements to Bourdieu's field theory, let alone to other permutations of it (Fligstein and McAdam 2012; Swartz 1997, 2013), the theory can be divided into two equally important, mutually shaping segments: structure and practice. Although the interrelated nature of both segments will quickly become clear, each is addressed individually, starting at the level of practice.

Elements of Practice

One of field theory's greatest strengths as an analytical toolkit is the particular emphasis it places on analysis at the mezzo level. This requires a clear consideration of the dialectical relationship between practical matters of social action on the micro-level and more macro-level structural relations. Bourdieu theorized about how sociological dynamics operate at the level of practice, which led to a variety of conceptual categories, including what he called capital, habitus, and doxa (Bourdieu 1977, 1990, 1993). I refer to these concepts as *elements of practice* because they function as fundamental components of Bourdieu's theory of practice (see Fig. 3.1). None of the components are wholly unique or independent of the others, and their interaction constitutes sociological dynamics that are far greater than each individual part. That is, their combination defines the structure of fields, thus shaping the practices that occur within them.

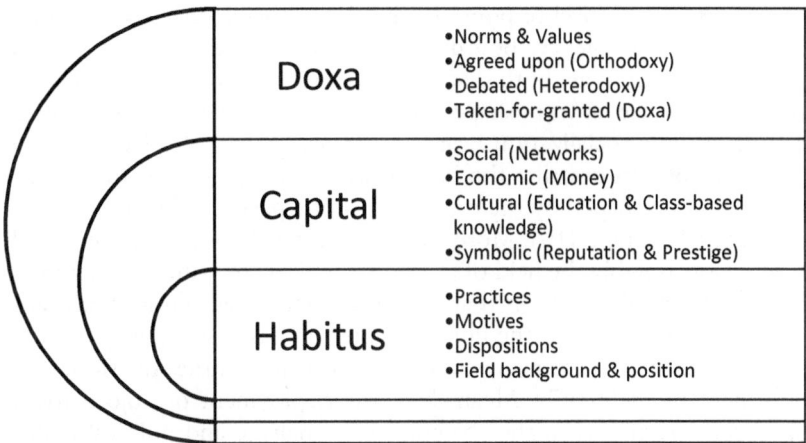

Fig. 3.1 Elements of practice

One basis of social action within fields occurs through the exchange of various types of capital. The concept of capital signifies the various aspects of power and privilege that "governs success in the field and the winning of the external or specific profits … which are at stake in the field" (Bourdieu 1993, p. 30). There are four primary types of capital in Bourdieu's (1993) framework (see also Swartz 1997). *Economic capital*, signified by monetary resources, allow its possessor access and influence that far exceeds those with less. *Cultural capital*, or class-based knowledge, tastes, and resources, is primarily attained through institutionalized forms of socialization (education, family, media, etc.) and can provide its possessor the kinds of cultural resources necessary for social interaction and mobility. *Social capital* represents one's ties to other social actors as well as the potential, realized or not, they hold for various opportunities. *Symbolic capital* denotes the status or recognition social actors receive, which imbue its possessor with increased influence (i.e., symbolic power). Seen in this light, it is clear how each type of resource represents a form of relational and discursive power (Reed 2013).

Relatedly, one's capital is combined with their experience and position in the field to (re)produce their habitus. According to Bourdieu's (1990, p. 53) conception, the *habitus* is a system of "durable, transposable dispositions, structured structures predisposed to function as structuring structures." As a novel response to the classic sociological consideration of structure and agency, Bourdieu's theorizing makes clear how social actors' dispositions are both shaped by social structures, while their application in practice, in turn, shapes social structures. The concept's consideration of how socialization bears upon social action also led Bourdieu (1990, p. 66) to describe the habitus as having a "feel for the game," which is often shaped by the expectations of a particular field (Bourdieu 1998, p. 81; Song 2010). Moreover, social actors' positioning among all fields, most notably the field of power, structures the habitus and imbues it with varying dispositions that, in turn, shape social action. For example, journalists' belief in the norm of objectivity is based largely on their socialization within the profession of journalism, and the American public sphere more broadly. Meanwhile, the deployment of objectivity, in practice, contributes to the shaping of journalistic and political reality. More specifically, Ida Willig's (Schultz 2007, p. 194) discussion of the journalistic habitus and its many iterations associated with particular subfields, like the "investigative reporter habitus," "editorial habitus," and "television habitus," also illustrates the shared nature of field-specific dispositions. Given today's hybridized field context, I theorize that a "networked habitus" is emerging throughout much of the journalistic and political fields (see Chap. 4).

The dynamics of practice and power within a field are inevitably tied to normative structures that guide and help define social action. Bourdieu (2005, p. 37) referred to a field's normative structure as *doxa*, which he defined as "the universe of tacit presuppositions that we accept as the natives of a certain society." In other words, doxa are a field's taken-for-granted values that go largely undiscussed and undisputed (Bourdieu 1977). In comparison to doxa, Bourdieu offered the concepts of *heterodoxy* and *orthodoxy* to signify values that are up for discussion and debate (heterodoxy), as well as those that are not (orthodoxy). Willig (Schultz 2007, p. 194) defined a distinctly *journalistic doxa* as "a set of professional beliefs which tend to appear as evident, natural and self-explaining norms of journalistic practice." Altogether, these concepts make up much of Bourdieu's theoretical model. Thus, as actors are socialized into a field, they start acquiring field-specific capital, forming a situated habitus, and eventually become accustomed to the various doxa of that field.

Practice is a product of the interaction between capital and habitus in consideration of the field as additional, but integral, context. Bourdieu (1984, p. 101; Swartz 1997, p. 141) offered this equation:

$$\left[(habitus)(capital)\right] + field = practice$$

While this formulation may have been a satirical critique of positivism rather than a serious theoretical clarification (Savage and Silva 2013, p. 115), it is a useful expression of the basic terms on which practice occurs. Furthermore, this formulation helps to articulate the overarching contention of field theory: practice is a dialectical process in which structuring structures are continuously (re)produced. This is as true for the journalistic and political fields as it is for any other, although recent shifts in journalism's structural and practical elements raise particular questions about how the process will work in an age of mediatization, which will be discussed shortly. Each of the concepts outlined above serves an elemental purpose in the functioning and makeup of social fields, and will be examined in greater depth later in the book, especially in Chap. 4.

Structural Dynamics

If the elements of practice are part and parcel of a field's structure, then they inevitably shape the dynamics of power and position that come to define and dominate any particular field. Nevertheless, the structure of social relations within and across fields may vary greatly, especially when power is contested. The political, economic, and cultural fields tend to hold sway over the nature of social relations, including shaping the orthodox norms and values in less influential fields (Swartz 2013). Accordingly, Bourdieu came to refer to this arrangement as the field of power, which is actually a meta-field that cuts across and exceeds all other fields (Couldry 2012). Each field has enough autonomy for social action to play out on relatively distinct but varying terms. At the same time, field relations are somewhat predictable, taking on patterned trends that shape action and transformation. Thus, the structural makeup of a field is contingent on a number of key components—including, but not limited to, the history of its initial formation, its relations with other fields, as well as processes of distinction and boundary maintenance. Each of these factors will be addressed individually.

Field Formation and Professionalization

The long journey toward the formation and professionalization of the journalistic field took place over the course of numerous epochs. What started as citizens engaging politically by publishing information and distributing it as far as the technology and market would afford, slowly grew into a professional field with its own distinct set of practices. While such professionally structured relations were not yet prominent in the days of the early American republic, where the publishing of news was still first and foremost a political act, the Gilded Age and the oncoming boom of the newspaper business provided an ideal-typical context for a distinctly journalistic field to take shape. As Jean Chalaby (1998, p. 1) explained:

> [T]he profession of the journalist and the journalistic discourse are the products of the emergence, during the second half of the nineteenth century, of a specialized and increasingly autonomous field of discursive production, the journalistic field. The formation of the journalistic field had a tremendous impact on the discourse produced by the press. The relations of production which began to prevail within this emerging field originated new discursive practices and strategies, new discursive norms and new discursive phenomena. Only when these new discursive practices emerged did the press begin to produce a discourse that is distinct from other discursive forms and peculiar to the journalistic field.

As the formation of the journalistic field continued, growth and specialization also increased within news organizations.

By the Progressive Era, the parameters of the journalistic field had developed and an emphasis was increasingly placed on professionalization. According to Michael Schudson and Susan Tifft (2005, p. 18), professionalization is "the differentiation of journalists as a distinct occupational group with distinctive norms and traditions and, depending on the time and place, some degree of autonomy from political parties and publishers." Indeed, although many journalistic practices can be dated back much further, the decades-long progression toward an autonomous, professionalized institution with formal organizations, norms, and values is said to have begun in the 1860s and 1870s (Krause 2011).

If the Gilded Age was the time when the journalistic field was formed, the Progressive Era was when the field went through the most obvious stages of professionalization (McChesney 2008, p. 29; Schudson 1978). According to Monika Krause (2011, p. 93):

> The period between 1890 and 1914 brought a rapid expansion of the newspaper industry and a consolidation of journalism as a distinct area of practice. In this time, we see a rise in professional journalistic education, associations and awards, which mark the consolidation of a field with a set of stakes and status internal to it.

While journalism was not yet established as a professional field in the early twentieth century, "professionalizing tendencies were at work" (Schudson and Tifft 2005, p. 24). Walter Williams, the founder of the country's first journalism school at the University of Missouri, opened the school primarily as a reaction to the political-economic shifts shaping the practice of journalism (Weinberg 2008, pp. 13–14; see also Krause 2011, p. 94). At the same time, journalism schools were also being formed at other universities around the country and beyond.

Other examples of developments congruent with the formation and professionalization of the journalistic field during the Progressive Era include the development of a code of ethics, special prizes, formalized training, national conferences, and various professional associations (Krause 2011; Mott 1962). These efforts helped to transform American journalism from a craft, learned primarily through apprenticeship, into a profession with formalized training. Thus, from the perspective of field theory, journalism is not merely "the business or practice of producing and disseminating information about contemporary affairs of general public interest and importance" (Schudson 2003, p. 11), but rather, a collective of agents and practices that structure the products and processes of news work. Such institutionalization played an integral role in the formation of "journalistic rules," which helped define journalism as a professional field (Kumar 2009, p. 140).

During this time, journalists gained even greater autonomy, formed professional associations, and began uniting around an evolving set of norms and practices. Workplace organization also continued its evolution, as the growth of the news business, implementation of new technologies, and further professionalization led to an increasingly specialized field with emergent subfields. Although the journalistic field's structure and practices remained in motion for much of the next century, its basic foundation was set during the 50-year span of the 1860s to the 1910s. This time period served as what many historical sociologists refer to as a "switch point," where the future of the profession was inextricably shaped.

Inter-Field Relations (a.k.a. Autonomy and Heteronomy)

Media scholars have long been concerned with how economic pressures bear on the practices and profession of journalism. The tension between the news and business "desks" has existed, and persisted, since the birth of news organizations. Despite this fact, the field of professional journalism was founded largely in the name of political and economic interests.

Indeed, the influence of political and economic factors runs so deep that journalistic autonomy is often seen as having been granted by the owners and operators of early journalistic institutions, rather than by journalists granting rights to owners in selling their labor (McChesney 2008). The fact that history is rarely written from the latter perspective is telling, in and of itself, of the power and influence wielded by political and economic forces within the journalistic field.

Beyond the primacy of political and economic influences throughout American journalism's history, technological and cultural factors have also played a significant role in the field's structural relations. Not only have communication technologies afforded new capabilities with each innovation, but cultural developments have also provided an important context for journalistic practices to occur. For example, consider the nature of newswork today, which often entails a growing expectation of being present and engaging on social media. Institutional policies on social media engagement vary, with some preferring web-first, while others are accepting of social-first practices, where content from live-blogging and other forms of public note-taking can be polished and published later. However, all of these policies are shaped by competing goals to drive traffic to their stories (i.e., revenue to their institution) while adhering to journalistic norms such as verification and objectivity. This pressure to produce more content, and to "do more with less," which is discussed at greater length in Chaps. 4 and 9, serves to erode journalists' autonomy.

Of course, other indicators point to strain at the borders of the journalistic field. Roughly a century after its formation, the field of American journalism began another time of reformation. An era of rapid cultural and technological revolution came along with the market crisis of 2008, which was marked by economic instability from declining and unreliable revenue streams. This led to the failure or downsizing of many papers, and thus, a loss of hundreds of thousands of newspaper jobs since 1990 (Greenslade 2016). Blogging had become a standard publishing format for the web, and social media platforms were growing in popularity, thus offering unparalleled opportunity for instant dissemination and public engagement. This age of transformation, spurred by the instability of the media market, provided opportunities for—and in many cases, required—nonelite members of the field to adapt new practices for producing and distributing journalism. It also lowered barriers to entry, thus "open[ing] up the field of possibility" (Butler 2006, p. viii) for new actors to help shape the field. But the problem of limited resources remains a constant constraint on newswork, regardless of professional status.

The question of autonomy—or the extent to which an individual or collective can act without constraint—has long been of interest to sociologists, as evidenced by the field's emphasis on the dialectic of structure and agency. Indeed, it is a key factor in understanding the terms on which social action occurs. Thus, the journalistic field's level of autonomy or heteronomy, and thus, its structural composition, is determined in no small part by its relation to other fields. For example, Krause (2011, p. 91) summarized American journalism's autonomic eras as they relate to economic and political conditions:

> Under favorable economic and political conditions, during two periods of high autonomy, 1890 to 1914 and 1945 to 1970, reporting practices, including local and investigative reporting, flourished. In two other periods, 1915 to 1945 and 1970 to 2000, the field's autonomy was challenged and local and investigative reporting declined.

Journalism's ties to economic, political, technological, and cultural fields can explain much of this variance. Indeed, the extent to which one field is reliant (heteronomous) or not (autonomous) on others will bear importantly on its structure as well as the practices it normalizes. Although the majority of journalists rely on the values of objectivity as the profession's primary barrier, designed as an attempt to control for the inevitable heteronomy felt by their integral personal and institutional ties to other fields, most citizen journalists find themselves in a very different position. With relatively few formal ties to the political and economic fields, little to no institutional oversight, lower standards for objectivity, and a distinctly different habitus, the subfield of citizen journalism is generally defined by much greater autonomy.

While most professional journalists enjoy relative autonomy in their everyday practices, many external constraints still bear on them. The political and economic interests of their employers play an important role in the work they do, whether in the form of story assignment and framing, diminishing funding for investigative work, increased workload, or otherwise. Many reporters have become accustomed to doing more with less, and many who have not are struggling to piece together a salary while juggling multiple freelance assignments. As Nicole Cohen (2015, p. 100) made clear, traditional journalism companies are under pressure to cut costs and maximize efficiencies through a variety of strategies, including "outsourcing, unpaid labor, metrics and measurement, and automation."

While some of these pressures may be enabled or amplified by the affordances of new technologies themselves (Paulussen 2012), they fall squarely in line with the longstanding institutional imperatives of capitalist institutions. In a field that has long been driven and defined by profit orientation, it makes little sense to assert that new technologies play a unique and alienating role in contemporary newswork. More generally, workers' relationship with technology has long been tumultuous, as in the infamous case of the Luddites, who feared a deskilling of their work, and thus a devaluing of their labor. Nevertheless, in a profession of civil service and an age of networked individualism (Rainie and Wellman 2012), there are ample reasons to question the (negative) deterministic effects of technologies on the labor process. If digital journalists began incorporating Twitter into their daily routines long before their institutions were ready to adopt—let alone mandate—its use, then it is worth considering why, and to what effects. At the same time, a great many of today's digital journalists now have little choice but to maintain a social media presence, at least to help publicize stories and provide a semblance of public engagement. In this sense, the added work of managing social media accounts is partly a consequence of economic pressure, whether externally from their employers, or internally as a means to greater journalistic capital.

Furthermore, the appearance of autonomy from the political field should not be confused for genuine autonomy. The journalistic value of objectivity and its attainment of doxic status throughout much of the American professional field noted at the beginning of this chapter, provides a powerful smokescreen that has been most successful at masking the latent political ideologies of journalistic acts and accounts. Jay Rosen's pointed criticisms of the "view from nowhere" (2003) and "he said, she said" journalism (2009) make clear just how distorting and politically effective so-called objective reporting can be. Although most legacy news institutions in the United States are no longer owned and operated with explicitly political goals, most are still at the least implicitly promoting them. Fox News provides an ideal-typical illustration of how political ideology can combine with economic motive to produce influential, if largely distorting, media content.

Given these constraining factors, journalistic autonomy remains a key component in the field and necessary for its actors to have the ability to practice the kind of reporting for which the field was founded and on which American democracy largely depends (McChesney 2000). In order to ensure relative autonomy, especially from the political and economic fields,

American journalists spent decades erecting "walls" between the news and business offices and drawing "lines" between facts and opinion. Nonetheless, "the strongest of walls and the boldest of lines bring journalists no closer to the levels of control where forces beyond the newsroom and even beyond journalism define the limits of journalistic autonomy" (Glasser and Gunther 2005, p. 390). This is where the growing number of new actors entering the journalistic field, both through traditional (professional) and nontraditional (citizen) paths, become increasingly relevant.

Beyond the more or less explicit forms of censorship mentioned earlier, many journalists simply become socialized to the realities of the heteronomous field in which they reside. The result is often an implicit disposition toward stories that are less likely to challenge the status quo or the interests of powerful individuals and institutions (Alterman 2003; Jensen 2015). Despite the challenges facing legacy journalists, countless instances of critical, public service journalism persist. And despite numerous obstacles, many legacy organizations still fund real, investigative journalism. These cases are made possible by suitable funding models where the firewall separating "church and state" remains intact (McChesney 2008). Notable portions of this work are supported by not-for-profit funding models, such as ProPublica and First Look Media, who have consciously constructed less penetrable buffers from such heteronomy.

These inter-field relations have undergone various changes throughout recent history, and thus, the journalistic field's autonomic and heteronomic dynamics have also varied significantly. The reformation of citizens' journalistic habitus, or what Adrienne Russell (2016) referred to as "hacktivist sensibilities" provide new opportunities for influence via collaboration and competition, as the values, practices, and boundaries increasingly overlap with those of the traditional journalistic field. Field theory has shown that the dynamics of the journalistic field do not transpire within a vacuum of journalistic elites. Rather, the journalistic field is situated among the broader network of fields (power, political, economic, cultural, etc.), which all have the potential to influence each other in various ways (Benson and Neveu 2005).

Boundary Maintenance and Reformation at the Intersection of Practice and Profession

Much is at stake in the battle to control the borders of the journalistic field. While droves of dedicated amateurs may not be lining the sidewalks outside of media employment offices, their overwhelming presence at journalism's gates—the practices and processes through which information becomes news—is cause for much conflict. Beyond the obvious power that comes with the rights to broadcast media, another type of power is at stake: symbolic power. This type of power entails the capacity to produce and transmit symbolic forms, which is a result of having amassed significant symbolic capital, and thus, field position (Thompson 1995, p. 17; see also Bourdieu 1991; Tang and Yang 2011). Symbolic power is traditionally a tool of elite institutions (media, government, corporations), and thus wielded by elite actors to shape the norms, values, and ideologies of particular groups. Therefore, it is applicable here as a force that defines (il) legitimate journalistic action. This concept will also be used later in the book to help explain the growing ability of networked publics to exercise counter-power using media such as Twitter.

Such dynamics of legitimation are also increasingly shaped by what Nick Couldry has termed "media meta-capital" (2003, 2012, 2014). If *media-(related) capital* refers to the resources social actors draw on that are tied to various forms of media influence, and *meta-capital* refers to a super-ordinate capability to influence other forms of power (capital) across fields, then *media meta-capital* refers to the capacity of media to "exercise power over other forms of capital" (Couldry 2014, pp. 59–60). In other words, media meta-capital is an emergent form of networked capital that, due in large part to the growing ubiquity and symbolic power of media, can fundamentally alter relations of power and competition in other fields. This dynamic can be seen at work in many of the cases examined throughout the book, including the journalistic field's ongoing battles of legitimation.

As described earlier, American journalism has its own history of field formation and institutionalization, but it has never been so formal as to officially define and regulate card-carrying members. Thus, while the question of *who* is a journalist may seem trivial to many, its significance has grown increasingly important. The entire endeavor of boundary policing leads to contentious conclusions about who deserves this label, and who does not, most notably when a press pass is required. This may also include debating what constitutes "fake news," which pundits and publishers rely on slanted half-truths, or what to make of "advocacy journalism" with verified facts but a clear political bias. Needless to say, "*What* is journalism?" is a much better question, since it is shaped less by a pressure to police boundaries and more by efforts to define and operationalize the work of a practice and profession from a diverse set of positions (Jarvis 2013).

The political and juridical fields have an obvious form of symbolic power in this instance: their policies, rhetoric, and rulings on where the *de jure* and de facto boundaries of journalism begin and end could bear greatly on the legal courses of action the state may take to prosecute bloggers, activists, and whistleblowers. For example, based on where an actor is positioned in the journalistic field according to the views held within political or juridical fields, consequences may be different for leaking or publicizing revealing information about the horrors of war or illegal spying programs. It is from this position that Senator Dick Durbin argued, "Journalists should have reasonable legal protections to do their important work. But not every blogger, tweeter or Facebook user is a 'journalist'" (Preston 2013, para. 1). If media shield laws protected everyone who committed acts of journalism in the public interest, then it would be significantly harder for the state to help perpetuate the status quo. This demonstrates the dual significance of symbolic power and media meta-capital in this instance: first, to define the legitimacy of the journalistic actor, and thus their right to be heard; and second, to help shape public opinion through acts of journalism.

Much of what is at stake within fields has to do with the power to define who and what constitutes membership and action in said field. Thus, the subfield of large-scale production, including educational and legacy media institutions, tends to seek a monopoly over the right to define acceptable journalistic acts and actors. While occupying a dominant position within the field often means possessing various forms of capital required to successfully control this definition, countless challenges to this authority are increasingly emerging. The "bloggers vs. journalists" dynamic is a prime example of this contentious relationship. The emergence of the blogosphere in the mid-2000s provided citizens the opportunity to wield much greater influence within the journalistic field. As Schudson and Tifft (2005, p. 41) put it, "Historically, the press had mobilized citizens; now, it was citizens who mobilized the press." One important way bloggers engage journalists is by donning the "self-appointed role as watchdogs of the watchdogs" (Singer 2007, p. 89; Vos et al. 2012). Or, as Stephen Cooper (2006) put it, this increasingly networked body of citizens functions as a "fifth estate" who keep watch over how the media's "gates" are functioning, and what flows through them (Bruns 2005). The prominence of this self-appointed role will emerge as a common theme throughout many of the case studies presented in this book. Nevertheless, the growth of citizens' role in the journalistic field, and the changes that ensue, should also be seen as an expression of media meta-capital.

As boundaries continue to blur between politics and journalism, reporting and (micro)blogging, producing and consuming, some of those most dedicated to journalistic traditions have begun working even harder to guard the gates to the field. Throughout my years of digital-ethnographic experiences on Twitter, I encountered countless instances of journalistic actors situated solidly within the field of large-scale production pontificating about the virtues of traditional journalism and the vices of journalistic acts carried out by nonprofessionals. Ironically, these rants were usually published in blog form. More broadly, many scholars have examined the ongoing tensions between professional and citizen journalism, the latter of which is often synonymous with blogging (Hirst and Treadwell 2011; Lowrey 2006; Singer 2003). Despite these ongoing struggles, "there is no other criterion for membership of a field than the objective fact of producing effects within it" (Bourdieu 1993, p. 42). Thus, by creating such a stir, those at the border of the journalistic field have, *ipso facto*, entered the field already.

Many scholars and media professionals have pointed out the ongoing and remarkable shift toward a journalistic field more open to influence from nonprofessional actors (Deuze 2007; Lennett et al. 2011; Reese et al. 2007; Rosen 2006; Ross 2011). The Open Society Foundations have produced a number of reports that detail the extent to which "old boundaries of the journalistic profession are ... being challenged" (Lennett et al. 2011, p. 53). As Nadine Jurrat (2011, p. 8) explained:

> The audience is not only connected vertically to people in power, such as editors and politicians, but also horizontally to each other, enabling them to mobilize. The flow of information is no longer controlled from the top. Readers are becoming reporters, citizens and journalists share one identity.... [I]n principle, anyone with access to the internet can influence the news agenda.

Of course, the growing potential for citizens to act within the journalistic field does not mean that all, or even most, will actually do so. In addition to the requisite economic capital (time and money) and cultural capital (education and technical literacies), many other forms of journalistic, intellectual, and politically oriented capital and dispositions serve as necessary conditions for entrance into the journalistic field.

Still, there is ample reason to view American journalism as a distinct field, especially given the criticism of the profession as overly rigid, exclusionary, and increasingly committed to furthering many of its already doxic distinctions. C.W. Anderson (2011, para. 12) summarized the criticism this way, "Professions are monopolistic guilds designed to raise barriers to entry in order to maintain professional privilege at the expense of the public good." This is partially true, evidenced by how the vast majority of professional journalism institutions have reacted to the changing structure of the news environment over the past couple decades by appearing to adapt while clinging to old and increasingly inadequate strategies (Zuckerman 2017). It is increasingly clear that the journalistic field of today, and especially tomorrow, will continue to feel the pull of nonprofessional journalistic actors. As the title of this book suggests, the citizens are at the gates.

Recent work on the "boundaries of journalism" has demonstrated the importance of examining what happens at the edges of the journalistic field, especially as it crosses over into the political realm (Carlson and Lewis 2015; Kreiss et al. 2015). As the remaining chapters will show, these boundaries overlap in many instances. An examination of what is occurring in such spaces necessarily entails a consideration of various structural and practical consequences following (de)professionalization and their synthetic counterpart: hybridization. Within this context, such analyses also shed light on the myriad ways that media meta-capital bear on field dynamics.

Given all the conflicts inherent within the tensions between professional and citizen journalists, it is easy to overlook the essential ties that bind the two groups together. However invisible, this common ground begins not with particular acts of journalism, but rather, with the "collective belief in the game" (Bourdieu 1996, p. 230). This shared belief, which Bourdieu termed *illusio*, is a necessary precondition for action in any field, and is "simultaneously the precondition and the product of the very functioning of the game" (Bourdieu 1996, p. 230). Indeed, Bourdieu's view of social action emphasizes the importance of conflict and competition as definitively (re)structuring the field and (re)locating its agents.

A field's collective decision-making process about how to manage their boundaries is central to its shape and trajectory. Writing about the structure of the artistic field, Bourdieu (1996, p. 230) explained how the *nomos*, or the "principle of legitimate vision and division" is what permits "the separation between art and non-art, between the 'true' artists, worthy of being publicly and officially exhibited, and the others, condemned to oblivion by the rejection of the jury." Therefore, this source of conflict is frequently the field's equivalent of "picking winners and losers" before the next game even begins. Of course, this is a highly consequential process, as equally affirming for the winners as it is dejecting for the losers of this meta-game.

Fields undergo change based on various internal and external dynamics. Shifts in the definition, value, and possession of differing forms of capital can lead to profound changes in a field's makeup. While changes within fields can clearly come as a result of outside influence, a careful examination of the dynamics at play in or around a field's borders are at least as significant as those occurring externally. Most notably, it is often new entrants to a field who regularly challenge taken-for-granted norms and serve, *ipso facto*, as agents of innovation. According to Bourdieu (1996, pp. 239–240):

> It is true that the initiative for change can be traced back, almost by definition, to new (meaning younger) entrants. These are the ones who are also the most deprived of specific capital, and who (in a universe where to exist is to be different, meaning to occupy a distinct and distinctive position) only exist in so far as—without needing to want to—they manage and assert their identity (that is, their difference) and get it known and recognized ('make a name for oneself') by imposing new modes of thought and expression which break with current modes of thought and hence are destined to disconcert by their 'obscurity' and their 'gratuitousness'.

Countless other examples could be given of such new, innovative entrants in today's journalistic field. Many are operating at the margins of the field, on Twitter and beyond, producing work that often pushes the boundaries of journalism, advocacy, and activism, thus contributing to journalism's ongoing reformation (Lindner and Larson 2017). As the remaining chapters in this book will show, boundary actors include both professional and citizen journalists, many of whom also intersect notably with the political field, on Twitter and beyond.

MIXING IN MEDIATIZATION

Despite the analytical strengths of field theory, it is somewhat limited by its lack of emphasis on media as well as its compartmentalization of social action into distinct fields. While much of Bourdieu's theorizing has proven to be widely applicable, withstanding the test of time, it is not entirely suited to account for the transformative effects of the twenty-first-century technological revolution (Couldry 2014, p. 59). Thus, this book retains the theoretical bases established by Bourdieu's field theory, mixing in insights from mediatization to adopt or adapt concepts that adequately address the nature of contemporary social relations.

Today, in a "post-factual" society driven more and more by echo chambers and algorithmically shaped, homophilious social networks, it is easier to succumb to confirmation bias (willingly or not) than it is to engage in diverse and rational dialogue. Furthermore, in an age when networked individuals are able to do the work of publishers, the trends of sharing, amplification, and rapid-response reaction are ever-evolving. This, among other political, cultural, and technological shifts, leads to an emergent media logic where power is increasingly contingent upon individual and collective abilities to command attention and guide action using information and communication technologies.

Such an expression of media meta-capital is just one example of the role media play in the changing structures and practices of social fields. As Couldry (2012) explained, recent techno-cultural transformations have led many scholars to contend with the possibility of a new "media logic." This was meant to highlight the ways in which the ubiquity of media led to patterned social experiences, and thus, increased social influence, across media platforms and formats. Building off of David Altheide and Robert Snow's (1979) initial formulation, many have questioned whether or not the concept of "logic" captures the essence of social change in mediatized worlds, let alone whether or not such effects are universal (Couldry 2012; Hepp and Krotz 2014). Given the diversity of media platforms and publishers, as well as the extent to which they are constantly being reworked and (re)constructed, it is clear that they do not all follow a universal logic.

As many have suggested, the ongoing convergence of technologies and collapsing of contexts seen so frequently in networked environments has ushered in new dynamics of social relation that require new concepts and perspectives to fully explain and examine. That is, while the term "logic" may be too abstract, the more specific concepts from field theory—habitus, capital, doxa, and practice—can be seen as taking on new forms in increasingly mediatized field contexts. Thus, in the following chapters, I develop and advance the concepts of "networked habitus" and "mediatized superstructure." *Networked habitus*, which can be thought of as the socially constructed practices and dispositions displayed by individual actors, provides a lens to examine the micro-level articulations of mediatization. Additionally, *mediatized superstructure* is used to explain macro-level flows of information and social relations in an increasingly mediated society.[1] Furthermore, in addition to drawing on field theory's traditional conceptual toolkit, I occasionally adapt and deploy Couldry's conception of *media meta-capital* to account for emergent forms of power that operate across fields.

Wheras Bourdieu preferred to refer to power operating as a "field," it is not, and never was, a field in the traditional sense, but rather, a meta-field that surrounds all social relations. While Bourdieu's conceptualization of "symbolic power," or the "power of constructing [social] reality," was a step in this direction, it was developed prior to the onslaught of a hyper-mediated society (Bourdieu 1990, p. 166; Couldry 2012, p. 138). Nonetheless, field theory is indeed adaptable to the study of communication in the twenty-first century, as it has been for the study of journalism over the last two decades (Benson 1999; Benson and Neveu 2005), on par with the similar tradition of neo-Marxian adaptations (Fuchs 2017). Indeed, this book aims to examine how societal-level shifts in media alter the dynamics of the journalistic field. Additionally, though the specific relations may differ, a similar argument could be made of nearly all other fields today. However, as the conceptual framework outlined above suggests, accomplishing this task requires the help of additional compatible theoretical tools.

Scholars of mediatization contend that what is happening is a result of more than a shift in logic; it is fundamentally transforming the form and function of modern social relations. For example, recent studies on the intersections of culture and mediatization define it as "the process whereby culture and society to an increasing degree become dependent on the media and their logic" (Hjarvard 2013, p. 17), or as "cultures that are 'moulded' by the media" (Hepp 2013, p. 2). While the forces of mediatization are far from deterministic, the language used makes it clear that the influence of media is expanding to the point of being ubiquitous. In an increasingly mediatized society, channels for participation and influence are more open, making room for greater opportunity to disrupt the doxa of a given field. Others have taken less optimistic positions, of course, whether minimizing the impact of technologies, emphasizing negative implications (Morozov 2012; Turkle 2012), or linking these changes back to other fields of origin (McChesney 2013). The position taken throughout this book is that the ongoing technological and communicative revolutions are altering the way field dynamics work, in ways that are disruptive to institutional power, and which often—though not always—result in a net benefit for networked individuals.

Andreas Hepp and Fredrich Krotz (2014, p. 3) outlined two schools of thought within studies of mediatization. According to the *institutionalist* tradition, the concept "refers to the adaptation of different social fields or systems like politics or religion, for example, to these institutionalized rules." Alternatively, the *social-constructivist* perspective "moves the role of various media into the foreground as part of the process of the construction of social and cultural reality" (p. 4). Thus, mediatization "refers to the process of a construction of socio-cultural reality by communication," and mediatization studies analyze "the status of various media within this process" (p. 4). In other words, it refers to the "changed dimensionality of the social world" due to the growing ubiquity of new media forms and content across fields (Couldry 2014, p. 58).

This book aims to synthesize both approaches to mediatization. This is done by applying a broad analytical framework that examines both practical and institutional dynamics at the boundaries of journalism as they manifest on Twitter. Whereas the focus on professional journalism through the lens of field theory clearly signals the significance of the institutionalist framework, interest in the particular role of Twitter as well as the norms, practices, and data/objects produced on it requires a consideration of processes of media's role in the social construction of reality. As Couldry (2012) suggested, the concept of mediatization is not universally applied, and as such, it is flexible enough to accommodate a wide range of applications. At the same time, field theory is adaptable enough to accommodate mediatization as an emergent social process (Couldry 2014). Couldry's concern, and one that guides this work, is with developing a more general conception capable of explaining how media-shaped logics can shape practice across fields, while also remaining consistent with Bourdieu's theorizing.

This is precisely why Couldry developed the concept of media meta-capital to explain media's growing, yet not universal or deterministic, influence on matters occurring within and across field boundaries. But given the apparent ontological disagreements between field theory and some currents of mediatization research, Couldry argues that a true form of *media capital*, which is a super-ordinate capital based on media influence and not bound to particular fields, is not yet possible because its influence does not yet operate according to a singular logic across all fields. However, "in the future, media capital, as a new basic form of capital, *might* emerge, from the spreading influence of media meta-capital across more and more separate fields" (Couldry 2014, p. 59). At the time of this writing, it is fair to say that media meta-capital has indeed spread throughout a variety of fields. As the following chapters will demonstrate, the growing saturation of social media such as Twitter throughout pivotal fields like journalism and politics is helping solidify the significance of such media and ushering in an advanced stage of mediatization.

The focus on Twitter is not meant to overemphasize or isolate the role of particular technologies, nor to suggest that Twitter itself is a deterministic or even primary variable. It also does not deny the many downsides to the fields' growing reliance on digitally mediated communication, including pressure to work longer hours and produce more content on a variety of platforms, increased marginalization for members of historically oppressed groups, and the ability to shirk the work of traditional social movement organizing (Russell 2016). In fact, the book will consider each of these concerns. Instead, *Citizens at the Gates* is focused on teasing out some of the key transformations occurring at the boundaries of a mediatized journalistic field by examining certain objects of journalism (Anderson and De Maeyer 2015) and activism produced by some of the fields' most networked practitioners. The cases examined throughout the book highlight a variety of implications for the ongoing trends of mediatization and field transformation, in general, and for the shifts at the boundaries of networked journalism and political activism, specifically.

Like the political implications of journalism, the theme of nontraditional political actors (a.k.a. "average citizens") engaging in politics is not new. However, the reach of their voices and the way in which their influence resonates within and translates across a variety of fields demonstrates the significance of media meta-capital and a mediatized superstructure. Under a mediatized superstructure, the nature of social relations is couched in the logics of communicative action, where influence can grow and spread in a more rhizomatic and less institutionalized manner (Castells 2015). Thus, a *mediatized superstructure* is an assemblage of networked individuals, techniques, and technologies that, once populated by a critical mass, provide a relatively stable and persistent mechanism for the vetting and spreading of information. This has also given rise to what danah boyd (2014, p. 8) referred to as *networked publics*, or "publics that are restructured by networked technologies. As such, they are simultaneously (1) the space constructed through networked technologies and (2) the imagined community that emerges as a result of the intersection of people, technology, and practice." What boyd's conception helps illustrate is a dynamic seen throughout much of the book: an array of networked individuals working to collectively hold media and political institutions accountable.

It has long been said that the structure of the journalistic field is in a state of transition, given the ongoing mediatization of the profession, as well as of society writ large. Whereas the journalistic field of previous decades was dominated by a shrinking number of media conglomerates, the emergence of the web and social networks has, to an extent, altered the course of media history. While legacy news institutions still control the core of the media market, members of the networked public are playing an increasingly significant role in workings of the field. One significant and highly visible way they do this is through the use of Twitter and other web-based platforms. Whether by creating original content, commenting, or sharing others' accounts, many engaged members of networked communities play an important role in creating or shaping media coverage (Bruns 2014).

While traditional journalistic structures remain in place, the growth of opportunities for nonprofessional actors to shape the traditional gatekeeping processes marks a notable shift in the everyday structure and functioning of the journalistic field. Indeed, as Bourdieu (1996, p. 225) explained:

> The great upheavals arise from the eruption of newcomers who, by the sole effect of their number and their social quality, import innovation regarding products or techniques of production, and try or claim to impose on the field of production ... a new mode of evaluation of products.

This book is devoted to unpacking just how networked publics perform this function, and what implications these evolving practices have for the journalistic field.

THE FIFTH ESTATE? ACTION AT JOURNALISM'S GATES

If we accept Rosen's (2006) assertion that "the people formerly known as the audience" have entered the journalistic field, then we might ask: what are they up to? In other words, what is going on at journalism's gates, and what role is the networked public playing? Because there are still few studies that have addressed this question empirically, this book aims to help fill the gap.

Stephen Cooper (2006) explained that much of the networked public's efforts can be found in the battle over framing and gatekeeping. If gatekeeping entails deciding which facts and views are included in the news, then framing is about deciding the context in which those facts and views are placed (Entman 1993; Shoemaker and Vos 2009). Given the tendency for legacy media to rely on elite sources (Artwick 2014) and to therefore frame stories with a bias toward the status quo (Bennett et al. 2004), then there is reason to believe that networked publics have an interest in contesting the stories and frames regularly deployed in legacy media (Bruns and Highfield 2015).

William Dutton (2009) expanded Cooper's consideration of bloggers as a monitor of the journalism establishment to theorize their role as a "fifth estate." While professional journalists and journalism organizations perform key democratic functions by providing necessary information and facilitating dialogue, they are not alone in being able to serve this role.

Despite the apparent competition between legacy media and networked publics, it is a mistake to assume that the growth of the latter necessitates competition with, or a replacement of, the former. Indeed, professional and nonprofessional journalists alike can contribute to the flow of news and news criticism with little risk of crossing wires. At the same time, the burgeoning of citizen journalism practices can help diversify the news, and even improve accountability through public forms of media criticism (Dutton 2009, p. 9). These goals can be accomplished through many avenues.

Axel Bruns' (2014, p. 231) notion of "gatewatching," which "largely focuses on the republishing, publicising, contextualisation and curation of existing material rather than the development of substantial new journalistic content [sic]" is one important example. Even more proactive users, which Bruns (2014) termed "gatecrashers," have been known to create and distribute content of their own, often through social media channels. Although Bruns' conception of gatewatching has emphasized the role of "produsers"—a now-common hybridizing of producer and user—in republishing existing content on news aggregation sites, the practice has broadened to include broader functions of media criticism (Bruns 2005). Given the longstanding watchdog tradition in journalism, as well as the public's civic duty to "watch the watchers," I seek to reconsider the work of networked publics who amplify and critique media coverage. Thus, if *gatekeeping* signifies professional media workers' responsibility and relative autonomy to decide what becomes news, and *gatewatching* entails observation, amplification, and criticism of professional media work with an emphasis on holding publishers accountable to the public, then *gatecrashing* is the process of citizens taking media work into their own hands.

If networked publics were forming and starting to serve fifth-estate functions using the blogosphere of the early 2000s, then the structural transformation of the web around social media platforms beginning in the late 2000s provided an opportunity for the fifth estate to grow a more public face. Not only were these acts more visible on the social networks, they were also more spreadable and searchable (boyd 2014). Furthermore, the growth of cultures and practices of civic participation on Twitter and elsewhere helped redefine parts of these platforms, and of the fields of journalism and politics more broadly, to better account for the concerns of networked publics. In other words, the fifth estate has been mediatized.

At the same time, professional journalists, a group tasked with serving the public, are also plugged into the network. Their work is inevitably shaped by the social conditions of mediatization, from the freedoms of filing a story from home to the growing pressure to do so. Of course, the pressures journalists face are not solely institutional—many now have the "sensibilities," or sticking with the lexicon of field theory, the "habitus" native to the networked world (Powers and Vera-Zambrano 2017; Russell 2016). Despite the striking directive, "tweet or be sacked," which serves as the title of Chap. 4, few digital journalists have to be told to tweet. Just as newspaper editors were socialized to find salacious quotes for headlines, and cable news producers to hunt for sound bites, many digital journalists know that the news will be (re)tweeted, and they respond accordingly, whether as an author, marketer, follower, or news curator. Accordingly, attention will now turn to examine the significance of Twitter in the everyday practices of professional journalists.

NOTE

1. The term "superstructure," inspired by a Marxian conceptualization of power dynamics beyond the political-economic "base," is meant to signal the ubiquity of mediated communication, and by extension, the endless reach of its influence throughout all spheres of society.

REFERENCES

Alterman, E. (2003). *What liberal media?: The truth about bias and the news.* New York: Basic Books.

Altheide, D. L., & Snow, R. P. (1979). *Media logic.* Beverly Hills, CA: SAGE.

Anderson, C. W. (2011, November 10). The Jekyll and Hyde problem: What are journalists, and their institutions, for? *Neiman Foundation at Harvard.* Retrieved November 16, 2017, from http://www.niemanlab.org/2011/11/the-jekyll-and-hyde-problem-what-are-journalists-and-their-institutions-for/.

Anderson, C. W., & Maeyer, J. D. (2015). Objects of journalism and the news. *Journalism, 16*(1), 3–9. https://doi.org/10.1177/1464884914545728.

Artwick, C. G. (2014). News sourcing and gender on Twitter. *Journalism, 15*(8), 1111–1127. https://doi.org/10.1177/1464884913505030.

Bennett, W. L., Pickard, V. W., Iozzi, D. P., Schroeder, C. L., Lagos, T., & Caswell, C. E. (2004). Managing the public sphere: Journalistic construction of the great globalization debate. *Journal of Communication, 54*(3), 437–455. https://doi.org/10.1111/j.1460-2466.2004.tb02638.x.

Benson, R. (1999). Field theory in comparative context: A new paradigm for media studies. *Theory and Society, 28*(3), 463–498. https://doi.org/10.1023/A:1006982529917.

Benson, R., & Neveu, E. (2005). *Bourdieu and the journalistic field.* Malden, MA: Polity.

Bourdieu, P. (1977). *Outline of a theory of practice.* Cambridge: Cambridge University Press.

Bourdieu, P. (1984). Distinction: *A social critique of the judgement of taste.* Cambridge, MA: Harvard University Press.

Bourdieu, P. (1990). *The logic of practice.* Stanford, CA: Stanford University Press.

Bourdieu, P. (1991). *Language and symbolic power.* Cambridge, MA: Harvard University Press.

Bourdieu, P. (1993). *The field of cultural production: Essays on art and literature.* New York, NY: Columbia University Press.

Bourdieu, P. (1996). *The rules of art: Genesis and structure of the literary field.* Stanford, CA: Stanford University Press.

Bourdieu, P. (1998). *Practical reason: On the theory of action.* Stanford, CA: Stanford University Press.

Bourdieu, P. (2005). The political field, the social science field, and the journalistic field. In R. Benson & E. Neveu (Eds.), *Bourdieu and the journalistic field* (pp. 29–47). Malden, MA: Polity.

boyd, d. (2014). *It's complicated: The social lives of networked teens.* New Haven, CT: Yale University Press.

Bruns, A. (2005). *Gatewatching: Collaborative online news production.* New York: Peter Lang.

Bruns, A. (2014). Gatekeeping, gatewatching, real-time feedback: New challenges for journalism. *Brazilian Journalism Research, 10*(2 EN), 224–237.

Bruns, A., & Highfield, T. (2015). From news blogs to news on Twitter: Gatewatching and collaborative news curation. In S. Coleman & D. Freelon (Eds.), *Handbook of digital politics* (pp. 325–339). Cheltenham: Edward Elgar.

Butler, J. (2006). *Gender trouble: Feminism and the subversion of identity.* New York: Routledge.

Carlson, M., & Lewis, S. C. (Eds.). (2015). *Boundaries of journalism: Professionalism, practices and participation.* New York: Routledge.

Castells, M. (2015). *Networks of outrage and hope: Social movements in the Internet Age* (2nd ed.). Malden, MA: Polity.

Chalaby, J. (1998). *The invention of journalism.* New York, NY: Palgrave Macmillan.

Cohen, N. S. (2015). From pink slips to pink slime: Transforming media labor in a digital age. *The Communication Review, 18*(2), 98–122. https://doi.org/10.1080/10714421.2015.1031996.

Cooper, S. D. (2006). *Watching the watchdog: Bloggers as the fifth estate.* Spokane, WA: Marquette Books.

Couldry, N. (2003). Media meta-capital: Extending the range of Bourdieu's field theory. *Theory and Society, 32*(5/6), 653–677.

Couldry, N. (2012). *Media, society, world.* Cambridge: Polity.

Couldry, N. (2014). When mediatization hits the ground. In A. Hepp & F. Krotz (Eds.), *Mediatized worlds: Culture and society in a media age* (pp. 54–71). New York: Palgrave Macmillan.

Deuze, M. (2007). *Media work.* Malden, MA: Polity.

Dutton, W. H. (2009). The fifth estate emerging through the network of networks. *Prometheus, 27*(1), 1–15. https://doi.org/10.1080/08109020802657453.

Entman, R. M. (1993). Framing: Toward clarification of a fractured paradigm. *Journal of Communication, 43*(4), 51–58. https://doi.org/10.1111/j.1460-2466.1993.tb01304.x.

Fligstein, N., & McAdam, D. (2012). *A theory of fields* (Reprint ed.). New York: Oxford University Press.

Fuchs, C. (2017). Marx's capital in the information age. *Capital & Class, 41*(1), 51–67. https://doi.org/10.1177/0309816816678573.

Glasser, T., & Gunther, M. (2005). The legacy of autonomy in American journalism. In G. Overholser & K. Hall-Jamieson (Eds.), *The press* (pp. 384–399). Oxford: Oxford University Press.

Greenslade, R. (2016, June 6). Almost 60% of US newspaper jobs vanish in 26 years. *The Guardian.* Retrieved November 16, 2017, from http://www.theguardian.com/media/greenslade/2016/jun/06/almost-60-of-us-newspaper-jobs-vanish-in-26-years.

Hepp, A. (2013). *Cultures of mediatization.* Malden, MA: Polity.

Hepp, A., & Krotz, F. (Eds.). (2014). *Mediatized worlds: Culture and society in a media age.* New York: Palgrave Macmillan.

Hirst, M., & Treadwell, G. (2011). Blogs bother me: Social media, journalism students and the curriculum. *Journalism Practice, 5*(4), 446–461. https://doi.org/10.1080/17512786.2011.555367.

Hjarvard, S. (2013). *The mediatization of culture and society.* New York: Routledge.

Jarvis, J. (2013, July 11). Who is a journalist? Manning trial poses question of vital public interest. *The Guardian.* Retrieved November 16, 2017, from https://www.theguardian.com/global/2013/jul/11/who-is-journalist-bradley-manning-trial.

Jensen, R. (2015, June 10). American journalism's ideology: Why the "liberal" media is fundamentalist. *ZNet.* Retrieved November 16, 2017, from https://zcomm.org/znetarticle/american-journalisms-ideology-why-the-liberal-media-is-fundamentalist/.

Jurrat, N. (2011, July 12). Mapping digital media: Citizen journalism and the internet. *Open Society Foundations.* Retrieved November 16, 2017, from https://www.opensocietyfoundations.org/reports/mapping-digital-media-citizen-journalism-and-internet.

Krause, M. (2011). Reporting and the transformations of the journalistic field: US news media, 1890–2000. *Media, Culture & Society, 33*(1), 89–104. https://doi.org/10.1177/0163443710385502.

Kreiss, D., Meadows, L., & Remensperger, J. (2015). Political performance, boundary spaces, and active spectatorship: Media production at the 2012 Democratic National Convention. *Journalism, 16*(5), 577–595. https://doi.org/10.1177/1464884914525562.

Kumar, A. (2009). Looking back and looking ahead: Journalistic rules, social control, social change, and relative autonomy. *Journal of Media Sociology, 1*(3/4), 136–160.

Lennett, B., Clark, J., Glaisyer, T., Meinrath, S., & Napoli, P. (2011). Mapping digital media: United States. *Open Society Foundations.* Retrieved November 17, 2017, from https://www.opensocietyfoundations.org/reports/mapping-digital-media-united-states.

Lindner, A. M., & Larson, R. P. (2017). The expansion and contraction of the journalistic field and American online citizen journalism, 2000–2012. *Poetics, 64*, 40–52. https://doi.org/10.1016/j.poetic.2017.08.001.

Lowrey, W. (2006). Mapping the journalism–blogging relationship. *Journalism, 7*(4), 477–500. https://doi.org/10.1177/1464884906068363.

McChesney, R. W. (2000). *Rich media, poor democracy: Communication politics in dubious times.* New York: The New Press.

McChesney, R. W. (2008). *The political economy of media: Enduring issues, emerging dilemmas.* New York: Monthly Review Press.

McChesney, R. W. (2013). *Digital disconnect: How capitalism is turning the internet against democracy.* New York: The New Press.

Morozov, E. (2012). *The net delusion: The dark side of internet freedom* (Reprint ed.). New York: PublicAffairs.

Mott, F. L. (1962). *American journalism: A history, 1690–1960* (3rd ed.). New York: Macmillan.

Paulussen, S. (2012). Technology and the transformation of news work: Are labor conditions in (online) journalism changing? In E. Siapera & A. Veglis (Eds.), *The handbook of global online journalism* (pp. 192–208). Malden, MA: Wiley-Blackwell.

Powers, M., & Vera-Zambrano, S. (2017). How journalists use social media in France and the United States: Analyzing technology use across journalistic fields. *New Media & Society*, Advance online publication. https://doi.org/10.1177/1461444817731566.

Preston, B. (2013, July 2). Democrat sen. Dick Durbin wants government to decide who qualifies as a real journalist. *PJ Media*. Retrieved November 16, 2017, from https://pjmedia.com/blog/democrat-sen-dick-durbin-wants-government-to-decide-who-qualifies-as-a-real-journalist/.

Rainie, L., & Wellman, B. (2012). *Networked: The new social operating system*. Cambridge, MA: MIT Press.

Reed, I. A. (2013). Power: Relational, discursive, and performative dimensions. *Sociological Theory, 31*(3), 193–218. https://doi.org/10.1177/0735275113501792.

Reese, S. D., Rutigliano, L., Hyun, K., & Jeong, J. (2007). Mapping the blogosphere: Professional and citizen-based media in the global news arena. *Journalism, 8*(3), 235–261. https://doi.org/10.1177/1464884907076459.

Rosen, J. (2003, September 18). The view from nowhere. *PressThink*. Retrieved November 16, 2017, from http://archive.pressthink.org/2003/09/18/jennings.html.

Rosen, J. (2006, June 27). The people formerly known as the audience. *PressThink*. Retrieved November 16, 2017, from http://archive.pressthink.org/2006/06/27/ppl_frmr.html.

Rosen, J. (2009). He said, she said journalism: Lame formula in the land of the active user. *PressThink*. Retrieved November 16, 2017, from http://archive.pressthink.org/2009/04/12/hesaid:shesaid.html.

Ross, P. (2011). Is there an expertise of production? The case of new media producers. *New Media & Society, 13*(6), 912–928. https://doi.org/10.1177/1461444810385393.

Russell, A. (2016). *Journalism as activism: Recoding media power*. Malden, MA: Polity.

Savage, M., & Silva, E. B. (2013). Field analysis in cultural sociology. *Cultural Sociology, 7*(2), 111–126. https://doi.org/10.1177/1749975512473992.

Schudson, M. (1978). *Discovering the news: A social history of American newspapers*. New York, NY: Basic Books.

Schudson, M. (2003). *The sociology of news*. New York: Norton.

Schudson, M., & Tifft, S. (2005). American journalism in historical perspective. In G. Overholser & K. H. Jamieson (Eds.), *The press* (pp. 17–46). New York: Oxford University Press.

Schultz, I. (2007). The journalistic gut feeling. *Journalism Practice, 1*(2), 190–207. https://doi.org/10.1080/17512780701275507.

Shoemaker, P. J., & Vos, T. (2009). *Gatekeeping theory.* New York, NY: Routledge.

Singer, J. B. (2003). Who are these Guys?: The online challenge to the notion of journalistic professionalism. *Journalism, 4*(2), 139–163. https://doi.org/10.1177/146488490342001.

Singer, J. B. (2007). Contested autonomy. *Journalism Studies, 8*(1), 79–95. https://doi.org/10.1080/14616700601056866.

Song, F. W. (2010). Theorizing web 2.0. *Information, Communication & Society, 13*(2), 249–275. https://doi.org/10.1080/13691180902914610.

Swartz, D. (1997). *Culture and power: The sociology of Pierre Bourdieu.* Chicago, IL: University of Chicago Press.

Swartz, D. L. (2013). *Symbolic power, politics, and intellectuals: The political sociology of Pierre Bourdieu.* Chicago, IL: University of Chicago Press.

Tang, L., & Yang, P. (2011). Symbolic power and the internet: The power of a "horse". *Media, Culture & Society, 33*(5), 675–691. https://doi.org/10.1177/0163443711404462.

Thompson, J. (1991). Editor's introduction. In P. Bourdieu (Ed.), *Language and symbolic power* (pp. 1–31). Cambridge, MA: Polity Press.

Thompson, J. (1995). *The media and modernity: A social theory of the media.* Stanford, CA: Stanford University Press.

Turkle, S. (2012). *Alone together: Why we expect more from technology and less from each other.* New York: Basic Books.

Vos, T. P., Craft, S., & Ashley, S. (2012). New media, old criticism: Bloggers' press criticism and the journalistic field. *Journalism, 13*(7), 850–868. https://doi.org/10.1177/1464884911421705.

Weinberg, S. (2008). *A journalism of humanity: A candid history of the world's first journalism school.* Columbia, MO: University of Missouri Press.

Zuckerman, E. (2017, January 18). It's journalism's job to save civics. *Medium.* Retrieved November 16, 2017, from https://medium.com/@EthanZ/its-journalism-s-job-to-save-civics-2b31f46092e4#.lj8xyv4zi.

"Tweet or Be Sacked": Hybridity and Shifts in (Professional) Journalistic Practice

In 2010, BBC *Global News* Director Peter Horrocks addressed his staff and directed them to "tweet or be sacked." While Horrocks later clarified that the directive was more a statement about the need to understand social media than a literal command to the members of his newsroom, it was also a clear expression of the zeitgeist of the moment (Miller 2011). By 2011, use of Twitter by journalists had become normalized, and indeed, engagement on the platform was increasingly expected of many professionals. *The Boston Globe* even installed a "Twitter board" in the heart of its newsroom to encourage its staff to keep up with news as it spread on the platform (Ellis 2011). Since that time, studies have shown a steady growth in journalists' adoption of social media (Chadha and Wells 2016; Santana and Hopp 2016).

While it is not possible to determine how many journalists are on Twitter at any point in time, which means that a clear way to create a population sample does not exist, there are a variety of mechanisms for approximating the platform's popularity and influence in the profession. Professional journalists' use of Twitter has grown substantially over time,

A previous version of this chapter was published as: Barnard, S. R. 'Tweet or be sacked': Twitter and the new elements of journalistic practice. *Journalism*, 17(2), 190–207, Copyright © 2016, SAGE Publications. Reprinted by permission of SAGE Publications. Available at: http://journals.sagepub.com/doi/abs/10.1177/1464884914553079.

61

as illustrated by a study of 553 reporters from 15 countries, which found that Twitter usage grew from 47% in 2012 to 59% in 2013 (Irvine 2013). In the United Kingdom, 10,630 full-time professional journalists had known (i.e., registered) Twitter accounts at the time of this writing ("UK journalists" 2017). Although no such equivalent exists for American journalists, one study of 1080 US journalists estimated that "more than half (53.8%) ... regularly use microblogs such as Twitter for gathering information and reporting their stories" (Willnat and Weaver 2014, p. 21). Furthermore, a survey of 480 American newspaper reporters found that a similar majority (51.7%) "indicated that Twitter was either important or very important professional tool for the creation of news," and just over 70% worked for organizations with formal policies governing Twitter usage (Santana and Hopp 2016, p. 396). Twitter's rising popularity among professional reporters over the years is reflected in many other accounts of the platform's journalistic significance, many of which will be examined in this chapter. While Twitter's growth curve may have flattened out in recent years, its journalistic significance remains.

Journalistic uses of Twitter vary greatly, from advocacy and activism on one end of the spectrum, to more traditional "objective" journalism and information dissemination on the other. By observing journalists' everyday use of Twitter and analyzing their meta-journalistic tweets in greater detail, a greater understanding of the meaning and significance of Twitter-based journalistic practices may come to light. This chapter's focus on the hybridity of practices and practical elements (e.g., norms, values, dispositions, and means of distinction) demonstrates the extent to which action within the journalistic field is being reshaped to better fit the mediatized, networked era.

A PRACTICE AND PROFESSION IN TRANSITION

Twitter's growing acceptance within the field of journalism marks a notable turning point in some of the profession's values and practices. Nevertheless, as the previous chapters make clear, this shift began amid a slew of broader transformations in and beyond the journalistic field, from political and economic to cultural and technological. While the implications for these developments are immense across the spectrum, American journalism is one field where such transformations are most profound.

The rise of new information and communication technologies, along with the networked effects of social media services, has ushered in a new era of mediated relations. While powerful new media platforms continue to grow and evolve, Twitter is one platform where major shifts are occurring. As a streamlined, short-form communication platform embedded within the larger context of the web, Twitter allows users to create their own personalized, interactive "awareness system" (Hermida 2010) that can be accessed anywhere with an internet connection. Its journalistic value increases exponentially as other fields embrace it as well.

The work of journalists has changed considerably since the proliferation of digital media technologies. Due, in part, to a loss of professional reporting jobs as well as a tightening of budgets, many throughout the journalistic field are expected to do "more with less" (McChesney and Nichols 2010, p. 23), and work quickly to make news "direct" and "in real time" (Champagne 2005, p. 53). Furthermore, this burgeoning of digital journalism contributes to increased workloads and "limit journalists' ability to pursue stories" (Chadha and Wells 2016, p. 1032; Ternes et al. 2017). Not surprisingly, the mediatization of journalistic work has contributed to a shift in reporters' work-related attitudes, which are often contradictory (Comor and Compton 2015; Weaver and Willnat 2016). On the one hand, many reporters find their use of social media to be valuable for information gathering and added accountability (Weaver and Willnat 2016). On the other hand, a recent survey of American newspaper journalists found that reporters were expected to take on new roles and responsibilities, work faster, and even cut corners to make up for staffing cuts as well as the increased demand for online content, whether on social media or news organizations' websites (Ternes et al. 2017).

These pressures have manifested in a whole array of new(s) practices that networked journalistic actors—professional and not—perform in the process of identifying, producing, distributing, and responding to news. Beyond the growth of Twitter and other social media for journalistic practices (Bentivegna and Marchetti 2017; Lasorsa et al. 2011), these networks are also used for the production and reproduction of journalistic norms (Lasorsa 2012). Furthermore, the "triple revolution" of communication technologies following the proliferation of mobile, online social networks (Rainie and Wellman 2012) has helped usher in new articulations of journalism, citizenship, and democracy (Papacharissi 2009).

Altogether, these developments facilitate a number of important changes to the structural and practical dynamics of American journalism. A number of recent studies have helped shed light on how the increased acceptance of Twitter has changed the institutional culture, power relations, and practice of professional journalism (Canter 2015; Chadha and Wells 2016; Compton and Benedetti 2010; Hellmueller et al. 2013;

Krause 2011; Kunelius and Ruusunoksa 2008; Lawrence et al. 2014; Molyneux et al. 2017; Papacharissi and Easton 2013; Russell 2013; Santana and Hopp 2016; Schultz 2007; Vos et al. 2011; Wiik 2009). Still, significant gaps exist in understanding how cultural and technological—in combination with political and economic—shifts can transform the practical dynamics of the journalistic field. This chapter seeks to help fill these gaps through an analysis of journalistic (inter)action on Twitter.

According to Alfred Hermida (2010, 2012), Twitter has given journalists a new "awareness system" to keep abreast of and verify the latest news and potential sources. Former National Public Radio (NPR) "social media strategist" Andy Carvin is a prime example, as his work on Twitter allowed him to curate crowd-sourced news from the Arab Spring live and in groundbreaking fashion (Carvin 2012). Similar strategies have been employed by professional journalists covering place-based news events, such as the 2011 UK riots (Vis 2013), Occupy and Ferguson protests (Araiza et al. 2016; Guerrini 2013), among countless others (Russell 2016). Examples like these illustrate the logic behind the journalistic field taking to Twitter with such force, given how effective a crowd of networked individuals can be for the practice of journalism across vast distances and in real time (Hermida et al. 2014). Indeed, the journalistic potential of the medium is so compelling that by 2011, studies showed that Twitter had become "normalized" throughout the field (Lasorsa et al. 2011; cf. Bentivegna and Marchetti 2017; Santana and Hopp 2016). As the title of this chapter suggests, this shift creates a climate where abstention from the Twitter community may have a negative impact on individual journalists and their institutions.

As the above discussion makes clear, growing bodies of literature are investigating the transformative potential of digital media, with some studies focusing specifically on the dynamics of the journalistic field (Siapera and Spyridou 2012). For example, an international, comparative analysis of media system changes brought on by digital innovations yielded notable findings about the structure and products of the journalistic field and the varying role that internet technologies may play in it (Benson et al. 2012). Contrastingly, more mezzo-focused studies have developed measures of journalistic capital and doxa that suggest ongoing changes in light of web-influenced practices (Hellmueller et al. 2013). Despite the strength and importance of these studies, there is still much to learn about the role Twitter plays in the transformation of journalistic practice, and the field writ large. Therefore, this chapter focuses on journalistic practice and meta-discourse on Twitter to identify relevant norms, dispositions, and capital at stake in the practice of networked journalism. As such, the chapter addresses this principal research question: in what ways does journalistic meta-discourse on Twitter demonstrate new logics and relations of practice in the networked era?

Professional Journalists on Twitter: Individual Practices and Elements of Practice

In order to address this guiding question, this chapter analyzes journalists' reflexive use of Twitter in 2011 to discuss the platform's role in the reporting process. As evidenced by the growth of literature examining journalists' use of the platform during that time period, Twitter had reached doxic status in the profession by 2011 (Hermida 2010, 2012; Lasorsa 2012; Lasorsa et al. 2011; Vis 2013). Similar conclusions are reached by examining Google Trends data, which measures Google search history and serves as a proxy for public interest in a topic. According to Google Trends, interest in "twitter journalism" was substantial as early as 2009 and grew steadily until early 2011, where it remained high before peaking in April 2013 ("Google trends" 2017). These observations would hardly surprise Twitter users from that time period, given how prominent a role reporting practices, and discussions thereof, played on the platform. While journalists' relationship to social media has evolved and grown more complex in recent years, studying Twitter's journalistic field during this formative time provided an opportunity to uncover the profession's emergent practices on the platform, as well as their underlying logics.

Given this study's focus on journalistic practice and meta-discourse on Twitter, it is necessary to consider the relationship between speech and action. As C. Wright Mills (1940) made clear, speech is more than vocalized motive; it is an act in itself (cf. Gubrium and Holstein 2008). Thus

> To speak is inevitably to situate one's self in the world, to take up a position, to engage with others in a process of production and exchange, to occupy a social space. *In its structure and use language is one of the central vehicles of habitus.* (Hanks 1993, p. 139) [emphasis added]

Bourdieu repeatedly emphasized that social action includes an exchange, most often measureable through specific forms of capital. Furthermore, "motives may be considered as typical vocabularies having ascertainable functions in delimited societal situations" (Mills 1940, p. 904). Stated in Bourdieu's terms, Mills' "ascertainable functions" can be seen in the exchange of *capital*, reflection of *habitus*, and delineation of *doxa* that occur within separate fields of social action. Accordingly, analysis of meta-discourse offers a revealing window into the elements of practice (Scheuer 2003; Scollon 2001), and can be especially revealing when combined with techniques of participant-observation (Gubrium and Holstein 2008).

Accordingly, the research presented in this chapter is based on a mixed-method approach that I have termed digital ethnographic content analysis (DECA), which incorporates insights from sustained participant-observations into more systematic analysis of relevant Twitter content. Participant-observation of journalistic (inter)action on Twitter between 2009 and 2011 revealed a number of hashtags commonly used by journalists, and snowballing from this initial list yielded a greater number of relevant search terms. The hashtags "journalism," "journchat," and "wjchat" were selected for analysis because each represent meta-discourse from Twitter's journalistic field in a unique manner. For example, "wjchat," an abbreviation of "web journalist chat," and "journchat" were selected because both hashtags were utilized in regular "tweetups," or live Twitter chats, frequented by journalists and other media professionals interested in discussing the challenges of and sharing strategies for doing the work of journalism in the digital age. Accordingly, as will become clear in the remainder of this chapter, a notable portion of these discussions addressed the profession's evolving values and practices, particularly as they pertained to Twitter. By contrast, "journalism" was a keyword and hashtag more likely to be used when nonprofessionals discussed the field. Thus, it provided a broader array of perspectives that, while frequently less relevant to this study, also allowed for a more diverse pool from which to draw insights. While the methodology prevents drawing conclusions about the profession as a whole, these discourses yielded a variety of notable insights about the practices employed by journalists, as well as broader themes emerging from their collective uses of Twitter. Both avenues are explored based on results from this study.

Eight Journalistic Practices on Twitter
A recursive coding process focusing on themes and frames in the content yielded eight primarily journalistic practices of the platform. Although they are not mutually exclusive, each is discussed individually and in no particular order:

Information Collection

The challenge of efficient information collection has long been of central importance for journalists, as well as members of the public. Twitter's logic of selectively "following" individual accounts and discursive topics allows users to customize the theme(s) of their feed based on their fields of interest. Thus, Twitter can help journalists keep up with a wide variety of news, an affordance the platform excels at, while also loosening their reliance on legacy media outlets. For example, multiple #journchat participants tweeted about "routinely leav[ing] hashtag searches open in their Twitter client" to cast their news net beyond the margins of their personal network. This theme clearly resonates with other research demonstrating how Twitter functions as a modern "awareness system," which helps users both collect and disseminate information (Hermida 2010).

News Dissemination

One of the most leveraged and visible of Twitter's journalistic affordances is the sharing of information. The medium's character limit provides just enough space for a tweet to contain a grabbing quote or headline and a link to a longer-form story, though more savvy users may post "tweet-storms" that allow for greater storytelling by stringing together multiple tweets in succession. As discussed in Chap. 2, the structure of the Twitter network provides an ideal system for sharing information with "followers" and other curious members of the public. Many of the journalists' tweets examined for this chapter provided a clear illustration that they took advantage of this affordance. For example, one #wjchat contributor emphasized Twitter's news dissemination affordances thusly: "I think breaking news is where the importance of your having established presence/personality on Twitter shines most." Direct authorship is not even required, as Twitter's "retweet" function allows users to curate and share content written by others. Furthermore, given the mobility and ubiquity of smartphones as well as Twitter's nearly seamless convergence with other photo and video services, it affords nearly all users the ability to disseminate (often breaking) news to an increasingly networked public with great efficiency.

Sourcing

Similar to the process of information collection, many journalists have long used Twitter as a means of connecting with potential sources. This research found discussions about using Twitter and other social media tools for sourcing were a common theme among the hashtag discourse analyzed. These included ideal-typical examples provided by the likes of Carvin, winner of the 2012 Shorty Award for best journalist using social media. While cases like Carvin's illustrate how new media tools allow the most tech-literate journalistic actors to find information and sources for important events across the world, the majority of journalists using Twitter simply integrate these practices into their diverse reporting repertoire. Indeed, many #wjchat participants responded to Carvin's explanation of his Twitter sourcing practices with interest and intent to begin utilizing some of his methods. Likewise, after explaining how much they learned about leveraging Twitter for sourcing purposes during a #wjchat, one participant tweeted, "Wish my sources were on twitter #smalltownblues." Another explained, "My SM reporting on breaking means using twitter as the source for Qs and tips that I verify."

Public Note-Taking

Another common theme for journalistic uses of Twitter is as an outlet for public note-taking. Similar to the practice of live-blogging events, Twitter-journalists have leveraged the medium to similar ends. Thus, in addition to serving as a personal record of quotes and sources to inform longer-form stories, these tweets make this information public. Live events such as political speeches and sporting events are ideal instances where journalistic actors employ live-tweeting practices. However, despite the significance of this practice, there was little explicit talk of it in the Twitter chats analyzed for this project. Nonetheless, a few chat participants did discuss the practical and ethical issues surrounding live-tweeting of events. And although it may pose potential conflicts for journalists affiliated with the Associated Press, BBC, or other institutions with similarly restrictive social media policies, live-tweeting is an increasingly common practice among citizens and professionals.

Public Engagement

Today's networked journalism affords, and all but requires, much greater engagement between journalists and the public. This theme was highly visible in much of the tweets analyzed for this chapter, especially during a #wjchat discussion over which social media platform the users preferred. As one contributor explained, "If you want to engage, in terms of conversation, Twitter makes everyone accessible." Similarly, another stated, "Definitely Twitter. I have more conversations with a wider range of people on different topics. Best engagement hands down." And yet another observed, "It says something about engagement that we chat on Twitter instead of G+, Facebook, Tumblr, etc." Moreover, Carvin chimed in to emphasize that his "Twitter followers interact w/each other." Thus, beyond the lowering of barriers to entry to the journalistic field and facilitating greater public engagement with journalists, Twitter's interactive affordances have also given rise to greater interaction across fields.

Journalistic Meta-Discourse

While many of the practices discussed above arose in the distinct production of journalistic content, others served different functions, such as producing and participating in field meta-discourse. This often took the form of journalistic criticism or reflexivity that explored, explained, or called into question the structural and practical realities of the field. For example, much of the Twitter discourse analyzed for this research addressed various norms, ethics, and practices in networked journalism. As demonstrated below, discussions of these themes often turned into debates over whether journalistic orthodoxy should be preserved, or if newer heterodox norms and values might better suit the new media ecology. Although these discussions were rarely central to the actors' professional practice, save for journalism scholars, they did contribute to the production of various forms of journalistic capital.

Other Professional (Inter)Actions

In addition to those named above, countless other professional interactions commonly took place on Twitter. Many of these practices often served social functions, such as sharing and making recommendations, chatting, asking for advice, and so on. Twitter content analyzed from the #journalism hashtag revealed numerous instances of users offering and requesting practical advice on how to leverage the medium's affordances for journalistic purposes. For example, one #journalism contributor tweeted about his plan to teach others in his organization about Twitter and asked for input, "Talking to the copy desk today about how to use Twitter. Any advice for new people I should include?" Another tweeted a link to a story on "Why is Twitter a great resource for #journalism and #journalists?" Due in large part to Twitter's brevity and conversational structure, professional interactions on Twitter were often less formal than other professional exchanges, but this theme differs distinctly from personal (inter)actions because these interactions stayed on the topic of journalism. Furthermore, beyond the various manifest functions served by these (inter)actions, they also serve many latent functions, including the exchange of capital.

Personal (Inter)Actions

Countless scholars and journalists have noted the many benefits from allowing journalists to be more personal and relatable in public interactions, especially those occurring online. Thus, it is common for journalism professionals to leverage Twitter and other social media to occasionally show a human face. From brief details about a user's personal life, to a friendly exchange between two or more users, and even voicing personal opinions, many journalistic actors on Twitter leveraged the medium for purposes that were not strictly business-related. While some users went as far as creating separate accounts for personal and professional tweeting, most found some way to integrate their personal and professional selves. In general, Twitter-journalists regularly engaged in personal inter(actions), although these tweets made up a minority of most feeds.

Elements of Practice

Journalists' discussion of the platform also revealed a variety of broader implications for how the professional culture—and by extension, the journalistic field more broadly—was responding to these shifts in practice. I refer to these key components of the field as elements of practice because they make up the breadth of practical matters that together constitute the terms of action within a field (see Chap. 2). Each of these elements is discussed in detail below.

Capital

Twitter's prominence as a medium for journalistic (inter)action means that various forms of journalistic capital flow swiftly throughout the network. Most directly, Twitter can help journalists amass *social capital* by establishing ties with other actors in the field. This was a common theme in both #journchat and #wjchat discourses, which frequently emphasized the importance of the Twitter network as a kind of modern rolodex. Indeed, many in the field saw Twitter as so pertinent to social capital that a conference panel was held on the subject (Laucius 2011).

One central avenue to *economic capital* via Twitter is by driving web traffic to sites monetized with advertising and/or paywalls, which generate revenue by charging visitors a fee to access content. This issue was discussed on both the #journalism and #journchat hashtags, much of it prompted by a #journchat moderator's question about "who should own journalists online identities" in light of a case where the "BBC lost 60k Twitter followers to its competitor" (Bergman 2011). Despite the central importance of economic issues to the journalistic field, only a small portion of the discourse analyzed for this chapter addressed this theme, likely because of Twitter's continued role as an indirect source of revenue. Nonetheless, as is shown below, Twitter-journalism practices can also help build other forms of capital, which may later be converted to economic capital.

Perhaps the most visible instances of journalistic *cultural capital* exchanged on Twitter come in the form of commentary and field meta-discourse. The personal (inter)actions that take place on Twitter help to facilitate the kinds of clever, intellectual commentary that were rarely visible to audiences prior to the rise of the participatory web. There may be no greater example of Twitter's relevance to cultural capital than the practices of Carvin and other journalistic actors deeply engaged on Twitter. Carvin's professional routine not only centers around gaining knowledge of distant events through Twitter, such as political movements in the Arab world, but he also uses the medium to share advice and therefore help others in the field build social media skills. Moreover, the public engagement Twitter facilitates helps journalists increase the impact of their reporting, thus assisting in the accumulation of other forms of cultural capital.

Journalism's most tech-savvy thought leaders also illustrate how powerful Twitter can be in helping build *symbolic capital*. Carvin is an obvious, if recurring, example of symbolic capital because he has earned a reputation as a "Twitter journalist" who leverages the medium proficiently in reporting on international news events. Additionally, many chat participants used Twitter for promotional purposes by sharing headlines and linking to stories. More broadly, many used Twitter to promote (i.e., tweet about) others' work. Each of these practices demonstrates Twitter's role in building and maintaining status as a journalist. When amassed in the context of mediatization, this status can manifest in a form of media meta-capital that affords its possessor(s) influence across social fields (Couldry 2014).

Habitus

Twitter's significance to the journalistic habitus is becoming increasingly apparent throughout the field. Accordingly, much of the discourse analyzed for this chapter provided explicit examples of Twitter's place within journalistic practices and dispositions. For example, a #wjchat participant explained how new media technologies like Twitter fit into his journalistic practice, "My social media discussions are largely an outlet for my work. Real reporting can be done via #Twitter. But not all of it." The habitus exemplified in this tweet illustrates the hybridity that is now so common of the modern journalistic disposition. It is explicit about the importance of social media's journalistic affordances, but also about the fact that the profession's more traditional role has not disappeared. Furthermore, a #journalism contributor tweeted about "using Twitter to collaborate on investigations," which embodies the open and participatory nature that has become a trademark of the networked era. Similar themes were also common among #journchat participants.

The journalistic habitus is integrally tied to actors' positions and dispositions, so it is important to consider specific practices (e.g., the eight discussed above) as well as the field location of Twitter-journalists. In this case, most journalists contributing to the discourse analyzed for this chapter worked for a professional media organization and were also active in the journalistic subfield of Twitter. As some chat participants noted, Felix Salmon, a journalist and former blogging editor for Reuters, said the journalistic value of Twitter was so high that he would pay $1000 annually for the service (Macnicol 2012). Such assertions clearly attest to Twitter's journalistic importance and indicate its influence on the hybrid positions and dispositions of networked journalists.

Doxa

Along with shifts in journalistic practices and dispositions come significant strains to the field's values, which are often identifiable in discursive exchanges. Accordingly, much of the Twitter discourse analyzed for this chapter was frequently framed around heterodox debates, like the costs and benefits of new media. These debates often concerned values of accuracy and credibility, prompted by the speeding pace of the news cycle. For example, while some users were concerned about tweets being viewed as comparable to, and sometimes even a replacement of, more traditional forms of journalistic practice, many others celebrated Twitter's journalistic potential. As one #wjchat participant tweeted, "Don't be afraid to run with a story you've found from Twitter. Twitter is here to help you, not hurt you."

Many chat participants agreed that retweeting breaking news was a useful act even if the information it contained was not yet verified. In a post that was retweeted many times, one #wjchat user declared, "Not journalistic sin to pass along rumors in new newsroom called Twitter." The framing of these accounts illustrates the extent to which journalistic doxa is in motion due to the kind of field disruption facilitated by Twitter and the participatory web. However, many Twitter-journalists recognized a notable difference between running with unconfirmed rumors through traditional media and passing them along via social media. As one user stated in regard to recent instances of Twitter inaccuracy that were a central point of debate, "Being wrong on #Twitter (lasts only seconds) #Future of #Journalism."

Despite such heterodox discourse, numerous other chat participants remained dedicated to traditional, orthodox journalistic norms such as accuracy and objectivity, and did not consider digital platforms like Twitter an exception. For example, a #wjchat participant emphasized that passing on rumors via Twitter was a "sin," stating, "You'd be pressed to publish a rumor in an article/blog post—how's twitter different?" Similarly, another #wjchat participant tweeted, "Even if I saw it on Twitter or in social media, it still needs verification. that aspect of journalism hasn't changed." Thus, orthodox values still remain strong among a significant portion of journalists on Twitter. Nonetheless, many chat participants framed accounts through a synthesis of orthodox and heterodox values. As one #wjchat participant tweeted, "Same rules of traditional journalism apply. Twitter isn't meant to loosen those rules, just more opportunities to find truth." The diversity of this discourse illustrates how the tension between traditional and digitally driven journalistic values may slowly be approaching synthesis.

Making Sense of Journalistic Practice (on Twitter)

Overall, the Twitter data analyzed for this chapter reveal significant application of the medium's journalistic affordances as well as a keen awareness of the various ways the field is shifting, due in part to the affordances of the participatory web. First and foremost, a shift in practice is underway. This chapter has established a typology of eight *practices* employed by journalistic actors on Twitter: information collection, news dissemination, sourcing, public engagement, brief note-taking, field meta-discourse, other professional (inter)actions, and personal (inter)actions. A large portion of legacy journalists contributing to the discourse analyzed for this chapter appeared to use Twitter primarily as a means of sharing content and staying current on news. Additionally, many of the most dedicated

Twitter journalists used the medium to find sources and engage with the public, while a broader swath also leveraged Twitter as a means of journalistic criticism. Furthermore, Twitter's journalistic subfield plays host to countless other professional as well as personal (inter)actions, further illustrating the hybridity it facilitates. As Carvin candidly put it, "I don't just have Twitter followers. You're my editors, researchers & fact-checkers. You're my newsroom" (Zamora 2012).

These examples illustrate the broad array of implications stemming from the normalization of Twitter and other digital tools within American journalism. It also illustrates that key transformations are taking place at the deeper levels of Bourdieusian practice, the most apparent of which can be found in the dispositions, or *habitus*, of the field's actors. As journalistic practices continue to evolve with the proliferation of new media tools, the ways journalistic actors view the world also begin to shift. For example, journalistic notions of interactivity and engagement tend to follow the patterns of hybridity and convergence modeled by the technologies themselves. Compare what is expected today to what one study found in the late 1990s, when many newspaper reporters were "horrified at the idea that readers would send them email about a story they wrote and might even expect an answer" (as cited in Steensen 2011, p. 317). As this study demonstrates, field relations are shifting as a growing number of journalists adapt to the interactive world of networked journalism. The journalistic field is undergoing significant transformation, resulting in the emergence of a hybrid *networked habitus*.

As introduced in Chap. 3, the term "networked habitus," is meant to highlight the growing acceptance of digital, interactive values and practices throughout much of the field (see Dahlgren 1996; Deuze 2007; Song 2010). According to Clóvis Filho and Sérgio Praca's (2009, p. 19) analysis of the changing structure of Brazil's journalistic field, "The new journalistic structures such as blogs and twitter provide the feeling of augmented 'agency' and journalistic independence. However, they are still bound by the norms and practices of the companies." Thus, journalistic actors are progressively fashioning a hybrid habitus that incorporates many networked values and dispositions. While the skills of traditional journalism remain essential (Herrera and Requejo 2012, p. 88; Thompson 2010), they are increasingly overlapping with digital skills, many of which rely heavily on networked values.

While the findings in this chapter suggest that networked technologies can play a highly significant role in structuring today's journalistic habitus, such an assertion is not entirely new. Technologies are "subsets of habitus" whose place in the field serves to inform and influence the dispositions of actors (Sterne 2003, p. 370). Thus, as with many other technologies and practices, Twitter and the web are increasingly becoming a part of the journalistic habitus. This argument shares many similarities with Zizi Papacharissi and Emily Easton's (2013) theorizing of a "habitus of the new," in that both emphasize the significance of discourse, technology, and convergence in the formation of a hybrid habitus. However, the field convergence and normalization of networked practices as seen on Twitter, which are characteristics that make up the journalistic "networked habitus," differ greatly from Papacharissi and Easton's broader notion of a habitus of the new, which suggests general trends in dispositional hybridity "via a state of permanent novelty" facilitated by dynamics of new media (p. 172).

Since the rise of the web and the growing crisis in the newspaper industry, journalistic *capital* exists increasingly in an online, or at least augmented, world. Given profound technological advancements, opportunities for the exchange of social, cultural, symbolic, and even economic capital continue to grow. One of the most obvious and compelling forms of capital available on Twitter is *social capital*. However, as is true for all forms of capital, the emphasis is not simply on the connections themselves, but rather, the sum of potential power and opportunity facilitated by this set of relations (Bourdieu and Wacquant 1992; Swartz 1997). While connections made on Twitter may remain strongest there, the steady collapse of the divide between digital and face-to-face realms has meant that social capital most often transfers to other contexts (Couldry 2014; Jurgenson 2011).

Twitter has arguably made the largest impact in the areas of symbolic and meta-capital, which is amassed through (inter)actions that publicly elevate an actor's status in the field. Capital may be transferred to the form of (symbolic) power when the sum of an actor's known capital influences their (inter)actions within the field, which it does regularly. Whereas legacy journalists have been most likely to build symbolic and cultural capital by reporting on important public issues that "enhance their prestige and moral positions among audiences" (Kumar 2009, p. 153; see also Champagne 2005), networked technologies provide new opportunities for the exchange of capital. For example, Twitter's increasingly normative status within the field (Lasorsa et al. 2011) has helped it grow into a leading digital space where journalistic reputations are made and maintained. The sheer number of journalistic actors and audiences present on Twitter allows reporters to build a meaningful reputation, positive or negative, through their (inter)actions.

Bourdieu's notion of *doxa* highlights the taken-for-granted norms and values of a particular field, which can (and often do) undergo change along with shifts in practice. Values can gain or lose acceptance through exchanges between actors taking orthodox and heterodox positions. Another important factor is the broader stability of the field, given that crises are a necessary but not sufficient condition for shifts in doxa to occur (Bourdieu 1977, p. 169). Crisis manifests for the journalistic field in the form of economic and technological shifts, which have ushered in the kinds of practical transformations discussed in this chapter.

As discussed in the previous chapter, the sum of these changes requires a deeper consideration of the manner in which field processes shift in the age of mediatization. Thus, rather than conceiving of networked publics as being made up of atomized individuals, this book considers how the dynamics of mediatization are shaping the structure and practice of the journalistic field. The journalistic uses of Twitter by professionals and citizens alike are, on the macro level, contributing to the ever-growing *mediatized superstructure* whereby members across the networked public populate and make possible an ambient and accountable news system. That is, networked publics play an integral role in the work of journalism, on Twitter and off. They do so, in part, by serving as sources that help gather, share, and verify information and make information more freely available. As will become evident in later chapters, those operating at the margins of the journalistic field pose challenges that have the potential to strengthen the fourth estate, whether by attempting to create and share news, call attention to underreported stories, or hold legacy media accountable to public concerns. By hosting and facilitating much of this work, platforms like Twitter have the ability to amplify the voices of these actors to the point that they can no longer be ignored.

According to the data collected for this chapter, one of the field's primary issues of debate on Twitter and the web concerned the values of truth and verification, as well as the distinction between professional and citizen journalism, which is a tension that will be visible throughout this book. Whereas a vocal minority of Twitter-journalists sought to uphold traditional values, many more took hybrid positions that synthesized traditional and digitally driven values. While debate continues, the fact that such contention is itself manifested through new media suggests that a transition toward doxic status may be further along than some traditionalists might hope. Indeed, "such deliberations may be had over a cultural and ideological shift that has already occurred and whose logic is finally simply playing itself out in our technological and social institutions" (Song 2010, p. 270). As adaptation to these values and practices continues within the context of mediatized fields, Twitter usage by professional (and citizen) journalists is steadily becoming more doxic.

Conclusion

From the telegraph, to the telephone, to Twitter, the proliferation of new media technologies has had a profound impact on many fields and practices, especially those related to journalism.

While the scope of this analysis focused primarily on professional journalists' use of Twitter between 2009 and 2011, a close examination of Twitter's place in the field during this formative time provides an important foundation on which later developments rest. Drawing on digital-ethnographic and textual data, this chapter analyzed Twitter's affordances and practical implications for the journalistic field. Although a notable portion of the field remained skeptical about the implications of Twitter and other new media tools for journalistic practice, a clear majority of Twitter-journalists found the medium to be a great asset. Reasons cited included its speed, conciseness, interactivity, and potential for engagement, made possible by its ubiquity and popularity in the field.

Nonetheless, as Twitter-journalism practices spread across the field, the capital and dispositions of the field's actors begin to reflect this normalization, thus affecting how they practice and perceive journalism. Accordingly, the field is undergoing a notable shift in the habitus of many networked journalists; as traditional and digital practices converge, journalists are becoming normalized to this hybrid relationship. The result is a combination of dispositions integrating many of the norms and values typical of the participatory web. This development is interpreted as the emergence of a networked habitus, where journalistic actors are increasingly disposed toward technological and participatory practices from hybridized field positions. As later chapters will illustrate, it is this hybridity—the dense connections between networked individuals from across the field spectrum—that makes possible a mediatized superstructure where networked publics engage in a wide variety of journalistic practices.

As journalistic capital and habitus undergo change, so do journalism's norms and values (i.e., doxa). This was illustrated by the taken-for-granted values inherent within statements of many Twitter-journalists. By analyzing journalistic meta-discourse on Twitter, many of the field's orthodox (accepted) and heterodox (debated) values were shown to be consistent with networked values of openness, participation, and convergence. Since the field's elements of practice come to constitute the field itself, the ongoing transformations documented here are highly significant for American journalism and those seeking to understand it. But as the remaining chapters will demonstrate, the journalistic uses and implications of Twitter are far from monolithic. Indeed, who uses Twitter, how, and to what ends, varies greatly, depending on the users' location and disposition within mediatized fields.

REFERENCES

Araiza, J. A., Sturm, H. A., Istek, P., & Bock, M. A. (2016). Hands up, don't shoot, whose side are you on? Journalists tweeting the Ferguson protests. *Cultural Studies ↔ Critical Methodologies, 16*(3), 305–312. https://doi.org/10.1177/1532708616634834.

Benson, R., Blach-Ørsten, M., Powers, M., Willig, I., & Zambrano, S. V. (2012). Media systems online and off: Comparing the form of news in the United States, Denmark, and France. *Journal of Communication, 62*(1), 21–38.

Bentivegna, S., & Marchetti, R. (2017). Journalists at a crossroads: Are traditional norms and practices challenged by Twitter? *Journalism*, Advanced online publication. https://doi.org/10.1177/1464884917716594.

Bergman, C. (2011). How the BBC lost 60,000 Twitter followers to ITV. *The Wall Blog*. Retrieved September 3, 2014, from http://wallblog.co.uk/2011/07/25/how-the-bbc-lost-60000-twitter-followers/.

Bourdieu, P. (1977). *Outline of a theory of practice*. Cambridge: Cambridge University Press.

Bourdieu, P., & Wacquant, L. (1992). *An invitation to reflexive sociology*. Chicago, IL: University of Chicago Press.

Canter, L. (2015). Personalised tweeting: The emerging practices of journalists on Twitter. *Digital Journalism, 3*(6), 888–907. https://doi.org/10.1080/21670811.2014.973148.

Carvin, A. (2012). *Distant witness: Social media, the Arab Spring and a journalism revolution*. New York, NY: CUNY Journalism Press..

Chadha, K., & Wells, R. (2016). Journalistic responses to technological innovation in newsrooms. *Digital Journalism, 4*(8), 1020–1035. https://doi.org/10.1080/21670811.2015.1123100.

Champagne, P. (2005). The 'double dependency': The journalistic field between politics and markets. In R. Benson & E. Neveu (Eds.), *Bourdieu and the journalistic field* (pp. 48–63). Cambridge: Polity.

Comor, E., & Compton, J. (2015). Journalistic labour and technological fetishism. *The Political Economy of Communication, 3*(2), 74–87. Retrieved from http://www.polecom.org/index.php/polecom/article/view/59.

Compton, J. R., & Benedetti, P. (2010). Labour, new media and the institutional restructuring of journalism. *Journalism Studies, 11*(4), 487–499.

Couldry, N. (2014). When mediatization hits the ground. In A. Hepp & F. Krotz (Eds.), *Mediatized worlds: Culture and society in a media age* (pp. 54–71). New York: Palgrave Macmillan.

Dahlgren, P. (1996). Media logic in cyberspace: Repositioning journalism and its publics. *Javnost – The Public, 3*(3), 59–72.

Deuze, M. (2007). *Media work*. Cambridge: Polity.

Ellis, J. (2011, August 2). Boston Globe creates a Twitter board for the newsroom. *Neiman Foundation at Harvard*. Retrieved November 17, 2017, from http://www.niemanlab.org/2011/08/boston-globe-creates-a-twitter-board-for-the-newsroom/.

Filho, C. D. B., & Praca, S. (2009). Ethics in old and new journalism structures. *Brazilian Journalism Research, 5*(2), 5–21.

Google trends. (2017). Google. Retrieved November 21, 2017, from https://trends.google.com/.

Gubrium, J. F., & Holstein, J. (2008). *Analyzing narrative reality*. London: SAGE.

Guerrini, F. (2013). Newsroom curators and independent storytellers: Content curation as a new form of journalism. *Reuters Institute for the Study of Journalism – Fellowship Paper*. Retrieved November 20, 2017, from http://reutersinstitute.politics.ox.ac.uk/our-research/newsroom-curators-and-independent-storytellers.

Hanks, W. F. (1993). Notes on semantics in linguistic practice. In C. J. Calhoun, E. LiPuma, & M. Postone (Eds.), *Bourdieu: Critical perspectives* (pp. 139–155). Chicago, IL: University of Chicago Press.

Hellmueller, L., Vos, T. P., & Poepsel, M. A. (2013). Shifting journalistic capital? *Journalism Studies, 14*(3), 287–304.

Hermida, A. (2010). Twittering the news: The emergence of ambient journalism. *Journalism Practice, 4*(3), 297–308.

Hermida, A. (2012). Tweets and truth. *Journalism Practice, 6*(5), 1–10.

Hermida, A., Lewis, S. C., & Zamith, R. (2014). Sourcing the Arab spring: A case study of Andy Carvin's sources on Twitter during the Tunisian and Egyptian revolutions. *Journal of Computer-Mediated Communication, 19*(3), 479–499. https://doi.org/10.1111/jcc4.12074.

Herrera, S., & Requejo, J. L. (2012). 10 good practices for news organizations using Twitter. *Journal of Applied Journalism & Media Studies, 1*(1), 79–95.

Irvine, D. (2013, June 14). Study: Majority of journalists use Twitter. *Accuracy in Media*. Retrieved December 7, 2017, from http://www.aim.org/don-irvine-blog/study-majority-of-journalists-use-twitter-2/.

Jurgenson, N. (2011, February 24). Digital dualism versus augmented reality. *Cyborgology*. Retrieved November 17, 2017, from http://thesocietypages.org/cyborgology/2011/02/24/digital-dualism-versus-augmented-reality/.

Krause, M. (2011). Reporting and the transformations of the journalistic field: US news media, 1890–2000. *Media, Culture & Society, 33*, 89–104.

Kumar, A. (2009). Looking back and looking ahead: Journalistic rules, social control, social change, and relative autonomy. *Journal of Media Sociology, 1*(3), 136–160.

Kunelius, R., & Ruusunoksa, L. (2008). Mapping professional imagination: On the potential of professional culture in the newspapers of the future. *Journalism Studies, 9*(5), 662–678.

Lasorsa, D. (2012). Transparency and other journalistic norms on Twitter. *Journalism Studies, 13*(3), 402–417.

Lasorsa, D., Lewis, S. C., & Holton, A. (2011). Normalizing Twitter. *Journalism Studies, 13*(1), 19–36.

Laucius, J. (2011, July 23). Twitter buffs talk tweets at Social Capital, an Ottawa social media conference. *The Ottawa Citizen*. Retrieved November 17, 2017, from http://liveworkplay.ca/media/citizen-socapott-july-23-2011.pdf.

Lawrence, R. G., Molyneux, L., Coddington, M., & Holton, A. (2014). Tweeting conventions. *Journalism Studies, 15*(6), 789–806. https://doi.org/10.1080/1461670X.2013.836378.

Macnicol, G. (2012, May 4). Juan Williams misses NPR; Ben Smith competes with Taco Bell Health Channel. *Politico*. Retrieved November 17, 2017, from https://www.politico.com/media/story/2012/05/juan-williams-misses-npr-ben-smith-competes-with-taco-bell-health-channel-000465.

McChesney, R. W., & Nichols, J. (2010). *The death and life of American journalism: The media revolution that will begin the world again*. New York, NY: Nation Books.

Miller, C. (2011, May 11). #bbcsms: Changing journalists' social media mindset. *BBC College of Journalism Blog*. Retrieved November 17, 2017, from http://www.bbc.co.uk/blogs/collegeofjournalism/entries/c25df279-74ed-3174-8db0-6d7a38613499.

Mills, C. W. (1940). Situated actions and vocabularies of motive. *American Sociological Review, 5*(6), 904–913.

Molyneux, L., Holton, A., & Lewis, S. C. (2017). How journalists engage in branding on Twitter: individual, organizational, and institutional levels. *Information, Communication & Society*, Advanced online publication. https://doi.org/10.1080/1369118X.2017.1314532.

Papacharissi, Z. (2009). *Journalism and citizenship: New agendas in communication*. New York, NY: Routledge.

Papacharissi, Z., & Easton, E. (2013). In the habitus of the new: Structure, agency, and the social media habitus. In J. Hartley, J. Burgess, & A. Bruns (Eds.), *A companion to new media dynamics* (pp. 171–184). Malden, MA: Wiley-Blackwell.

Rainie, L., & Wellman, B. (2012). *Networked: The new social operating system*. Cambridge, MA: MIT Press.

Russell, A. (2013). Innovation in hybrid spaces: 2011 UN Climate Summit and the expanding journalism landscape. *Journalism, 14*(7), 904–920.

Russell, A. (2016). *Journalism as activism: Recoding media power*. Malden, MA: Polity.

Santana, A. D., & Hopp, T. (2016). Tapping into a new stream of (personal) data: Assessing journalists' different use of social media. *Journalism & Mass Communication Quarterly, 93*(2), 383–408. https://doi.org/10.1177/1077699016637105.

Scheuer, J. (2003). Habitus as the principle for social practice: A proposal for critical discourse analysis. *Language in Society, 32*(2), 143–175.

Schultz, I. (2007). The journalistic gut feeling: Journalistic doxa, news habitus and orthodox news values. *Journalism Practice, 1*(2), 190–207.

Scollon, S. (2001). Habitus, consciousness, agency and the problem of intention. *Folia Linguistica, 35*(1/2), 97–129.

Siapera, E., & Spyridou, L. P. (2012). The field of online journalism: A Bourdieusian analysis. In E. Siapera & A. Veglis (Eds.), *The handbook of global online journalism* (pp. 77–97). Malden, MA: Wiley-Blackwell.

Song, F. W. (2010). Theorizing web 2.0. *Information, 13*(2), 249–275.

Steensen, S. (2011). Online journalism and the promises of new technology. *Journalism Studies, 12*, 311–327.

Sterne, J. (2003). Bourdieu, technique and technology. *Cultural Studies, 17*(3–4), 367–389.

Swartz, D. (1997). *Culture & power: The sociology of Pierre Bourdieu*. Chicago, IL: University of Chicago Press.

Ternes, B., Peterlin, L. J., & Reinardy, S. (2017). Newsroom workers' job satisfaction contingent on position and adaptation to digital disruption. *Journalism Practice*, Advanced print publication. https://doi.org/10.1080/17512786.2017.1318712.

Thompson, J. (2010, January 4). Ten things every journalist should know in 2010. *Journalism.co.uk*. Retrieved November 17, 2017, from http://blogs.journalism.co.uk/2010/01/04/ten-things-every-journalist-should-know-in-2010/.

UK journalists on Twitter. (2017). *Journalism.co.uk*. Retrieved November 17, 2017, from https://www.journalism.co.uk/prof/.

Vis, F. (2013). Twitter as a reporting tool for breaking news. *Digital Journalism, 1*(1), 27–47.

Vos, T. P., Craft, S. C., & Ashley, S. (2011). New media, old criticism: Bloggers' press criticism and the journalistic field. *Journalism, 13*(7), 850–868.

Weaver, D. H., & Willnat, L. (2016). Changes in U.S. journalism. *Journalism Practice, 10*(7), 844–855. https://doi.org/10.1080/17512786.2016.1171162.

Wiik, J. (2009). Identities under construction: Professional journalism in a phase of destabilization. *International Review of Sociology/Revue Internationale de Sociologie, 19*(2), 351–365.

Willnat, L., & Weaver, D. H. (2014, May). *The American journalist in a digital age: A first look*. Paper presented at the International Communication Association Annual Conference, Seattle, WA. Retrieved November 13, 2017, from http://news.indiana.edu/releases/iu/2014/05/2013-american-journalist-key-findings.pdf.

Zamora, J. (2012, March 26). "I don't just have Twitter followers. You're my editors, researchers & fact-checkers. You're my news room." – @acarvin." *@jczamora*. Twitter. Retrieved from https://twitter.com/jczamora/statuses/184493751794806784.

The Pros and Cons of Pro-Am Journalism: Breaking News During the #BostonMarathon Bombing and Beyond

As runners in the 2013 Boston Marathon steadily streamed toward the finish line, two bombs exploded nearby. The blasts not only induced panic amid the sea of participants, spectators, and volunteers at the scene, but also upon the constant stream of news and information. Reports of the attack spread like wildfire across media channels of all kinds—broadcast, online, print, and social networks. Beyond the obvious shock and awe flowing from the scene, a group of networked journalists—both professional and amateur—began using their respective media channels to get the word out about this breaking news event and to begin the process of "sorting-out" what happened and who was behind it (Kovach and Rosenstiel 2007).

Like many engaged members of the networked public, I was furiously wading through a sea of Twitter posts, seeking a glimpse of what had happened and searching for links to longer-form stories that could provide a more detailed picture. In addition to being filled with updates about the breaking news events, my Twitter feed was also packed with journalistic meta-discourse—reflections about how well (or not) professionals and citizens had covered the news. This theme was facilitated in part by the hashtag discussions surrounding the 2013 International Symposium for Online Journalism (ISOJ), held on that same day.

News updates of the event were shared over a broad media ecosystem via live television broadcasts, blogs, social media posts, as well as many other platforms. In addition to the flow of news from professional

© The Author(s) 2018
S. R. Barnard, *Citizens at the Gates*,
https://doi.org/10.1007/978-3-319-90446-7_5

reporters, countless spur-of-the-moment updates were posted by "the people formerly known as the audience" (Rosen 2006). Eye-witness updates in the form of text, pictures, and videos were shared on Facebook, YouTube, Tumblr, Instagram, and blogs, many of which were later republished by news organizations. Not surprisingly, many posts were little more than reactions from relatively uninformed members of the public. For example, Twitter was flooded with vast speculation about which social group the perpetrators might be behind the attack. And, in a somewhat predictable manner, many jumped to blame Arab Muslims, North Koreans, and even Boston's gay community ("Public Shaming" 2013).

Despite the all-too-common lack of civility in public discourse, it was the lack of factuality that posed the greater threat in this case. While the Boston Marathon bombing may seem like an extraordinary case, the flow of news following the bombing was far from atypical. The falsities and distortions (re)presented on social media channels appeared to grow almost exponentially, leading many to lambast them for facilitating more chaos than order (Schultz 2013). Most infamously, the multiday response of many members of the Reddit community was so misguided that the site's general manager issued a public apology for the community's role in "fueling online witch hunts" (Kaufman 2013). A simple web search for "Boston Marathon bombing AND social media" yields two distinct kinds of stories: those that lambast social media users for contributing to the confusion, and those that praise them for meaningful contributions to the public record and response efforts.

Indeed, concerned citizens committed many laudable acts in the aftermath of the bombing. Some quickly switched from enjoying the race to documenting the tragedy, and even aiding the response efforts. Others not at the scene opted to create a list of runners who had already crossed the finish line, and were therefore purportedly safe. Professional journalists also turned to their usual media—especially television, radio, blogs, and Twitter—to tell the story as it unfolded (Rogers 2013). Many of these reports played an integral role in the spread of information across society. Yet, despite what were likely the best of intentions, many early reports were partially—if not utterly—false. This tension is not merely a matter of episodic mistakes; it is a fact of open journalism, and remains at the core of countless debates over how to foster truthful reporting in the age of mediatization.

With triumphant successes and epic failures on both sides, the work of professional and citizen journalists reporting on the Boston Marathon bombing provide a broad-ranging view of the media landscape from which many fruitful lessons may be harvested. Accordingly, this chapter is driven by three main questions: What were the successes and failures of the journalistic response to the bombings? What role did Twitter and other news media play in this response? What can this case tell us about the state of the American journalistic field?

To address these questions, a wide variety of media responses were examined as well as key actors' usage of Twitter and social media. In addition to seeking an explanation for what did and did not work in the media response to the bombings, this chapter aims to build a better understanding of how reporting from across the new media landscape can be leveraged to more effectively produce accurate and socially impactful histories of the present. At the same time, this chapter is also focused on addressing the evolving relations of the journalistic field.

TWITTER'S ROLE IN BREAKING NEWS

As discussed in Chap. 1, digital media tools are an increasingly prolific part of social life in the twenty-first century. Opportunities for networked sharing are abundant on the web, and such sharing appears increasingly likely when users possess the technology and capital to participate. Still, meaningful participation seems unlikely without the technologies, practices, and dispositions—let alone the meaningful experiences—needed to create news. Indeed, while a growing majority of those belonging to networked publics may be seen as "everyday newsworkers" (Gans 2007) given their proclivity for sharing information, their definition of the situation and of newsworthiness are both more likely to align with fields other than journalism. Nonetheless, the growing norm of social sharing can be just as applicable during a mundane experience as during an experience marred with tragedy.

Imagine the difference in social media timelines surrounding the 2012 and the 2013 Boston Marathon races. While the differences are obvious—with the former dominated by typical posts about the famous marathon, and the latter by atypical posts about the now infamous bombing near the finish line—the commonalities reflect users' experiences in that place and time. Thus, when news breaks in today's mediatized society, the networked public, armed with mobile devices, will play an important role in documenting and reporting on the events. Furthermore, the distributed, ambient nature of citizen reporting in the digital age helps to make up the mediatized superstructure that helps shape information flows.

While it is impossible to pin down the exact date Twitter became unquestionably critical to the breaking news process, by April 2013, the stage was already set for Twitter and other social media sites to play host to the real-time exchange of vital news and information (Bruns 2014; Murthy and Longwell 2013; Papacharissi and Oliveira 2012; Vis 2013). This new and growing flow of information not only enabled media producers near and far to tell their stories, but for members of the global public to participate in the exchange as well. While these affordances are leveraged to varying ends, depending on the case and context, the unifying trend has hued toward an evolving sorting-out process that is both quicker and messier than traditional journalistic practice, harnessing the power of technological convergence and privileging the fast-flowing information from sources outside the field's traditional gatekeepers. While the acts of sharing and commenting on existing news stories (gatewatching) and producing and disseminating their own (gatecrashing) may be more likely to spread factual errors, a more open journalistic field also provides opportunity for the sharing of valid perspectives not often seen in legacy media.

Throughout the 2011 Egyptian revolution, for example, Twitter served as an important site for both professional and citizen news actors. The news values held by these two groups appear more congruent than divergent, likely because citizen journalists "function based on what they have been socialized to recognize as accepted news values" (Papacharissi and Oliveira 2012, p. 273). However, as the next chapter illustrates, the networked public's heightened emphasis on instantaneity, crowd-sourced elites, solidarity, and ambience (Papacharissi and Oliveira 2012, p. 273) suggests a greater acceptance of networked news values than their professional counterparts. Indeed, citizen journalists' *illusio*, or "collective belief in the game," may differ slightly from professionals, given the latter group's more apparent commitment to the field's core values (Bourdieu 1996, p. 230). Whereas professional journalists are purportedly driven by their belief in the importance of civil discourse in service of the public good (Kovach and Rosenstiel 2007), citizen forays in the journalistic field, on the whole, are more advocative of particular political outcomes. Yet, as news values continue to spread beyond the professional core of the journalistic field, networked citizens are further internalizing those traditional media values and hybridizing them with others befitting of their (dis)position.

As the previous chapters have made clear, the rise of journalists' hybrid, networked habitus is ongoing, and is best illustrated by the field's pioneers, who might be thought of as part of a "media vanguard" (Russell 2016). In the early 2010s, Andy Carvin may have been the best example of hybrid journalism, as evidenced by the recent scholarship on his work (Hermida et al. 2014; Torres and Hermida 2017). Carvin's success in hybridizing the professional journalistic routine and combining it with a humanistic (and occasionally advocative) approach popularized by networked publics places him at an important journalistic boundary. This simultaneous embodiment of a journalistic and political habitus may be an example of the hybrid, networked habitus *par excellence*. As will be seen in the following sections, however, careful consideration is needed regarding what happens when such positions and dispositions are brought to bear within the context of the new media ecosystem.

Interlude: Lessons on Breaking News and Conflicting Reports from Yemen

Just as the response to the Boston Marathon bombing illustrates the dynamics of breaking news reporting in the time of mediatization, similar struggles to identify verifiable accounts of breaking news events can be found in comparable situations across the globe. Carvin (2013) wrote about his experience trying to make sense of conflicting reports coming out of Yemen during the 2011 "Arab Spring" protests and the deadly, state-sanctioned violence waged against citizens.

However surprising, one of Carvin's (2013, p. 164) most prominent early sources happened to be a "stay-at-home mom in New Jersey who doesn't speak Arabic" and who ran an influential blog dedicated to analyses of the revolution. Over time, he increasingly relied on information from Twitter and YouTube to find first-hand accounts from protestors and witnesses. Carvin's engagement with these sources was integral to his reporting, as well as to the broader public understanding of what happened. Indeed, Carvin's interventions into the flow of information, where he requested clarification or confirmation of statements, appeared to serve an important sorting-out function for Yemeni nationals as well as those following the events from abroad.

The reports flowing from the region via legacy media were so conflicting that they created even more confusion. At one point, Carvin (2013, p. 179) tweeted a summary of the deeply conflicting reports coming from television media, "So to summarize, Yemeni pres Saleh is/isn't/could be/perhaps is/supposedly/according to twitter/according to Reuters/sort of/who knows dead." By contrast, Carvin's strategy was not to retweet unverified rumors—he sometimes did this cautiously—but also to contextualize, clarify, and ask follow-up questions. For example, initial reports emerged that then-President Saleh had been taken to a Saudi hospital for treatment, which were quickly accompanied by an apparently doctored photograph of Saleh in a hospital bed looking gravely ill. The photo, initially circulated by a professional news organization, was later reported fabricated. Carvin responded by retweeting a link to the image along with a request for his followers to scrutinize the picture for evidence of (in)authenticity. As he explained, "A picture may speak a thousand words, but in this case it could have sparked a thousand rumors if we hadn't nipped it in the bud" (Carvin 2013, p. 183). Indeed, the race to provide quick updates often risks distorting the facts, thus soiling the public record, and therefore, public opinion.

Despite the potential damage done by erroneous reports, the online record is often set straight rather quickly, in a matter of minutes. Nevertheless, in a time of political polarization and network homophily, false reports can spread more rapidly than they can be corrected. In this case, and in many others, many engaged participants came together to investigate questionable claims and to share their findings with the rest of the network. Other examinations of networked news cycles have also shown that a small minority of key thought leaders typically drive the flow of information (Meraz and Papacharissi 2013; Tufekci and Wilson 2012). Indeed, at least with social news networks, public opinion may work much like it did nearly a century ago—driven by well-connected and trusted opinion leaders (Mills 1963). However, one key difference is the structure and scope of the network, which has grown far broader and more nimble in the age of mediatization. As this case demonstrates, however, greater influence for networked publics does not guarantee a more accurate and efficient communicative system. Rather, the outcome is often an array of conflicting reports coming from all across the media system. This is not unique to social news networks; as will be shown, the same can be said of professional reporting as well.

Triumphant Successes and Epic Failures: Media Coverage in the Aftermath of the Bombing

In just a decade or two, a central problem with the American media ecosystem has, in many regards, flipped to the opposite end of the spectrum. Whereas the challenge used to be about access to useful information, now, access to information is so great that it is hard to know where to begin. Thus, the new challenge becomes how to proceed effectively when information is so abundant, and often so conflicting, as to bring about a new kind of alienation?

While this problem is most often discussed in the context of individual news consumers, it also bears considerably on rank-and-file members of the journalistic field. Indeed, the steady flow of information through a growing array of channels requires that journalists both adapt to the new climate while remaining dedicated to the traditional practices of sourcing and verification. Pressures for speed and accuracy create a sort of paradox for journalists covering breaking news in the digital age. How can they be speedy and accurate without sacrificing one for the other? And what is lost when they try to do more with less? Their audience? Their credibility? Answers to these questions, as they relate to the Boston Marathon bombing, may be provided by first uncovering *how* media outlets responded and *why* the responses should be seen as successful, or not.

The public response through online media was a mixed bag of successes and failures. The same was true for professional news outlets' reporting of the events following the bombing. Some were extraordinary examples of how journalists should cover a crisis. Others were similarly extraordinary examples of what *not* to do. Consider the vast difference in coverage between the *New York Post* (*Post*) and the *Boston Globe* (*Globe*). On one hand, the *Post*'s coverage was characteristically sensational: they exaggerated the number of deaths, claimed that a key person of interest was Saudi, and ran a cover story with a photograph identifying two innocent witnesses as the suspected "bag men" (Shapiro 2013). As a result, the paper faced a lawsuit for defamation (Haughney 2013). On the other hand, the *Globe* was said to have "double coverage" of the bombing, with their publicly available Boston.com site dedicated to delivering "what you need to know" and the BostonGlobe.com paywalled site digging deeper into the subject with more "traditional reporting" accompanied by various multimedia (Ellis 2013).

On the whole, information flowed rapidly across the media landscape, and many news outlets were quick to weigh in with reports of varying credibility. The *Post*, for example, quickly claimed "a law enforcement source confirmed" that 12 people were killed and that a "Saudi Arabian national" was a suspected perpetrator (Kroll 2013; "Authorities ID" 2013). In actuality, only three victims were killed and the Saudi was a witness, not a suspect. As Johnathan Chait (2013, para. 7) put it:

> The *Post* is hardly the only news organization rushing fragments of pseudo-fact into the public domain and then retracting them. (The *Post* also errone-ously reported Monday that twelve people had died in the attacks.) But its recklessness displays an almost smarmy, legalistic disregard for its own swath of destruction. When the "Bag Men" scoop disintegrated, editor Col Allan replied, "We stand by our story. The image was e-mailed to law-enforcement agencies yesterday afternoon seeking information about these men, as our story reported. We did not identify them as suspects."

Reuters' Jack Shafer (2013, para. 12) similarly lambasted the *Post* for its wild disregard for responsible reporting:

> [T]he *Post*'s extreme, almost defiant inaccuracy has united America's arm-chair media critics like little else. It can hardly be denied that the racy *Post* has pointed the way for decades toward an info-entertainment hybrid that many have followed. This week, at least, in its stunning contempt for fact, it has defined the basement into which no media outlet that wants respect wishes to descend.

While the *Post* may stand out as the worst offender, with their obvious breaches of traditional journalistic norms, many more cases of reporting failures from legacy sources occurred. For example, CNN, Fox News, the Associated Press (AP), and the *Globe*, among many others, all misreported that an arrest had been made (Lichfield 2013; "Journalists talk" 2013). Although they worked swiftly to correct the record, the flawed informa-tion spread rapidly, especially among other professional news outlets. The *Globe*'s mistake, for example, was based on CNN's initial report.

Beyond the potential backlash from members of the public, misinfor-mation can also play a significant role in how public officials handle cases. The mounting pressure to be the first to publish breaking news may encourage looser verification standards, and this pressure can trickle down to the sources themselves, as evidenced by the false statements made by official sources in the aftermath of the bombing. For example, the decision to release photos of the two suspects was driven, in part, by a desire to counteract the misinformation proffered on Reddit and beyond (Greenfield 2013; Montgomery et al. 2013).

Although these examples are revealing, the counter-narrative about social media as a source for rumors and false reporting was also persistent. For example, as Gilad Lotan argued, "initial, mistaken information will be retweeted more than any subsequent information" (Skok 2012). This contention was based on a case study of an incorrect tweet by @NBCNewYork about the New York Police Department's (NYPD) response to the ongoing Occupy Wall Street protests (Silverman 2012). While Lotan (2012, para. 12) contended that misinformation is not necessarily any more likely to spread on Twitter than information that is verifiably accurate, he insisted that "the more sensationalized a story, the more likely it is to travel far." On the other hand, as Mark Jurkowitz pointed out just days after the bombing, "there is a self-correcting mechanism in journalism that's quicker than it's ever been" (as cited in Farhi 2013, para. 7). Both statements may be correct in their own right. As will be shown, it requires participation from a vast network of professional and amateur actors for the ambient news system to function properly.

Tweeting the #Manhunt

Initial reports of the bombing were followed by days of intense searching for the suspects, or as Twitter users referred to it, the "#manhunt." In addition to being a tragic and captivating news story, it was also a lesson in breaking news reporting, as the stream of updates from across the field were frequently rife with misinformation. Nevertheless, many excellent examples of citizen journalism also occurred. One of the most visible and illustrative examples was Andrew Kitzenberg, a Watertown, MA resident who happened to be in the right place at the right (or wrong) time, and decided to capture and live-tweet his experience. Like many other citizens committing acts of journalism, his perspective was so revealing that it got the attention of legacy and cable news outlets (Fitzgerald 2013; "Witness says" 2013). Indeed, in the days following the event, Kitzenberg served as both a witness and an ad hoc journalist for multiple news outlets.

Just minutes after midnight on April 19, 2013, while witnessing a shootout between police and the two suspects, Kitzenberg snapped photos on his phone and posted them to Twitter. His photo-driven tweets were also accompanied by text—the Twitter-journalist's version of captions—to help provide much-needed context. Indeed, while some pictures can "speak for themselves" and may be "worth a thousand words," at least aphoristically, Kitzenberg's required context. They were taken after midnight from his third-floor window, so they needed explanation if they were going to have their desired effect, which they certainly did. A mere 20 minutes later, Kitzenberg began receiving inquiries from journalists covering the story (Fitzgerald 2013). First, it was Ravi Somaiya from the *New York Times.* Later, it was Paul Walsh from the *Minneapolis Star Tribune*, and finally, NBC's Mara Schiavocampo. Within three months of the incident, Kitzenberg had "granted more than 50 interviews" (Fitzgerald 2013, para. 4).

Kitzenberg's swift rise to prominence as a source for professional reporters, and as an ad hoc reporter in his own right, had as much to do with his own actions as with their indisputable translatability into the professional journalistic field. He was a witness sine qua non, although this status had more to do with his public recognition than material condition. Indeed, while he was not the only eye witness that night, he was the most well-disposed to report on the night's events. NBC's Lester Holt attributed Kitzenberg with possessing "some of the best information we have about how the suspects behaved" (Fitzgerald 2013, para. 2). Or, as Kitzenberg himself put it, "I witnessed it, and had a lot of detail to describe what had happened. I think that brought more attention to me" (Fitzgerald 2013, para. 10).

Another likely factor contributing to legacy media gatekeepers' interest in Kitzenberg's account is the changing structure of the journalistic field. During times of crisis, legacy media outlets frequently loosen journalistic criteria to hasten the flow of breaking news by relying more heavily on citizen eye-witness accounts, which are increasingly collected and shared on platforms like Twitter (Bennett 2016). Rather than reflecting an explicit change in journalistic values, this trend is likely a response to the converging influence of market pressures and the normalization of Twitter, both of which were evident in the journalistic field by the time of the bombing in April 2013 (Bakker 2012; Lasorsa et al. 2012). Thus, the incorporation of (citizens') social media content in the news should be viewed as yet another step in the journalistic field's adaptation to the hybrid news environment.

New(s) Media Convergence in the Aftermath
of the Marathon Bombing

During his live interview with Schiavocampo, Kitzenberg reflected on the night's events and provided live narration of the continued response efforts to inspect for explosives. As Kitzenberg described, "Actually, as we speak, there is a bomb squad robot that is going into [the suspects'] green vehicle" ("Witness says" 2013, 4:11).

Why didn't NBC rely on their own staff to report from the scene? They had cameras there, wielded by qualified professionals. Did they not have another reporter who was qualified to stand on the other end of that camera with a microphone in hand? Or did they simply trust Kitzenberg enough to drop the mic and give him the opportunity to practice his skills as a journalist, however accidental? As with most historical events, the specific causal chain is likely complicated.

While the full story as to *why* Kitzenberg was granted such a coveted pass through so many of professional journalism's gates may never be known, an important lesson is hidden within the de facto press pass he possessed that night. Kitzenberg had no established credibility or symbolic capital in the field. Nevertheless, professional journalism's growing reliance on networked publics to provide ambient news coverage combined with legacy organizations' established media meta-capital to make Kitzenberg a temporary news celebrity (Couldry 2016). Indeed, NBC was drawn to Kitzenberg because he had a different, indisputable type of authority. He was *there*, on scene, and willing to share his knowledge with a captive, networked public. As Jay Rosen (2012, para. 2) put it, this kind of journalistic authority boils down to one simple axiom: "I'm there, you're not. Let me tell you about it."

However, with journalistic authority comes journalistic responsibility. And Kitzenberg did not let journalists, or the public, down. His actions demonstrated a savviness of journalistic conventions most amateurs (and too many professionals) would envy. He also appeared well-informed and capable of synthesizing this information to provide a pointed, contextualized analysis, even during live broadcasts ("Witness says" 2013). For example, Schiavocampo's live interview with Kitzenberg for MSNBC began with this attribution of journalistic capital:

> We have on the phone Andrew Kitzenberg, who was an eyewitness ... he gave his account to the *New York Times* and we have him on the line now. Andrew, in terms of all the accounts we've heard this evening, yours is by far

the most exhaustive. It sounds like you had, essentially, a front-row seat to everything that was happening. Describe what you saw this evening. ("Witness says" 2013, 0:01)

Whether or not he needed it, the vote of confidence worked and Kitzenberg went on to provide a detailed description of his eye-witness account. This successful pro-am collaboration is one small but illustrious example of the potential for members of the networked public to participate in the news-making process.

While this case study may be extreme, even approaching sensational, it is far from an outlier in terms of how the journalistic field handles breaking news in the digital age. Whether it is Kitzenberg's response to the #manhunt, Janis Krums' (2009) response to the plane in the Hudson River, or countless other cases where eye witnesses had a hand in shaping the story, these networked citizens took on roles that far exceeded the traditions of journalistic sourcing. It is this kind of hybridization that sets today's journalistic field apart from the one of decades past.

CONCLUSION

This chapter examined a small but visible portion of the American news media response in the aftermath of the 2013 Boston Marathon bombing. Much of the examples discussed comprise a variety of sources, including both new and traditional media. Most notable are the products and practices that arose from the collaborative effort put forth by networked journalists. These efforts were driven by a new kind of hybrid networked habitus that may be found in professional and amateur actors in the age of mediatization. Although some may view this trend as a threat to the orthodox traditions of American media, this convergence—of fields, actors, and practices—is an indispensable reality of the new media ecology.

Whether it is Carvin's trust in Twitter users to source his reporting on the Arab Spring or American media outlets tapping social media users to gather information about the manhunt as the news broke, traditional gatekeepers' reliance on the people formerly known as the audience is increasingly apparent. While both news events involved the initial publishing of errors, they occurred under different circumstances. On the one hand, Carvin shared (and when necessary, quickly corrected) information crowd-sourced through a vast network of citizen journalists. The use of Twitter to collect and verify this information provided a semblance of transparency, since much of the reporting process was conducted in public view. On the other hand, legacy media coverage of the Boston Marathon bombing, though relying on citizens' accounts shared on social media, was less transparent. Like the bulk of professional journalism, news outlets' coverage of the bombing included many stories that ran without much detail about the sources of their information or the manner in which it was collected.

Whatever the differences, the journalistic products and processes on display in the reporting of these breaking news events relied heavily on networked publics. For better or worse, these citizens and their use of networked communication technologies constitute a key part of the emergent mediatized superstructure, to which the profession of journalism is continuing to adapt. Although Carvin may have been an outlier in the extent to which he engaged with his network of amateur reporters, there is clear evidence to suggest that journalists are increasingly reliant on social networks, and indeed, their broad user base, to gather information (Santana and Hopp 2016). This trend is evidenced by television and online journalism outlets' increasing inclusion of citizens' social media posts as part of the news (Broersma and Graham 2013; Lefky et al. 2015).

Despite the journalistic affordances of Twitter and the glut of information it may contain, there are obvious reasons to question the network's effectiveness at sorting out fact from fiction. The "wisdom of the crowd" may not always be the best guide. By the same token, one must be careful not to rely too heavily on the first wave of information coming from legacy media channels either. This is especially true in breaking news situations, where adrenaline is pumping and the race to be first often gets in the way of what is otherwise a methodical process of gathering, verifying, and distributing information. As NPR Counterterrorism Correspondent Dina Temple-Raston put it, "The first information that you get is usually wrong.... It took us [NPR] half an hour to figure out that there were two explosions, and that, in fact, they had been bombs" ("Journalists talk" 2013, 37:57). To do this, NPR's verification process drew on a broad array of sources, found through both traditional and new channels.

As introduced in the previous chapter, a #wjchat contributor once tweeted, "real reporting can be done via #Twitter. But not all of it." Similarly, real reporting can be done by citizen journalists, but not all of it. Of course, posting breaking information—on Twitter or elsewhere—is not the same thing as "traditional" journalism, which contains verified, contextualized (and ideally, actionable) knowledge that is often the product of "gumshoe reporting." Doing this kind of important, yet painstaking, work takes time and capital, and not just the economic kind. Still, news consumers now have more and more opportunities to "crash the gates" and go straight to the source. Yet, it is not just average citizens who are more accessible; government officials are now an increasingly important part of the networked publishing cycle. For example, in the aftermath of 2017 hurricanes Harvey and Irma, emergency response personnel relied heavily on social media to gather information, coordinate evacuations, and keep the public informed of rapidly changing conditions (Gilmer 2017; Samuel 2017).[1]

Similar claims could be made about law enforcement following the Boston Marathon bombing. Four days after the blasts, when the search for the remaining suspect was over, Twitter users were the first to know about it. The news came straight from an official source: Boston Police Department. Their report was retweeted nearly 140,000 times and received nearly 47,000 favorites. It read: "CAPTURED!!! The hunt is over. The search is done. The terror is over. And justice has won. Suspect in custody" (Boston Police Department 2013).

NOTE

1. By contrast, Hurricane Maria, which hit many Caribbean islands including Puerto Rico, was so devastating that nearly all forms of telecommunication were rendered inoperable (Becker 2017).

REFERENCES

Authorities ID person of interest as Saudi national in marathon bombings under guard at Boston hospital. (2013, April 15). *New York Post.* Retrieved November 19, 2017, from http://nypost.com/2013/04/15/authorities-id-person-of-interest-as-saudi-national-in-marathon-bombings-under-guard-at-boston-hospital/.

Bakker, P. (2012). Aggregation, content farms and Huffinization. *Journalism Practice, 6*(5–6), 627–637. https://doi.org/10.1080/17512786.2012.667266.

Becker, R. (2017, September 29). Trying to communicate after the hurricane: "It's as if Puerto Rico doesn't exist." *The Verge.* Retrieved November 22, 2017, from https://www.theverge.com/2017/9/29/16372048/puerto-rico-hurricane-maria-2017-electricity-water-food-communications-phone-internet-recovery.

Bennett, D. (2016). Sourcing the BBC's live online coverage of terror attacks. *Digital Journalism, 4*(7), 861–874. https://doi.org/10.1080/21670811.201 6.1163233.

Boston Police Department. (2013, April 19). CAPTURED!!! The hunt is over. The search is done. The terror is over. And justice has won. Suspect in custody [Tweet]. Twitter. Retrieved November 19, 2017, from https://twitter.com/ bostonpolice/status/325413032110989313.

Bourdieu, P. (1996). *The rules of art: Genesis and structure of the literary field.* Stanford, CA: Stanford University Press.

Broersma, M., & Graham, T. (2013). Twitter as a news source. *Journalism Practice, 7*(4), 446–464. https://doi.org/10.1080/17512786.2013.802481.

Bruns, A. (2014). Social media and journalism during times of crisis. In J. Hunsinger & T. M. Senft (Eds.), *The social media handbook* (pp. 159–175). New York, NY: Routledge.

Carvin, A. (2013). *Distant witness: Social media the Arab Spring and a journalism revolution.* New York: Journalism press.

Chait, J. (2013, April 19). Profiles in profiling: From the appalling New York Post to the rest of us. *New York Magazine.* Retrieved November 19, 2017, from http://nymag.com/news/intelligencer/profiling-boston-bombers-2013-4/?mid=twitter_nymag.

Couldry, N. (2016). Celebrity, convergence, and the fate of media institutions. In P. Davidrshall & S. Redmond (Eds.), *A companion to celebrity* (pp. 98–113). West Sussex, UK: John Wiley & Sons, Inc. https://doi.org/10.1002/ 9781118475089.ch6.

Ellis, J. (2013). Double coverage: How The Boston Globe used its dual sites to cover the marathon bombing. *Nieman Foundation at Harvard.* Retrieved November 19, 2017, from http://www.niemanlab.org/2013/05/double-coverage-how-the-boston-globe-used-its-dual-sites-to-cover-the-marathon-bombing/.

Farhi, P. (2013, April 19). Mistakes in news reporting happen, but do they matter? *Washington Post.* Retrieved November 19, 2017, from https://www. washingtonpost.com/lifestyle/style/mistakes-in-news-reporting-happen-but-do-they-matter/2013/04/19/c89fbf6a-a926-11e2-a8e2-5b98cb59187f_ story.html.

Fitzgerald, B. (2013, July 25). What Watertown teaches us about sourcing in journalism. *The Morning News.* Retrieved November 19, 2017, from http:// www.themorningnews.org/post/one-persons-version.

Gans, H. J. (2007). Everyday news, newsworkers, and professional journalism. *Political Communication, 24*(2), 161–166.

Gilmer, M. (2017, August 29). During Harvey, social media rose to the challenge as a force for good. *Mashable.* Retrieved November 22, 2017, from http:// mashable.com/2017/08/29/social-media-harvey-rescues-force-for-good/.

Greenfield, R. (2013, April 19). How Reddit fueled the scanner-happy media to out innocent Boston 'suspects'. *The Wire*. Retrieved November 19, 2017, from http://www.thewire.com/technology/2013/04/reddit-police-scanner-innocent-boston-suspects/64384/.

Haughney, C. (2013, June 6). New York Post faces suit over Boston bomb article. *New York Times*. Retrieved November 19, 2017, from http://www.nytimes.com/2013/06/07/business/media/new-york-post-sued-over-boston-bombing-article.html?_r=0.

Hermida, A., Lewis, S. C., & Zamith, R. (2014). Sourcing the Arab Spring: A case study of Andy Carvin's sources on Twitter during the Tunisian and Egyptian revolutions. *Journal of Computer-Mediated Communication, 19*(3), 479–499. https://doi.org/10.1111/jcc4.12074.

Journalists talk covering terrorism stories [Video]. (2013, August 9). *C-SPAN*. Retrieved November 19, 2017, from https://www.c-span.org/video/?314488-1/journalists-talk-covering-terrorism-stories.

Kaufman, L. (2013, April 28). Bombings trip up Reddit in its turn in spotlight. *New York Times*. Retrieved November 19, 2017, from http://www.nytimes.com/2013/04/29/business/media/bombings-trip-up-reddit-in-its-turn-in-spotlight.html?_r=0.

Kovach, B., & Rosenstiel, T. (2007). *The elements of journalism: What newspeople should know and the public should expect*. New York: Random House.

Kroll, A. (2013). Question everything you hear about the Boston Marathon bombing: From Oklahoma City to 9/11 to Newtown, the aftermath of major tragedies is rife with misinformation. *Mother Jones*. Retrieved November 19, 2017, from http://www.motherjones.com/politics/2013/04/boston-marathon-bombing-misinformation-911-newtown.

Krums, J. (2009, January 15). http://twitpic.com/135xa – There's a plane in the Hudson. I'm on the ferry going to pick up the people. Crazy. [Tweet]. Twitter. Retrieved November 19, 2017, from https://twitter.com/jkrums/status/1121915133?lang=en.

Lasorsa, D. L., Lewis, S. C., & Holton, A. E. (2012). Normalizing Twitter. *Journalism Studies, 13*(1), 19–36. https://doi.org/10.1080/1461670X.2011.571825.

Lefky, T., Brewer, P. R., & Habegger, M. (2015). Tweets on television news: The nature and effects of campaign coverage of Twitter. *Electronic News, 9*(4), 257–269. https://doi.org/10.1177/1931243115604884.

Lichfield, G. (2013, April 20). Four ways the media failed in covering the Boston bombings, and one reason why. *Quartz*. Retrieved November 19, 2017, from http://qz.com/76668/boston-marathon-and-the-media/.

Lotan, G. (2012, March 5). A tale of three rumors. *Harvard University symposium Truthiness in Digital Media*. Retrieved November 19, 2017, from http://blogs.law.harvard.edu/truthiness/2012/03/05/541/.

Meraz, S., & Papacharissi, Z. (2013). Networked gatekeeping and networked framing on #Egypt. *The International Journal of Press/Politics, 18*(2), 138–166. https://doi.org/10.1177/1940161212474472.

Mills, C. W. (1963). *Power, politics, and people: The collected essays of C. Wright Mills*. New York: Oxford University Press.

Montgomery, D., Horwitz, S., & Fisher, M. (2013, April 20). Police, citizens and technology factor into Boston bombing probe. *The Washington Post.* Retrieved November 19, 2017, from https://www.washingtonpost.com/world/national-security/inside-the-investigation-of-the-boston-marathon-bombing/2013/04/20/19d8c322-a8ff-11e2-b029-8fb7e977ef71_story.html?utm_term=.2e6e8b7a97ab.

Murthy, D., & Longwell, S. A. (2013). Twitter and disasters. *Information, Communication & Society, 16*(6), 837–855.

Papacharissi, Z., & Oliveira, M. F. (2012). Affective news and networked publics: The rhythms of news storytelling on #Egypt. *Journal of Communication, 62*(2), 266–282.

Public shaming: Tweets of privilege. (2013, April 15). Tumblr. Retrieved November 19, 2017, from http://publicshaming.tumblr.com/post/48093470152/two-explosives-went-off-at-the-boston-marathon-on.

Rogers, S. (2013, July 10). The Boston bombing: How journalists used Twitter to tell the story. *Twitter Media Blog.* Retrieved November 19, 2017, from https://blog.twitter.com/2013/the-boston-bombing-how-journalists-used-twitter-to-tell-the-story.

Rosen, J. (2006, June 27). The people formerly known as the audience. *PressThink.* Retrieved November 19, 2017, from http://archive.pressthink.org/2006/06/27/ppl_frmr.html.

Rosen, J. (2012, March 27). I'm there, you're not, let me tell you about it. *PressThink.* Retrieved November 19, 2017, from http://pressthink.org/2012/03/im-there-youre-not-let-me-tell-you-about-it/.

Russell, A. (2016). *Journalism as activism: Recoding media power.* Malden, MA: Polity.

Samuel, N. (2017, September 24). Social media's impact during Irma. *Vero News.* Retrieved November 22, 2017, from http://veronews.com/2017/09/24/social-medias-impact-irma/.

Santana, A. D., & Hopp, T. (2016). Tapping into a new stream of (personal) data: Assessing journalists' different use of social media. *Journalism & Mass Communication Quarterly, 93*(2), 383–408. https://doi.org/10.1177/1077699016637105.

Schultz, C. (2013, October 24). In the wake of the Boston Marathon bombing, Twitter was full of lies. *Smithsonian Magazine.* Retrieved November 19, 2017, from http://blogs.smithsonianmag.com/smartnews/2013/10/in-the-wake-of-the-boston-marathon-bombing-twitter-was-full-of-lies/#.UmvfY_jB7Rw.twitter.

Shafer, J. (2013, April 18). Shameless paper in mindless fog. *Reuters.* Retrieved November 19, 2017, from http://blogs.reuters.com/jackshafer/2013/04/18/shameless-paper-in-mindless-fog/.

Shapiro, R. (2013, June 6). 'Bag men' sue New York Post over Boston Marathon bombing cover. *The Huffington Post.* Retrieved November 19, 2017, from http://www.huffingtonpost.com/2013/06/06/bag-men-sue-new-york-post-boston-marathon-bombing-cover_n_3395497.html.

Silverman, C. (2012, March 7). Visualized: Incorrect information travels farther, faster on Twitter than corrections. *Poynter.* Retrieved November 19, 2017, from https://www.poynter.org/news/visualized-incorrect-information-travels-farther-faster-twitter-corrections.

Skok, D. (2012, October 29). "The initial, mistaken information will be retweeted more than any subsequent correction." – @gilgul March 6, 2012 [Tweet]. Twitter. Retrieved November 19, 2017, from https://twitter.com/dskok/status/263100064900198401/photo/1.

Torres, E. G. d., & Hermida, A. (2017). The social reporter in action. *Journalism Practice, 11*(2–3), 177–194. https://doi.org/10.1080/17512786.2016.1245110.

Tufekci, Z., & Wilson, C. (2012). Social media and the decision to participate in political protest: Observations from Tahrir Square. *Journal of Communication, 62*(2), 363–379.

Vis, F. (2013). Twitter as a reporting tool for breaking news. *Digital Journalism, 1*(1), 27–47.

Witness says he saw 'pressure cooker bomb' [Video]. (2013, April 19). *MSNBC.* Retrieved November 19, 2017, from http://www.msnbc.com/msnbc/watch/witness-says-he-saw-pressure-cooker-bomb-26599491943.

Tweeting #Ferguson: Affective Publics, Boundary Maintenance, and Journo-Activism in a Mediatized Field

Michael Brown, an unarmed black teenager, was shot and killed by a white police officer in Ferguson, Missouri on August 9, 2014. The shooting was quickly shrouded in controversy, due in part to the contradictory accounts from dozens of witnesses (Santhanam and Dennis 2014). Public concern was compounded by a number of other factors, including the handling of Brown's body, the now well-documented, systemic injustices committed by police against Ferguson's mostly poor and black residents, as well as the use of force against demonstrators (Balko 2015; Berman and Lowery 2015). Protests were a regular occurrence throughout Ferguson in the months that followed, which at times resulted in violence, clashes with police, and destruction and looting of local businesses. Ferguson itself was described as a "powder keg" after the Justice Department found overwhelming evidence of racial discrimination in the department's policing ("Bigoted Ferguson" 2015). This included the use of an illegal quota system, along with other practices that resulted in a "disproportionate number of arrests, tickets, and use of force [stemming from] 'unlawful bias'" against African Americans (Berman and Lowery 2015, para. 7).

A previous version of this chapter was published as: Barnard, S. R. Tweeting #Ferguson: Mediatized fields and the new activist journalist. *New Media & Society,* Advanced online publication, Copyright © 2017, SAGE Publications. Reprinted by permission of SAGE Publications. Available at: http://journals. sagepub.com/doi/abs/10.1177/1461444817712723.

© The Author(s) 2018
S. R. Barnard, *Citizens at the Gates,*
https://doi.org/10.1007/978-3-319-90446-7_6

Beyond being a microcosm of the ongoing racial conflict in the United States, the case study serves as an ideal-typical example of networked journalism and activism in a time of mediatization. The #Ferguson hashtag emerged alongside #BlackLivesMatter and many others to signify calls for racial justice and criminal justice reform. In the days following Brown's death, the streets of Ferguson and the tweets of #Ferguson were shared by both professional and citizen journalists.[1] But many reporters would soon share more than physical and discursive space, as the increasingly militarized police forces began teargassing and arresting journalists and protestors alike.

This sharing of experiences and converging of networks contributed to a common identity and consciousness among many protestors and journalists, thus leading to episodes of media coverage that were more sympathetic to Ferguson activists (Araiza et al. 2016). While this relationship posed a unique opportunity for social movement activists, even the most considerate of media frames can pose challenges for movement organizers, who are constantly working to shape what gets covered, and how (Gitlin 2003; Sobieraj 2011). Although social movement activists face considerable challenges, the growing mediatization of everyday life provides new opportunities for members of the public to participate, and potentially shape political and journalistic discourses. Whereas uses of networked technologies for political and individual empowerment have been criticized for their lack of bearing on material realities (Barnard 2016a; Morozov 2014), alternative forms of expression on social media have grown popular in political-activist cultures. Social media is often used to call attention to a given cause and coordinate protest actions, therefore playing an important role in processes of social change. The case of Ferguson serves as an ongoing example of such reform, given the slow but notable changes in local, state, and federal policy, made possible in part by the persistence of networked activists (Shjarback et al. 2017; Wagner 2016).

The visibility and salience of #Ferguson has led scholars from a variety of fields to conduct research on the uses of networked technologies to document and respond to systemic racism (Araiza et al. 2016; Bonilla and Rosa 2015; Chaudhry 2016; Clark 2016; Freelon et al. 2016; Jackson and Welles 2016; LeFebvre and Armstrong 2016). These studies found that although traditional gatekeepers generally adhere to professional norms, Twitter functioned as a visible site of resistance and discursive influence for well-connected activists (Freelon et al. 2016; Jackson and Welles 2016; LeFebvre and Armstrong 2016). Furthermore, while studies of #Ferguson and similar events have revealed notable trends in the volume of coverage mainstream media outlets dedicated to the issue (Hitlin and Vogt 2014), few have offered an in-depth analysis of the Twitter discourse and how it maps onto the converging fields of journalism and activism. Accordingly, the research presented in this chapter seeks to fill this gap by providing a mezzo-level analysis of the content and context of networked journo-activism as seen on Twitter and beyond.

TWITTER, SOCIAL MEDIA AND THE NEW JOURNO-ACTIVIST FIELD

Drawing insights from field theory, Andrew Chadwick (2013, p. 12) detailed the ongoing hybridization of the journalistic and political fields, given the emergence of a media system defined by "struggles between older and newer media logics." While the journalistic and political fields are marked by clear differences in norms, values, and practices, like the use of objective versus persuasive styles of communication, trends toward hybridization and mediatization are also clear. This results in the emergence of shared media logics, both of field structures and practices. Many scholars have examined the relationship between these two fields in more traditional, institutional settings (Bourdieu 2005; Herman and Chomsky 2002; McChesney 2008; Starr 2005), but the relative publicness of digital communication provides a unique opportunity to reconsider such questions in light of recent shifts in technology and field dynamics. As the previous chapters have argued, Twitter provides one such space where the convergence of fields is most visible.

Many boundary spaces still remain despite the hybridity of mediatized journalistic and political fields, such as political conventions and highly visible hashtags. These boundary spaces present opportunities for "active spectatorship" among citizen-participants, (Kreiss et al. 2015) "reshaping the pattern of call and response relationship with mainstream media" (Russell 2013, p. 904). For example, Adrienne Russell (2013) examined how boundary work between journalists and environmental activists at a commingled UN Climate Summit revealed overlaps and fissures in the journalistic field. In addition to highlighting the hybrid yet distinctive positions and practices of networked actors, Russell's study also rendered visible the dual function of objectivity, which serves as both a bridge and a divide between "legacy" and activist-oriented media.

Although one of objectivity's latent functions is to foster processes of deliberative democracy through a separation of fact from value (Schudson 1981), instances where legacy journalism permits "affective news flows" can actually create "more space for critical interpretation of news events and issues" (Russell 2013, p. 918). In other words, allowing opinion and emotion to help render visible points of (dis)agreement about an issue, no matter how politicized or scientific, has the potential to strengthen democratic discourses, rather than hinder them. Given its mediatized structure and affordances, including its publicness, conversational structure, and popularity across a variety of fields, Twitter is well situated to lay bare the dynamics of political activism, journalism, and democracy (Maireder and Ausserhofer 2014). Scholars have become ever more attuned to Twitter's cultural (Brock 2012), political (Kreiss 2016), journalistic (Hedman 2015; Hermida 2010; Zeller and Hermida 2015), and activist (Tremayne 2014) implications. While it has already been mentioned that Twitter users still do not represent the "average" American, journalists and activists are two groups that are especially well represented on Twitter. So too are African Americans, given that 28% of Black internet users use Twitter, versus 20% of online Whites (Duggan 2015; Krogstad 2015). This overrepresentation may help explain the prominence of Black culture on Twitter, often referred to as "Black Twitter" (Brock 2012), and will be discussed in greater detail in Chap. 7.

According to an in-depth study of online discourse about police violence and racial injustice in Ferguson and Black Lives Matter more generally (Freelon et al. 2016), networked activists' use of Twitter brought significant attention to the issue and directly resulted in the mainstreaming of #BlackLivesMatter. Through their analysis of over 40 million public tweets, 21 million of which were from #Ferguson, researchers identified a variety of unique but interconnected communities, which included activists as well as mainstream news outlets that played a role in the #BlackLivesMatter movement. Furthermore, they discovered that both tweets and hyperlinks played an important role in disseminating information about the movement, particularly through gaining coverage from mainstream news sites (Freelon et al. 2016, p. 17).

As the #Ferguson events make clear, actors can now influence the gatekeeping process through numerous channels, whether they are located solidly within or at the boundaries of the (professional) journalistic field (Bruns 2003; Shoemaker and Vos 2009). While many journalists report an adherence to traditional doxa of independence, those working in more networked subfields are more likely to use social media in their selection and shaping of news (Raeymaeckers et al. 2015). Additional time spent in the same mediatized fields as professionals in politics or journalism provides additional opportunity for members of the public to influence reporting processes, including but not limited to helping shape what issues are covered as news (gatekeeping), and what aspects of those issues are discussed (framing). Given the growing potential for ties between networked journalists and journo-activists, the various modes of curation amount to new "flows" that often converge and influence one another despite hinging on different logics (Thorson and Wells 2015). Thus, the focus now turns to the role Twitter and mediatization play in shaping the flow of information from #Ferguson.

MEDIATIZATION IN THE FIELD: AFFECTIVE PUBLICS, SOCIAL NETWORKS, AND THE LINKS THAT CONNECT

The proliferation of networked technologies has ushered in significant shifts in the terms and consequences of communication. Mediatization, as introduced in Chap. 3, is more than a matter of scale, however. Indeed, the concept emphasizes the qualitative changes to communicative action brought about by hyper-mediation (Hjarvard 2013).[2] In mediatized fields, social action is not only bound by traditional institutional relations, but is also constantly augmented by media(ted) dynamics, which can amount to a fundamental shift in the form and function of fields (Barnard 2016b; Couldry 2014; Jurgenson 2012). The proliferation of #BlackLivesMatter—both as a hashtag and a networked social movement—illustrates how a hybrid, mediatized political-journalistic field can operate. In this case, networked publics' use of common platforms and hashtags to document, contextualize, and amplify cases of police violence against people of color helped link together individual cases, revealing an undeniable pattern explained only by structural racism. Many have argued that the mediatized field(s) and practices have significantly helped to popularize critical discourses like #BlackLivesMatter, without which the struggle for social justice would likely remain farther on the margins (Kidd 2017).

In addition to ushering in structural and theoretical shifts, the growth of mediatized relations has also facilitated emergent forms of communication. For example, the ability to live-tweet protests and political events contributes to the formation of affective publics. Accordingly,

Zizi Papacharissi (2014) examined the role of Twitter and other networked technologies in communicating affective expressions. While it has long been used in rather amorphous ways, the concept of *affect* seeks to highlight the emotive influence on decisions, expressions, and interactions (Himelboim et al. 2016). Despite the prominence of journalistic conventions like objectivity and independence, emotion and subjectivity inevitably seep into the reporting process. Although the historically private nature of reporting has rendered much of this affective labor invisible, the affective elements of communication are increasingly evident due to mediatization (Himelboim et al. 2016; Papacharissi 2014). Within the field of networked journalism, emerging forms of affective news blend objective information with opinion and emotion to create hybrid news frames (Meraz and Papacharissi 2013, p. 155). While activists and citizen journalists have long been known to engage in affective communication, mediatization has helped narrow divides between journalists and non-elite political actors, contributing to rising hybrid and affective reporting practices (Araiza et al. 2016; Poell and Rajagopalan 2015). By affording users the ability to live-tweet protests and political events in public, as illustrated by #Ferguson, mediatized spaces provide opportunities for the formation of affective publics (Papacharissi 2014).

Users also participate in the spread of affective news through sharing and linking (Molyneux 2015). Like other forms of (meta-)data, links are inherently locative: they convey a sense of meaning and context, which augment the interpretation of text (Carlson 2016). Links also have a quantitative component, as the more links a site or story receives, the more centrality and importance it is said to hold. While link analysis has been most frequently applied to traditional media and web content to examine cross-citation (Adamic and Glance 2005; De Maeyer 2013; De Maeyer and Holton 2015), social network analysis has largely been deployed to examine more robust engagement and interactional ties on social media (cf. Graeff et al. 2014; Meraz and Papacharissi 2013). Thus, network analysis offers a way to visualize discursive connections through engagement on social media, while link analysis provides a window into discursive patterns (Bruns and Burgess 2012).

When viewed in conjunction with the ties and characteristics exhibited by networked interactions on Twitter, links offer a way of locating social actors and understanding their practices. Despite the commonality of the "power law" phenomena, where a small number of users produce a disproportionate share of content, network structures do not universally privilege like-minded and powerful actors (Earl and Kimport 2011).

To the contrary, nonelite and nonpolitical sources carry increased influence in some online contexts (Freelon and Karpf 2015; Meraz and Papacharissi 2013). Overall, the tracing of network connections, whether through hyperlinks or interactional ties on social media, offers a means of mapping the structure of mediatized (sub)fields.

STUDYING PROFESSIONAL JOURNALISTS AND JOURNO-ACTIVISTS THROUGH #FERGUSON

In light of the context discussed in previous sections, tweets from an assortment of journalists and activists were collected and analyzed between August and November 2014, when discourse surrounding the protest movement was at a peak. Although the number of journalists' tweets were nearly equal to activists' tweets in the first few weeks following the event, activists' tweets made up a majority of the dataset (70%) overall (see Fig. 6.1).[3] Three main questions guided the research for this chapter. First, what themes and formats are apparent in tweets from #Ferguson? Are there similarities and differences between professional journalists and citizen journo-activists? Second, what is the structural composition of the field of actors tweeting #Ferguson? In what ways are journalists and journo-activists engaging in shared practices and experiences? Finally, to what extent is this contributing to the emergence of a new hybrid space, and what implications does this hold?

To address these questions, data were collected from a targeted sample of journalists and activists tweeting #Ferguson, using a combination of digital ethnography, content analysis, link analysis, and social network analysis. Like Chaps. 4, 7, and 8, the Twitter data collected for this chapter

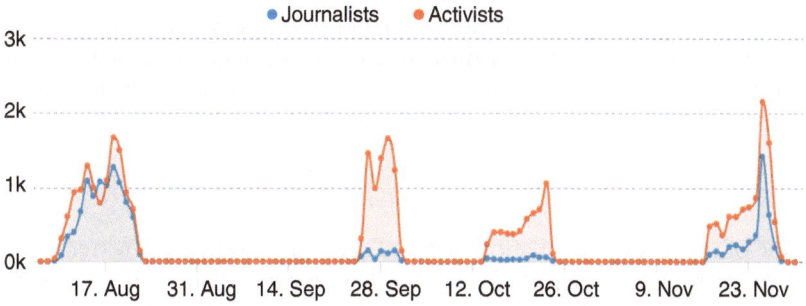

Fig. 6.1 Distribution of Ferguson tweets in sample

were analyzed using digital ethnographic content analysis (DECA), described in greater detail in the Appendix. While other studies have focused specifically on Twitter influencers through the "top tweets" function (Neuberg et al. 2014), this chapter examined all issue-related tweets by a set of users identified as influential in their respective networks (i.e., journalists and activists). This analysis yielded a variety of findings about how journalists and activists tweeted #Ferguson. Results are organized to correspond with the research questions stated above.

Themes: Similarity Across Difference

The first research question aimed to find similarities and differences between professional journalists and citizen journo-activists and to discover any themes apparent in their tweeting. After recursively examining the data, tweets were coded and analyzed and the following emergent themes were found.

Organizing

Activists regularly tweeted information about their whereabouts or protest action plans. Organizing tweets often included the time and place of protests, and were sometimes accompanied by additional information, such as newsletters or flyers, through links and images. For example, one prominent activist simply tweeted, "Walmart. Rock Road. St. Charles. #Ferguson." Others offered information about places to donate, safe places to rest, or the whereabouts and temperament of police. Many organizing tweets contained additional hashtags for added visibility (see below). Journalists typically refrained from using Twitter to organize in this way, likely because they either tended to work independently, or preferred more private forms of communication to coordinate travel and coverage. Overall, while organizing tweets often served a dual function of disseminating news about the planned actions, the organizing theme was distinguished by its explicit emphasis on providing support and direction to activists.

Amplifying

One of the predominant affordances of social media such as Twitter is the ability to spread messages to broader audiences beyond one's own network. This, of course, is the ideal-typical function of a hashtag. While the vast majority of tweets analyzed for this chapter (83%) contained the #Ferguson hashtag, many users also deployed other hashtags. For example, "Meet us on shaw and klemm tonight at 9pm!! #Ferguson #VonDerritMyers #shaw-shooting #MikeBrown #FergusonDecision." Other common secondary hashtags included #BlackLivesMatter, #FergusonDecision, #HandsUp, #DontShoot, #ShutItDown, and #STL, among countless others. The use of secondary hashtags functioned as a way to bridge parallel, but sometimes competing, discourses on a topic as well as to boost visibility. Expectedly, activists were far more likely to use hashtags in this context, given their motivation to inform the public and pursue systemic reforms. Occasionally, journalists also helped spread information with parallel hashtags, though this was often a latent function resulting from journalists retweeting activists' content.

News Dissemination

One obvious use of Twitter was to disseminate news. Journalists frequently opted to publicize their work by directing followers to their proprietary content platforms. For example, "turn on Fox News @ seanhannity—he has latest on #Ferguson—starts in 4 minutes!" or "BREAKING: @evanperez live on CNN with new details on #ferguson. Grand Jury didn't reach decision friday. Unclear when deliberations resume." Although such basic forms of sharing were common among all journalists, a larger portion appeared more Twitter-savvy, posting observations and explanations in formats that appeared more native to the platform. Not surprisingly, these more advanced methods of sharing news on Twitter (beyond posting links and headlines) were more likely to be employed by journalists working for digital news organizations. For example, "Still a lot happening in Ferguson, so we're still running our live blog for those of you not glued to Twitter: http://t.co/9Pirbv2eDL." Activists, on the other hand, were understandably less interested in self-promotion or driving traffic to other media sources, and instead, shared in ways similar to the more Twitter-savvy journalists. For example, one activist tweeted this update along with photos of the scene, "#Ferguson police has advanced to the other side of the street where protesters are standing." Although tweets ranged in focus and frame, this strategy of sharing information from a personal perspective was common among activist tweets.

Police Criticism

As expected, police criticism was a dominant theme and remained consistent over time. However, explicit criticisms increased in volume, tone, and visibility during or shortly after police actions. For example, one activist shared a local media story, "Cop in Ferguson Tweets Lies to Justify Tear-Gassing Protesters In Their Own Backyard http://t.co/1HbAGtf80y." Meanwhile, a journalist tweeted an original post with a more objective tone, "Here are photos of the Saint Louis County cop who assaulted me yesterday. #Ferguson http://t.co/z8Y7jrCrRd." This highlights a notable difference between such factual (i.e., objective) accounts of police violence and the more affective responses more likely to be seen from activists. For example, a sizeable number of tweets from activists directly criticized police actions, such as, "ONLY PPL RIOTING IN STL ARE THE POLICE. #STL #FERGUSON #FergusonMO," or "It's incredible how nobody talks about Mike Brown in these press conferences. But they talk about property. Tons. #Ferguson."

Media Criticism

A small but notable portion of the data (nearly 3%) explicitly referenced "media," and a clear majority of those tweets were focused on media criticism. While some criticisms were structural, most were episodic in nature. For example, one activist tweeted, "This is more than police-positive spin in #Ferguson… there are outright lies being released, and some media are reporting them uncritically [sic]." Around the same time, a journalist offered an illustration, "CNN incorrectly reporting there was no tear gas in #Ferguson tonight. I can still taste it. That said it was far, far, quieter." Although these posts were similar in message, their tone was notably different, falling in line with the normative frames of protestors' affectivity and journalists' objectivity. Other users offered even more targeted media criticisms, including instances where activists directly confronted reporters about their coverage, whether in person or on air. Most strikingly, a number of protesters were shown on live television chanting "fuck CNN" behind a CNN reporter, which was purportedly in response to coverage they deemed unfair and misleading (Feldman 2014).

Shared Experience

Despite activists' criticism of reporting on the movement, there was notable evidence of journalists' solidarity with protestors. Amid the fog of war, many journalists posted messages of shared experience, including instances of police threatening to arrest or otherwise punishing them for doing their job. For example, one journalist tweeted, "Police shooting tear gas directly at journalists now. Flashing lights so cameras can't record. #Ferguson #MikeBrown." Many others documented incidents of tear gas, rubber bullets, and other "less lethal" devices being used against journalists and activists alike. Some journalists tweeted images of police who "assaulted" or arrested them, but more commonly reported on the experiences of others. For example, another journalist tweeted, "Photo of reporter I believe to be @ryanjreilly being cuffed and put in a police van minutes ago in #Ferguson http://t.co/l6olRUPk13." The following day, the arrested journalist tweeted this message along with a photo, "Fellow reporter takes a lesson from my arrest, writes phone numbers on her arm #Ferguson http://t.co/KhFwfwTd9j." Additionally, like journo-activists, a number of journalists expressed hope for justice and reform. Some even shared messages of friendship and solidarity for the subjects of their reports, such as, "It wasn't all bad tonight. I made friends with at least a handful of folks who didn't threaten me with batons and tear gas. #Ferguson." This discovery of journalists tweeting with a more affective tone resonates with other studies investigating the shared experiences between journalists and activists in Ferguson (Araiza et al. 2016).

Meta-Discourse

Another commonality between tweets from journalists and activists was the use of Twitter to reflect on the significance of their practices and the role of social media in them. Approximately 1% of tweets directly referenced Twitter, while a greater number reflected more generally on media. Numerous posts described the contents of Vine videos or explained their importance to the cause. For example, one journo-activist offered a candid celebration of social media's informative function, "Make no mistake: if not for Twitter, Vine, Livestream etc, we'd have NO IDEA what was happening to protesters in #Ferguson. Police would lie." Another tweeted, "Were it not for Twitter, #Ferguson would have remained just another town no one outside of St. Louis ever heard of." Others reflected more on their networked community, tweeting messages of thanks to supporters for donations, as well as more generalized appreciation, including a picture of a chalk message reading "Thank You #Blacktwitter #Handsup #Dontshoot." Journalists, on the other hand, opted to reflect on their use of the platform, comment on its significance for members of the public, find crowd-sourced information, and occasionally, to find support from others in the network. For example, one journalist tweeted, "Not trying to persuade anyone on Twitter today, just letting #Ferguson #shawshooting protestors know our general approach to 2 incidents." Another posted, "Phone dying, tweets will stop. Chants of 'Hands up, don't shoot' and 'what if this was your town' will continue tonight in Ferguson." This mixture of commentary, community engagement, and reporting by journalists differed significantly from activists' meta-discourse containing media criticism and celebration of social media.

FORMAT: WHAT'S IN A TWEET?

On average, activists were more reactive and conversational, as measured by replies and retweets, while journalists were more authorial. Just over half of journalists' tweets were original posts (50.8%), whereas activists were more likely to reply and retweet (58.3%).[4] Similarly, journalists were a little more likely to link (18.9%) and share photos (27.8%), compared to activists (15.2% and 24.7%, respectively). Activists, on the other hand, were a little more likely to tweet videos (7.9%) and text-only (52.2%), compared to journalists (7.2% and 46.1%, respectively) (see Fig. 6.2). It is important to acknowledge, however, that usage of the formats often varied

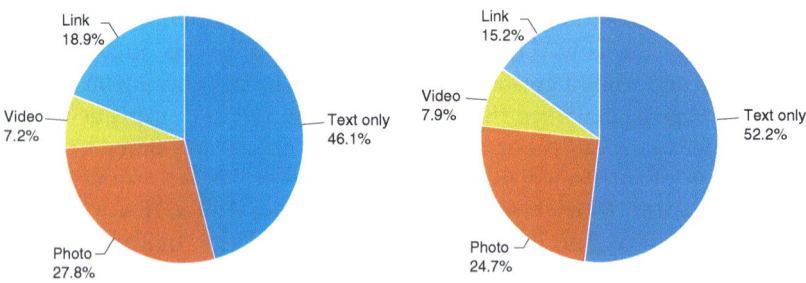

Fig. 6.2 Comparison of tweet formats for journalists (*left*) and activists (*right*)

more within comparison groups than across them, as some users were likely to use these functions extensively, while others did so rarely, if ever. Thus, while these differences are relatively minor, they illustrate how the technological affordances on Twitter shape the practices of professional and citizen journalists.

Discourse: Separate but Overlapping Communities

Journalists and activists largely exist in distinct but connected discursive communities.

By mapping discursive connections (i.e., retweets, replies, and links), it is possible to visualize the structural composition of journalists' and activists' subfields on Twitter. As Fig. 6.3 shows, professional journalists appeared less connected than activists, who were much more likely to engage with other users on Twitter. However, that engagement frequently crossed boundaries, as activists were also quite likely to retweet or reply to journalists (see Fig. 6.4). This is one indication of a hybrid, if episodic, field structure where convergence occurred either through shared experience or shared (discursive) space. Although the average journalist was more influential on Twitter than the average activist, as represented by the size of each node, activists had stronger and more numerous ties in #Ferguson.

As Twitter is a relatively open system, users act and interact in a variety of ways that span far beyond the platform, and the data created renders visible patterns of discursive connection. Table 6.1 depicts the 20 most frequently linked to sites from each group. Percentages are reported as the number of links to the site among all tweets with links from that group. As expected, professional journalists were somewhat more likely to link to legacy and digital news sites from national (e.g., *Washington Post, LA Times,* Buzzfeed, MSNBC, *Guardian,* etc.) and local sources (e.g., KSKD, KMOV, *Riverfront Times,* etc.). On the other hand, activists were more likely to link to social and alternative news sites, including Instagram, YouTube, and various livestreaming sites. Nevertheless, like the overlapping network maps, the commonality of links to legacy, digital, and social media sites across both groups illustrates the shared discursive ground as well as the convergence of journalist and journo-activist subfields.

Hashtags and keywords serve as another indicator of discursive community. While common trends were found across both groups, activists' tweets were much more likely to include the #Ferguson hashtag as opposed to the

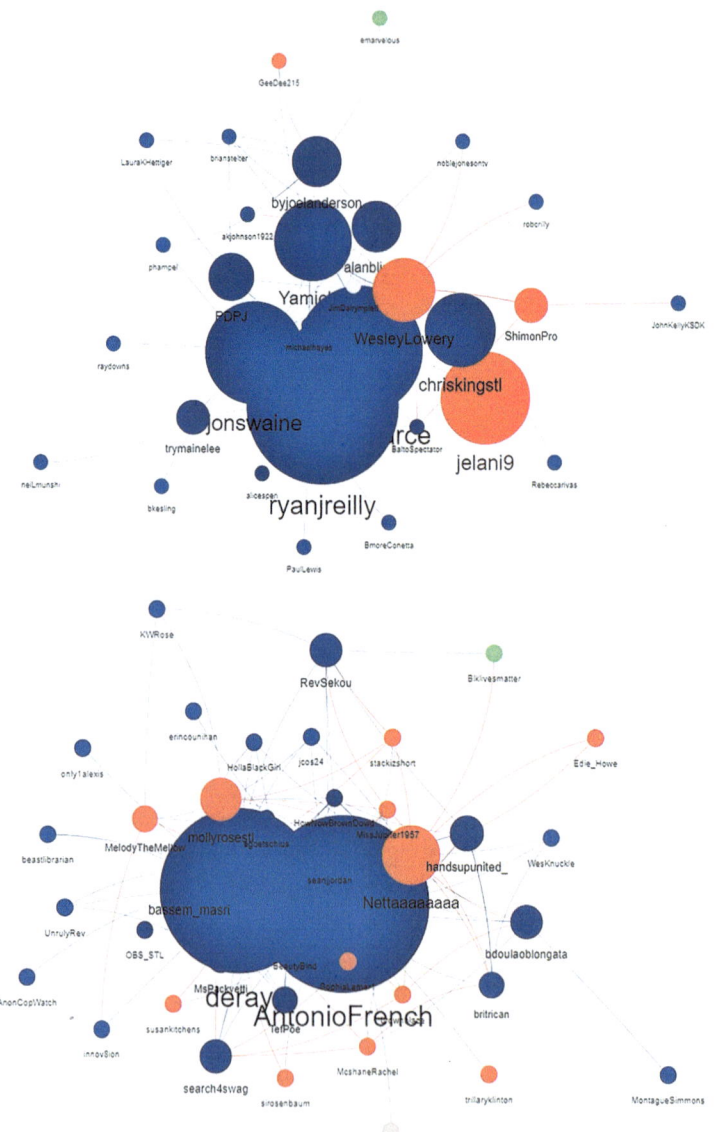

Fig. 6.3 Comparison of influencer networks for journalists (*top*) and activists (*bottom*)

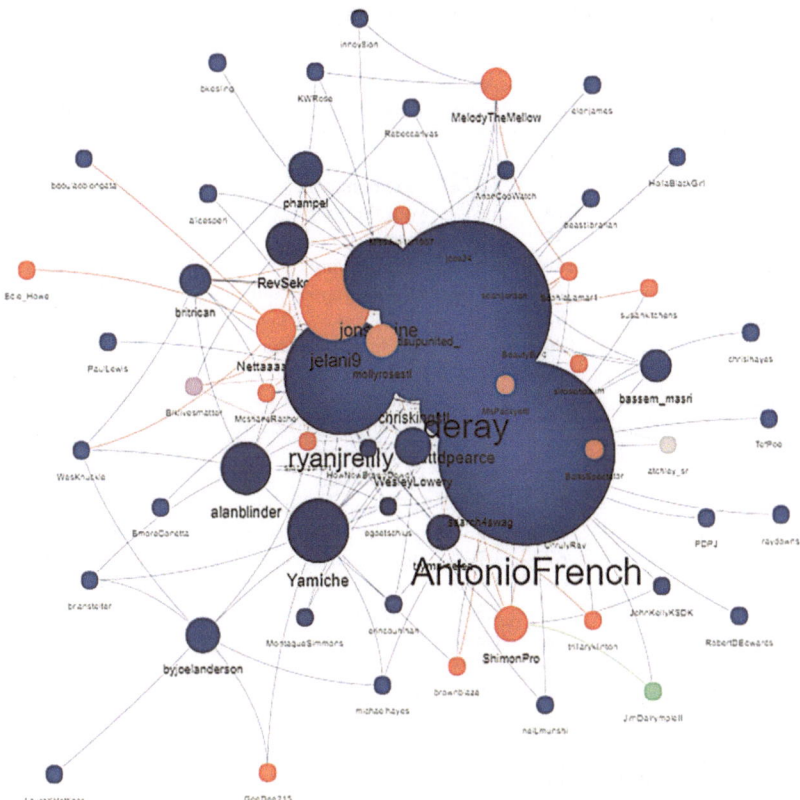

Fig. 6.4   Combined map of influencer network[5]

keyword "Ferguson" (ratio 6.3:1). Journalists also preferred the hashtag to the keyword (ratio 3.6:1). Thus, controlling for the number of tweets from each group, activists were nearly twice as likely as journalists to include the #Ferguson hashtag in their tweets than the keyword alone. Furthermore, activist users were significantly more influential on average; the top ten influential accounts in the dataset all belonged to activists. While it is clear that both journalist and activist users have a place in the discourse, the prominence of activist tweets in the dataset (just over 70%), the greater sociality of their tweets (i.e., hashtags, retweets, and replies), as well as their greater influence, suggests that activists had a deeper commitment to

Table 6.1   Number of top domain links by group

Journalists			Activists		
Domain	Count	Percent	Domain	Count	Percent
vine.co	786	20.33%	vine.co	1734	19.98%
instagram.com	281	7.27%	instagram.com	1252	14.42%
washingtonpost.com	213	5.51%	youtube.com	469	5.40%
buzzfeed.com	195	5.04%	twitter.com	236	2.72%
latimes.com	180	4.65%	stltoday.com	221	2.55%
stltoday.com	174	4.50%	huffingtonpost.com	202	2.33%
youtube.com	153	3.96%	ustream.tv	199	2.29%
huffingtonpost.com	134	3.47%	thisisthemovement.launchrock.com	150	1.73%
googleweblight.com	105	2.72%	scribd.com	130	1.50%
twitter.com	88	2.28%	washingtonpost.com	126	1.45%
ksdk.com	86	2.22%	livestream.com	107	1.23%
msnbc.com	85	2.20%	latimes.com	93	1.07%
kmov.com	73	1.89%	us5.campaign-archive2.com	91	1.05%
edition.cnn.com	67	1.73%	googleweblight.com	85	0.98%
wsj.com	67	1.73%	storify.com	83	0.96%
usatoday.com	64	1.66%	facebook.com	79	0.91%
news.vice.com	52	1.34%	ksdk.com	77	0.89%
theguardian.com	52	1.34%	secure.piryx.com	75	0.86%
livestream.com	42	1.09%	bambuser.com	74	0.85%
riverfronttimes.com	42	1.09%	msnbc.com	73	0.84%

tweeting #Ferguson. Finally, notable variance in user influence was also found, with a small minority of users responsible for a disproportionate number of tweets in the dataset. This finding falls squarely in line with many other studies of the web that found power law dynamics in digital discourse (Earl and Kimport 2011).

DISCUSSION AND CONCLUSION

Journalists' and activists' tweeting of #Ferguson revealed much about the ongoing mediatization of the journalistic field. Despite observable differences in themes, frames, communicative forms, and engagement in discursive communities, notable points of convergence were also found. In addition to clear connections within and across fields, both through (re)tweets and links, affective forms of reporting were found among both groups. Given that journalists have previously been found to use Twitter to share personal messages and connect with members of the public, it is not surprising to find journalists tweeting affectively on occasion. Nevertheless, given the experiences of #Ferguson journalists, many of whom were teargassed, arrested, or otherwise obstructed, one might also expect even less objective, more critical coverage. By contrast, while activists typically employed affective frames, they also borrowed reporting practices from the professional repertoire, often mixing objective (and occasionally, verified) information with opinion and emotion. Whether because of persistent engagement, shared experience, or the emergent mediatization of discursive space, the journalist and journo-activist fields of #Ferguson converged significantly on Twitter.

Expectedly, many of this chapter's findings resonate strongly with a previous analysis of social media posts from #Ferguson and beyond (Freelon et al. 2016). First, like that study, this chapter found notable ties between journalist and activist communities. Second, this chapter identified similar themes pertaining to news dissemination and amplification, criticism of media and police, as well as the tendency to engage in affective framing. These similarities appear to demonstrate the robustness of findings pertaining to trends in the use of social media for journalistic and activist ends. By contrast, this chapter's discovery of relevant meta-discourse, where Twitter users reflect directly on the significance of the platform for their practices, resonates with research particular to the journalistic field (Carlson 2015). Thus, it demonstrates another possible site of hybridity between journalist and activist practices. This finding, like those related to users' sharing of personal experiences as well as the variations in the format of their tweets, may be explained, in part, by the targeted nature of the sample, which included a closer examination of less influential tweets and users.

Another notable implication of this study relates to the transformation of journalistic practices. Like the research presented in Chap. 4, the analysis conducted for this chapter suggests that the elements of journalistic practice are experiencing a shift toward mediatized repertoires that demonstrate the centrality of digital technologies in the reporting process. Depending on organizational culture and policy, Twitter can play a central role in the creation and dissemination of news. This has obvious implications for the norms and values (doxa), dispositions (habitus) and measures of skill and status (capital) of the journalistic field (Bourdieu 1993). Whereas many of the professional journalists tweeting #Ferguson clearly operated under a Twitter-first motto, those working for legacy news organizations were more likely to use Twitter in a manner similar to traditional media by broadcasting proprietary content. While the latter strategy prioritizes more traditional means of accumulating capital—especially economic—through clicks and engagements, the decision to embrace the social nature of news allows for the generation of social, cultural, symbolic, and even economic capital. Furthermore, in a hybrid, mediatized field context, this capital is transferable—both to different forms of capital as well as different field contexts—due, in no small part, to the growing significance of media meta-capital (Couldry 2014). Indeed, active participation in the mediatized field can lead to opportunities in professional journalism and politics. For example, the prominent Black Lives Matter activist, Shaun King, was hired as a writer for the *New York Daily News*. Others like DeRay McKesson and Antonio French, both included in the cohort of journo-activists studied in this chapter, parlayed their media meta-capital into more traditional capital recognized in the political field, as evidenced by their individual campaigns for mayor in their home cities as well as the media attention they received.

Overall, these findings demonstrate the ongoing shift toward a mediatized journalistic field (Couldry 2014) characterized by more hybrid reporting practices and greater interaction between professional journalists and members of the public (Zúñiga et al. 2018). Of course, these observed shifts in structure and practice, whether pertaining to the journalistic or political fields, do not mark the end of traditional divides, as the majority of organizations and subfields still adhere to predominant (professional) norms. Furthermore, it is important to note that actors' field position and influence as seen on Twitter are not necessarily representative of the field as a whole. In fact, despite the visibility of action in mediatized fields, many journalists and activists shown to be influential in their Twitter subfields hold much less powerful positions in the broader journalistic and political fields. Thus, although these findings may not be fully representative, they are revealing of the current and unfolding state of networked journalism and are consistent with other studies of journalistic practice as it intersects with other fields (Araiza et al. 2016).

This chapter also has implications for the broader literature of mediatization and field theory, and it seeks to bolster greater conversation between them. While mediatization research has been applied mostly to analyses of traditional politics and journalism, this chapter demonstrates the importance of considering how the dynamics of mediatization could contribute to a diminished distinction between the two fields due to increasing hybridity and emergent media logics (Couldry 2014; Esser and Strömbäck 2014). Each field has retained its own structure, practices, and status markers, but the marginal positions and dispositions where they converge are increasingly visible and consequential in a mediatized context. The slippery nature of objective and affective frames, the overlapping of network ties, and the limited convergence of discourses as seen through links, each serve as illustrative examples. Yet, it is unclear—on Twitter, at least—whether the norms of journalistic engagement become complicated during controversies mired by racism and police violence against protestors and journalists alike. While the #Ferguson case may be exceptional in its representation of these issues, the extent to which it models the hybridity of journalism and activism could demonstrate a new normal in an increasingly networked, mediatized field context.

Although they are consequential, direct network ties are not a necessary condition for journo-activists to influence reporting and gatekeeping decisions. In #Ferguson, citizens took to the streets as well as to Twitter to perform gatewatching and gatecrashing roles, and they often built lucrative ties with professional journalists in these networked spaces. This may not always be the case, however, as the story of #Nerdland in the next chapter is quite different. There was much less interaction between gatewatchers and professional journalists than in this chapter, perhaps because activists' reactions were episodic and primarily digital in #Nerdland compared to the prolonged, real world actions of #Ferguson. Nevertheless, the outcomes were clearly similar, as the growth of public participation and media criticism appears to be reflected in the work of more traditional professional journalists. This dynamic will be examined in greater depth next.

Notes

1. Thus, the hashtag "#Ferguson" is broadly used to describe the discursive exchanges occurring on Twitter and the wider web. By contrast, "Ferguson" is used only to describe the events taking place on the ground in Ferguson, Missouri and the surrounding area.
2. Numerous studies have demonstrated the implications of mediatization for social relations, including journalism (Backholm et al. 2012; Rees 2012), activism (Mattoni and Treré 2014), politics (Strömbäck 2008), culture (Chen 2015; Hepp 2013) conflict, and memorialization (Cottle 2006; Lindgren 2012), and beyond (Couldry and Hepp 2013).

3. While searching explicit mentions of #Ferguson or "Ferguson" by specific users allowed for a targeted sampling, it missed similar tweets from all other relevant users as well as those that did not include the search terms. Furthermore, the reliance on Twitter data rendered invisible professional journalists' primary reporting on more mainstream media platforms, which likely differed in tone and tenor from their tweets.
4. All percentages are based on in-group comparisons, rather than the entire data set.
5. Node colors represent the Twitter users' self-defined country of origin (Blue = US; Purple = UK; Green = Laos; Gray = Italy; Red = unknown).

REFERENCES

Adamic, L. A., & Glance, N. (2005). The political blogosphere and the 2004 U.S. election: Divided they blog. *Proceedings from the 3rd international workshop on Link discovery* (pp. 36–43). Retrieved November 21, 2017, from http://dl. acm.org/citation.cfm?id=1134271.1134277.

Araiza, J. A., Sturm, H. A., Istek, P., & Bock, M. A. (2016). Hands up, don't shoot, whose side are you on? Journalists tweeting the Ferguson protests. *Cultural Studies ↔ Critical Methodologies, 16*(3), 305–312. https://doi. org/10.1177/1532708616634834.

Backholm, K., Moritz, M., & Björkqvist, K. (2012). U.S. and Finnish journalists: A comparative study of roles, responsibilities, and emotional reactions to school shootings. In G. W. Muschert & J. Sumiala (Eds.). *School shootings: Mediatized violence in a global age* (pp. 141–160). Bingley: Emerald Group. Retrieved November 21, 2017, from http://www.emeraldinsight.com/doi/ abs/10.1108/S2050-2060%282012%290000007011.

Balko, R. (2015, July 2). Justice Department report: Police tactics in Ferguson created confrontation. *The Washington Post*. Retrieved November 21, 2017, from https://www.washingtonpost.com/news/the-watch/wp/2015/07/02/justice-department-report-police-tactics-in-ferguson-created-confrontation/?utm_term=.81e9e27e9725.

Barnard, S. R. (2016a). Spectacles of self(ie) empowerment? Networked individualism and the logic of the (post)feminist selfie. In L. Robinson, J. Schulz, S. R. Cotten, et al. (Eds.), *Communication and information technologies annual, studies in media and communications* (pp. 63–88). Bingley Emerald Group. Retrieved November 21, 2017, from http://www.emeraldinsight.com/doi/ full/10.1108/S2050-206020160000011014.

Barnard, S. R. (2016b). Digital sociology's vocational promise. In J. Daniels, K. Gregory, & T. M. Cottom (Eds.), *Digital sociologies* (pp. 195–210). Bristol: Policy Press.

Berman, M., & Lowery, W. (2015, March 4). The 12 key highlights from the DOJ's scathing Ferguson report. *The Washington Post*. Retrieved November 21, 2017, from https://www.washingtonpost.com/news/post-nation/wp/2015/03/04/the-12-key-highlights-from-the-dojs-scathing-ferguson-report/.

Bigoted Ferguson was 'Powder Keg': Our View. (2015, March 4). *USA Today*. Retrieved November 21, 2017, from http://www.usatoday.com/story/opinion/2015/03/04/ferguson-civil-rights-justice-department-darren-wilson-editorials-debates/24397873/.

Bonilla, Y., & Rosa, J. (2015). #Ferguson: Digital protest, hashtag ethnography, and the racial politics of social media in the United States. *American Ethnologist, 42*(1), 4–17.

Bourdieu, P. (1993). *The field of cultural production: Essays on art and literature*. New York, NY: Columbia University Press.

Bourdieu, P. (2005). The political field, the social science field, and the journalistic field. In R. Benson & E. Neveu (Eds.), *Bourdieu and the journalistic field* (pp. 29–47). Malden, MA: Polity.

Brock, A. (2012). From the blackhand side: Twitter as a cultural conversation. *Journal of Broadcasting & Electronic Media, 56*(4), 529–549.

Bruns, A. (2003). Gatewatching, not gatekeeping: Collaborative online news. *Media International Australia, 107*(1), 31–44.

Bruns, A., & Burgess, J. (2012). Researching news discussion on Twitter. *Journalism Studies, 13*(5–6), 801–814. https://doi.org/10.1080/14616 70X.2012.664428.

Carlson, M. (2015). Metajournalistic discourse and the meanings of journalism: Definitional control, boundary work, and legitimation. *Communication Theory, 26*(4), 349–368.

Carlson, M. (2016). Embedded links, embedded meanings. *Journalism Studies, 17*(7), 915–924.

Chadwick, A. (2013). *The hybrid media system: Politics and power*. New York: Oxford University Press.

Chaudhry, I. (2016). 'Not so black and white': Discussions of race on Twitter in the aftermath of #Ferguson and the shooting death of Mike Brown. *Cultural Studies ↔ Critical Methodologies, 16*(3), 296–304.

Chen, W. (2015). Mediatizing the network model of cultural capital: Network diversity, media use, and cultural knowledge along and across ethnic boundaries. *Social Networks, 40*, 185–196.

Clark, L. S. (2016). Participants on the margins: Examining the role that shared artifacts of engagement in the Ferguson protests played among minoritized political newcomers on Snapchat, Facebook, and Twitter. *International Journal of Communication, 10*, 26.

Cottle, S. (2006). *Mediatized conflict: Understanding media and conflicts in the contemporary world*. New York, NY: McGraw-Hill Education.

Couldry, N. (2014). Mediatization and the future of field theory. In K. Lundby (Ed.), *Mediatization of communication* (pp. 227–245). Berlin: Walter de Gruyter GmbH.

Couldry, N., & Hepp, A. (2013). Conceptualizing mediatization: Contexts, traditions, arguments. *Communication Theory, 23*(3), 191–202.

De Maeyer, J. (2013). Towards a hyperlinked society: A critical review of link studies. *New Media & Society, 15*(5), 737–751.

De Maeyer, J., & Holton, A. E. (2015). Why linking matters: A metajournalistic discourse analysis. *Journalism, 17*(6), 776–794.

Duggan, M. (2015). *The demographics of social media users*. Pew Research Center. Retrieved November 21, 2017, from http://www.pewinternet.org/2015/08/19/the-demographics-of-social-media-users/.

Earl, J., & Kimport, K. (2011). *Digitally enabled social change: Activism in the internet age*. Cambridge, MA: MIT Press.

Esser, F., & Strömbäck, J. (Eds.). (2014). *Mediatization of politics: Understanding the transformation of western democracies*. New York: Palgrave Macmillan.

Feldman, J. (2014). Crowd of NY Ferguson protestors chants 'F*ck CNN!' on CNN. *Mediaite.com*. Retrieved November 21, 2017, from http://www.mediaite.com/tv/crowd-of-ny-ferguson-protestors-chants-fck-cnn-on-cnn/.

Freelon, D., & Karpf, D. (2015). Of big birds and bayonets: Hybrid Twitter interactivity in the 2012 presidential debates. *Information, Communication & Society, 18*(4), 390–406.

Freelon, D., McIlwain, C. D., & Clark, M. D. (2016). Beyond the hashtags: #Ferguson, #Blacklivesmatter, and the online struggle for offline justice. *Center for Media and Social Impact*. Retrieved November 21, 2017, from http://cmsimpact.org/resource/beyond-hashtags-ferguson-blacklivesmatter-online-struggle-offline-justice/.

Gitlin, T. (2003). *The whole world is watching: Mass media in the making and unmaking of the new left*. Berkeley, CA: University of California Press.

Graeff, E., Stempeck, M., & Zuckerman, E. (2014). The battle for 'Trayvon Martin': Mapping a media controversy online and off-line. *First Monday, 19*(2). https://doi.org/10.5210/fm.v19i2.4947.

Hedman, U. (2015). J-Tweeters. *Digital Journalism, 3*(2), 279–297.

Hepp, A. (2013). *Cultures of mediatization*. Malden, MA: Wiley-Blackwell.

Herman, E. S., & Chomsky, N. (2002). *Manufacturing consent: The political economy of the mass media*. New York: Pantheon.

Hermida, A. (2010). Twittering the news: The emergence of ambient journalism. *Journalism Practice, 4*(3), 297–308.

Himelboim, I., Sweetser, K. D., Tinkham, S. F., Cameron, K., Danelo, M., & West, K. (2016). Valence-based homophily on Twitter: Network analysis of emotions and political talk in the 2012 presidential election. *New Media & Society, 18*(7), 1382–1400.

Hitlin, P., & Vogt, N. (2014, August 20). *Cable, Twitter picked up Ferguson story at a similar clip.* Pew Research Center. Retrieved November 21, 2017, from http://www.pewresearch.org/fact-tank/2014/08/20/cable-twitter-picked-up-ferguson-story-at-a-similar-clip/.

Hjarvard, S. (2013). *The mediatization of culture and society.* New York: Routledge.

Jackson, S. J., & Welles, B. F. (2016). #Ferguson is everywhere: Initiators in emerging counterpublic networks. *Information, Communication & Society, 19*(3), 397–418.

Jurgenson, N. (2012). When atoms meet bits: Social media, the mobile web and augmented revolution. *Future Internet, 4*(1), 83–91.

Kidd, D. (2017). *Social media freaks: Digital identity in the network society.* Boulder: Westview Press.

Kreiss, D. (2016). Seizing the moment: The presidential campaigns' use of Twitter during the 2012 electoral cycle. *New Media & Society, 18*(8), 1473–1490.

Kreiss, D., Meadows, L., & Remensperger, J. (2015). Political performance, boundary spaces, and active spectatorship: Media production at the 2012 democratic National Convention. *Journalism, 16*(5), 577–595.

Krogstad, J. M. (2015, February 3). *Social media preferences vary by race and ethnicity.* Pew Research Center. Retrieved November 21, 2017, from http://www.pewresearch.org/fact-tank/2015/02/03/social-media-preferences-vary-by-race-and-ethnicity/.

LeFebvre, R. K., & Armstrong, C. (2016). Grievance-based social movement mobilization in the #Ferguson Twitter storm. *New Media & Society,* Advanced online publication. https://doi.org/10.1177/1461444816644697.

Lindgren, S. (2012). Collective coping through networked narratives: YouTube responses to the Virginia Tech shooting. In G. Muschert & J. Sumiala (Eds.), *School shootings: Mediatized violence in a global age* (pp. 279–298). Bingley: Emerald Group. Retrieved November 21, 2017, from http://www.emeraldinsight.com/doi/abs/10.1108/S2050-2060%282012%290000007017.

Maireder, A., & Ausserhofer, J. (2014). Political discourses on Twitter: Networking topics, objects, and people. In K. Weller, A. Bruns, J. Burgess, N. Mahrt, & C. Puschmann (Eds.), *Twitter and society* (pp. 305–318). New York, NY: Peter Lang.

Mattoni, A., & Treré, E. (2014). Media practices, mediation processes, and mediatization in the study of social movements. *Communication Theory, 24*(3), 252–271.

McChesney, R. W. (2008). *The political economy of media: Enduring issues, emerging dilemmas.* New York: Monthly Review Press.

Meraz, S., & Papacharissi, Z. (2013). Networked gatekeeping and networked framing on #Egypt. *The International Journal of Press/Politics, 18*(2), 138–166.

Molyneux, L. (2015). What journalists retweet: Opinion, humor, and brand development on Twitter. *Journalism, 16*(7), 920–935.

Morozov, E. (2014). *To save everything, click here: The folly of technological solutionism.* New York: PublicAffairs.

Neuberg, C., vom Hofe, H. J., & Nuernbergk, C. (2014). The use of Twitter by professional journalists: Results of a newsroom survey in Germany. In K. Weller, A. Bruns, J. Burgess, N. Mahrt, & C. Puschmann (Eds.), *Twitter and society* (pp. 345–357). New York, NY: Peter Lang.

Papacharissi, Z. (2014). *Affective publics: Sentiment, technology, and politics.* New York: Oxford University Press.

Poell, T., & Rajagopalan, S. (2015). Connecting activists and journalists. *Journalism Studies, 16*(5), 719–733.

Raeymaeckers, K., Deprez, A., De Vuyst, S., & De Dobbelaer, R. (2015). The journalist as a jack of all trades: Safeguarding the gates in a digitized news ecology. In T. Vos & F. Heinderyckx (Eds.), Gatekeeping in transition (pp. 104–119). New York: Routledge.

Rees, G. (2012). Afterword: Is mediatization a useful concept for informing practice in journalism? In G. W. Muschert & J. Sumiala (Eds.), *School shootings: Mediatized violence in a global age* (pp. 333–341). Bingley: Emerald Group. Retrieved November 21, 2017, from http://www.emeraldinsight.com/doi/abs/10.1108/S2050-2060(2012)0000007019.

Russell, A. (2013). Innovation in hybrid spaces: 2011 UN climate summit and the expanding journalism landscape. *Journalism, 14*(7), 904–920.

Santhanam, L., & Dennis, V. (2014, November 25). What do the newly released witness statements tell us about the Michael Brown shooting? *PBS NewsHour.* Retrieved November 21, 2017, from http://www.pbs.org/newshour/updates/newly-released-witness-testimony-tell-us-michael-brown-shooting/.

Schudson, M. (1981). *Discovering the news: A social history of American newspapers.* New York: Basic Books.

Shjarback, J. A., Pyrooz, D. C., Wolfe, S. E., & Decker, S. H. (2017). De-policing and crime in the wake of Ferguson: Racialized changes in the quantity and quality of policing among Missouri police departments. *Journal of Criminal Justice, 50*, 42–52. https://doi.org/10.1016/j.jcrimjus.2017.04.003.

Shoemaker, P. J., & Vos, T. (2009). *Gatekeeping theory.* New York: Routledge.

Sobieraj, S. (2011). *Soundbitten: The perils of media-centered political activism.* New York: NYU Press.

Starr, P. (2005). *The creation of the media: Political origins of modern communications.* New York: Basic Books.

Strömbäck, J. (2008). Four phases of mediatization: An analysis of the mediatization of politics. *The International Journal of Press/Politics, 13*(3), 228–246.

Thorson, K., & Wells, C. (2015). How gatekeeping still matters: Understanding media effects in an era of curated flows. In T. Vos & F. Heinderyckx (Eds.), *Gatekeeping in transition* (pp. 25–44). New York, NY: Routledge.

Tremayne, M. (2014). Anatomy of protest in the digital era: A network analysis of Twitter and Occupy Wall Street. *Social Movement Studies, 13*(1), 110–126.

Wagner, L. (2016, February 9). Ferguson approves police and courts overhaul – With some changes. *National Public Radio*. Retrieved November 21, 2017, from http://www.npr.org/sections/thetwo-way/2016/02/09/466221524/ferguson-approves-police-and-courts-overhaul-with-some-changes.

Zeller, F., & Hermida, A. (2015). When tradition meets immediacy and interaction: The integration of social media in journalists' everyday practices. *About Journalism, 4*(1), 106–119.

Zúñiga, H. G. d., Diehl, T., & Ardèvol-Abreu, A. (2018). When citizens and journalists interact on Twitter. *Journalism Studies, 19*(2), 227–246.

We Stand with #Nerdland: Gatewatching and Agenda-Building by the "People Formerly Known as the Audience"

From subscriber, follower, and click counts to other engagement metrics (Christin 2014), it is clear that news institutions have methods of watching and responding to the "people formerly known as the audience" (Rosen 2006). But in a mediatized world, the citizens themselves can, and often do, provide guidance to reporters and editors about what stories and issues are important. As discussed in previous chapters, while the agenda-setting power of media was previously a privilege only granted to elite institutions, today's most prominent social media platforms afford users with opportunities to collectively shape what news stories get covered, and how. This chapter examines the role Twitter can play in this agenda-setting process, as seen through the media coverage and public outcry following the unexpected cancellation of a popular cable TV news show.

Melissa Harris-Perry, an African-American political science professor and then cable TV host, publicly announced her discontent with her MSNBC employer on February 26, 2016. The email to her staff, which was shared on the popular blogging platform, *Medium*, detailed her abrupt exit from MSNBC after repeatedly being sidelined from appearing on air without any communication from company leadership (Smith 2016). The post prompted many fans of her show, which they affectionately called "Nerdland," to take to social media to express support for Harris-Perry as well as to put pressure on MSNBC to explain or address the situation. Initially, MSNBC spokespeople denied many of Harris-

© The Author(s) 2018
S. R. Barnard, *Citizens at the Gates*,
https://doi.org/10.1007/978-3-319-90446-7_7

Perry's claims, including the alleged efforts to intentionally take her off the air. Nevertheless, network executives later admitted they were parting ways with Harris-Perry, suggesting that she brought this on herself by being "challenging and unpredictable," and that their decision to limit her airtime was solely a response to MSNBC shifting priorities toward election coverage (Farhi 2016a).

Among the legacy cable television news institutions in the United States, MSNBC is typically placed toward the left of the American political spectrum. The network was founded in 1996 as a branch of NBC, which was owned by General Electric at the time and is now owned by Comcast. MSNBC has long marketed itself as a progressive alternative to the purportedly conservative Fox News (FOX) and centrist CNN (Bae 1999). Starting in 2013, this strategy meant making an effort to hire more minority reporters than what was typical of legacy news organizations (Christopher 2013). For example, a recent analysis revealed that MSNBC had a greater number of minority anchors, reporters, and guests compared to FOX and CNN (Christopher 2014; Maza 2016). This supports an earlier study that found diversity in news staff was related to more diversity in sources (Zeldes and Fico 2005). However, in recent years, the network has cut back on liberal talk shows, which often featured reporters of color, as part of an effort to rebrand itself due to a drop in ratings ("Melissa Harris-Perry" 2016; Farhi 2016b). In this context, the cancellation of Harris-Perry's show may be interpreted as part of the network's rebranding.

The perceived decline in diversity at MSNBC gave rise to a number of public efforts to raise awareness and seek redress. Such acts of media criticism, whether through traditional, institutionally sponsored channels such as ombudspersons, or alternative channels like (online) letter-writing campaigns, have yielded mixed results in terms of building accountability and audience trust (Jacobson 2013; Wurff and Schönbach 2014). Nevertheless, the #Nerdland debacle proved to be a galvanizing moment for Harris-Perry and fans of her show, who used networked tools like Twitter to create a media spectacle in hopes of saving (the diversity of) the program and its associated community of viewers.

HERE COMES (SOME OF) BLACK TWITTER

Within hours of Harris-Perry's announcement, #Nerdland was trending on Twitter, and for a short time, even ranked first among trending topics in the United States. This was likely due, in large part, to the concern displayed by the show's dedicated fan base, many of whom could be identified as participants in the online subculture known as "Black Twitter." Literature continues to grow on the cultural and political significance of Twitter and social media use by African Americans (Brock 2012; Florini 2014, 2017; Sharma 2013). In addition to journalists, African Americans are one of the most demographically overrepresented groups on Twitter. As noted in previous chapters, approximately 28% of Black internet users report using Twitter, while a resounding 40% of Blacks aged 18–29 report using the service (Duggan 2015; Smith 2014). With this growth in Twitter usage, networks and cultural practices have emerged that encourage community engagement and amplification of salient messages (Florini 2014). As a result, Black Twitter has been credited with disproportionate influence over Twitter's "trending topics" by thoughtfully leveraging the retweet, reply, and hashtag functions. This includes a notable history among Black Twitter contributors to intentionally amplify messages by using catchy, inviting hashtags as well as retweeting and replying to messages in mass, which increases reach and visibility. Thus, "blacktags" trend in part because of users' awareness of and ability to game the preferences written into Twitter's algorithms (Sharma 2013).

In the case of #Nerdland, many of Harris-Perry's fans and followers leveraged the affordances of their Twitter networks to mourn the loss of the program and to call attention to the perceived injustices that contributed to its downfall. While some offered alternative frames and counternarratives to those provided by network executives, others sought to gain visibility by participating in media spectacle—either to convince the network to revive the show or to attract the attention of other media outlets. For example, some viewers began using the hashtag #MSNBCsoWhite in an attempt to call attention to the network's perceived bias using sensational language. This strategy was effective in large part because it took advantage of a key component of mediatized society: the yearning for spectacle. As Douglas Kellner (2009, p. 76) explained, media spectacle "refers to technologically mediated events, in which media forms like broadcasting, print media, or the internet process events in a spectacular form." Spectacle occurs when events are presented in a sensational manner, maximizing the likelihood for audience interest—and thus, media attention. As this chapter shows, #Nerdland serves as an example of networked publics leveraging Twitter to engage in the practice of gatewatching, designed to attract, and ideally, to shape media attention.

GATEKEEPING, AGENDA-SETTING, AND THE MEDIATIZATION OF THE JOURNALISTIC FIELD

The gatekeeping literature has a longstanding notion of the individual and institutional factors that shape selection and curation criteria for what is treated as newsworthy, and how (Shoemaker and Vos 2009; Vos and Heinderyckx 2015). Questions of autonomy and journalistic influence are ubiquitous, hinging as much on professional norms as outside factors like political and economic influence (Benson and Neveu 2005; Hellmueller 2014; Raeymaeckers et al. 2015). Although journalists' institutional norms are fairly robust and resistant to direct influence, many other factors can shape the story throughout the gatekeeping process. This begins with selection and sourcing, proceeds through the editorial chain, and even persists beyond, as members of the public amplify and respond to news stories (Shoemaker and Vos 2009).

The digital age provides a growing number of opportunities for members of networked publics to influence reporting and gatekeeping processes. For example, as John Carr (2012, p. 2826) explained:

> By rapidly and massively circulating stories critical of conventional media providers, Internet users drove those providers to engage in 'forced reflexivity'—defined here as the sometimes unwilling coverage of events and critiques that expose and challenge their role in maintaining media hegemony.

Carr's account of Jon Stewart's appearance on CNN's *Crossfire*, which was cancelled after Stewart's pointed criticism went viral online, further illustrates the ability of networked publics to hold media institutions accountable. In the case of #Nerdland, the public's successful attempts to attract media attention from the *New York Times* (NYT) and *Washington Post*, among many other outlets, demonstrates the potential for news flows to be shaped from outside the media professions.

Although gatewatching and gatecrashing practices may not be formally acknowledged as media work, they can play an integral role in the functioning of the journalistic field. Nevertheless, many journalism professionals have become increasingly interested in audience participation and engagement as the public's contribution to the field grows. As Stephanie Craft, Tim Vos, and David Wolfgang (2016, p. 12) pointed out:

Commenting itself constitutes a kind of participation in journalism that places commenters at least within striking distance of the field. Because the cultural capital of journalism is defined by the roles, ethics, and epistemologies unique to that field, introducing social norms that are by definition broadly applicable to all members of society undercuts the field's unique capital and, therefore, represents a contestation of the traditional doxa of journalism that could act as a disruptive force on the field.

If the very presence of, and action from, nontraditional members of the journalistic field is seen as a disruption in itself, then an increase in journalistic influence is unquestionably unsettling to the stability and status quo of the field. Thus, while some studies have found public comments on news sites to be largely in agreement with journalistic doxa (Craft et al. 2016), this chapter considers whether less institutionalized patterns of discourse, which flow quickly and publicly on Twitter, are more critical of media organizations, and if these critiques play a role in shaping the frames and flows of news.

Many nontraditional actors are driven by motivations outside the journalistic field. That is, they are issue-driven and seek to raise awareness about a cause that is personal to them. To an extent, the aphorism "all press is good press" is fitting for many who seek media attention as a means of gaining public awareness about their cause. However, for political actors, the greatest challenge is not simply to get coverage, but to *shape* it (Gitlin 1980; Sobieraj 2011). The high concentration of networked journalists on Twitter appears to make that possible.

Recent scholarship on "intermedia agenda setting" and "network agenda setting" have examined real and potential effects of media products and participation on the flows and frames of published news stories (Meraz 2011; Groshek and Groshek 2013; Russell et al. 2015; Conway et al. 2015; Cushion et al. 2018; Guo and McCombs 2016). Similarly, studies of "agenda-building" have demonstrated the long-term influence of public social media posts on the gatekeeping processes of legacy news institutions (Parmelee 2014; Boynton and Richardson 2015; Russell et al. 2015) as well as on the agendas advanced by public officials (Camaj 2016). Together, these perspectives offer a unique and revealing window into the changes occurring within the structures of the journalistic field because they demonstrate the extent to which the flow of news is less the product of largely autonomous, legacy news institutions, and more a mutually shaping exchange between gatekeepers and members of networked publics.

Assessing Agenda-Building in #Nerdland

In light of changes in the gatekeeping literature (Bruns 2014; Shoemaker and Vos 2009), agenda-setting (Gitlin 1980; Kutz-Flamenbaum et al. 2012; Sobieraj 2011), and the mediatization of the journalistic field (Couldry 2014), this chapter examines the agenda-setting potential of social media on traditional media outlets. While many have applied time series analysis methods to statistically test correlation (Conway et al. 2015; Groshek and Groshek 2013; Meraz 2011, 2015), this method is less applicable to single-issue topics where comparisons are not feasible. Instead, this analysis examined intermedia agenda-setting by comparing the flows and frames of news on Twitter with those published on legacy news websites.

Accordingly, Twitter data from #Nerdland was compared and contrasted with online news reporting on Harris-Perry's exit from MSNBC, both in the weeks preceding and following her own public announcement. Previous studies have developed methods for examining the use, meaning, and consequences of links, hashtags, and retweets in Twitter posts (Weller et al. 2011). Others have assessed agenda-building and intermedia agenda-setting on Twitter using quantitative analyses (Russell et al. 2015) and journalist-audience interaction using network analysis (Larsson 2013). This chapter, like others in this book, incorporates elements from each of these methods into a mixed approach that also includes qualitative content analysis and digital ethnography (Altheide and Schneider 2012). By examining the themes, frames, discourse, and format of networked communication around a specific issue, this study assesses similarities and differences between social media and traditional media discourses as well as the relationships between them. When considered as part of a temporal order, trends in framing and publishing in the Twittersphere are shown to contribute to the flows and frames of news stories published by legacy and digital news organizations. Similarly, the format of a post, whether it is a text-only tweet, contains multimedia, or is (part of) a lengthy news story, conveys meaning in itself, including the publication's field location. Overall, by examining the ebbs and flows of information-sharing about Harris-Perry's email to her staff on Twitter, and the precipitant reporting on her abrupt exit from MSNBC, this analysis considers the potential agenda-building function of networked publics' use of social media.

From Tweet-Streams to the Mainstream

In the days following Harris-Perry's public announcement, thousands of supporters took to Twitter to express outrage over the loss and hope for the program's future. As Fig. 7.1 makes clear, the flow of news and reaction happened much quicker on Twitter than on individual publishing platforms. Of course, this was expected since news spreads quickly on Twitter, and many news agencies have adopted social-first policies. For example, on the day Harris-Perry's exit from MSNBC was made public, news sites published a mere three stories on the topic. Clearly, the news was bound to spread faster by journo-activists on the web, especially given that legacy media outlets took their time picking up the story.

In general, legacy media outlets produce relatively few stories on the workings of the US news industry, whether about this particular story or others. Thus, it was not surprising to find that the online legacy news coverage of Harris-Perry's abrupt exit from MSNBC was rarely original, even though the stories were published on hundreds of different sites. Of the most visible news stories, most were duplicates or near duplicates of

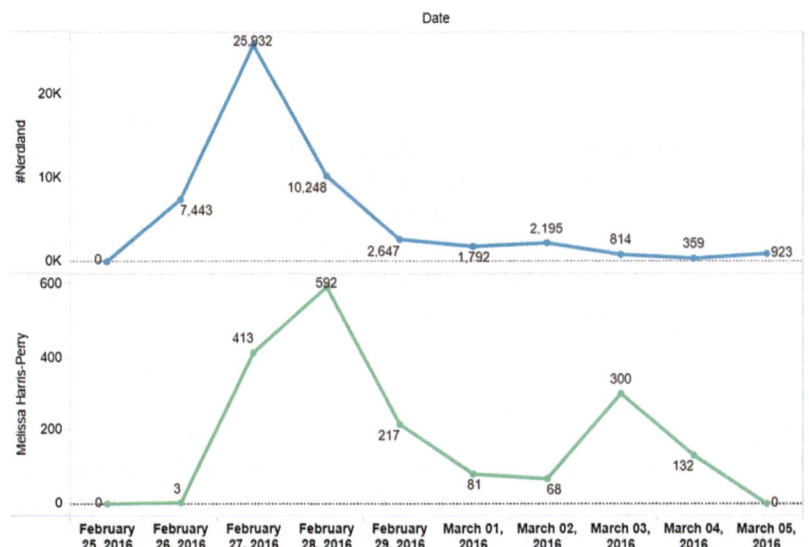

Fig. 7.1 Twitter mentions of #Nerdland *(top)* vs. news stories about "Melissa Harris-Perry" *(bottom)*

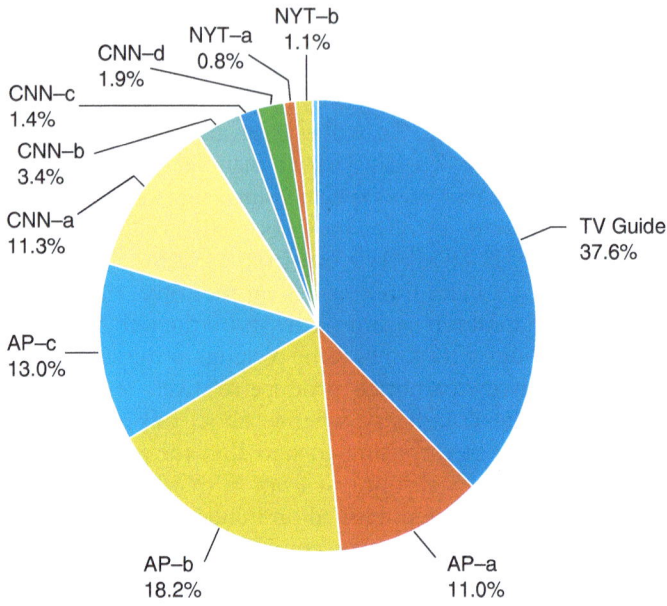

Fig. 7.2 Number of times influential news stories were republished (in percent)

other published news stories. For example, a mere 14 stories made up nearly 35% ($n = 635$) of the news dataset, and were distributed by one of four publishers (see Fig. 7.2). On average, each of these stories was republished 45 times, primarily on local or niche news sites such as broadcast network affiliates and conglomerate-owned local and regional newspapers. However, the number of times a legacy story was republished varied, from 240 times for a single *TV Guide* story, to only 2 times for a single NYT story (Fig. 7.3).

Given the profound concentration of ownership in the US media market, the republishing of identical stories on countless sites demonstrates the true potential of the (corporate) web to function as an echo chamber. Ironically, this is the charge often waged by members of the legacy media against citizen journalists, claiming that they rarely produce original content. While it is true that #Nerdland contributors produced less original journalism when compared to those seen in previous chapters for the #BostonMarathon bombing or #Ferguson, it would be a mistake to

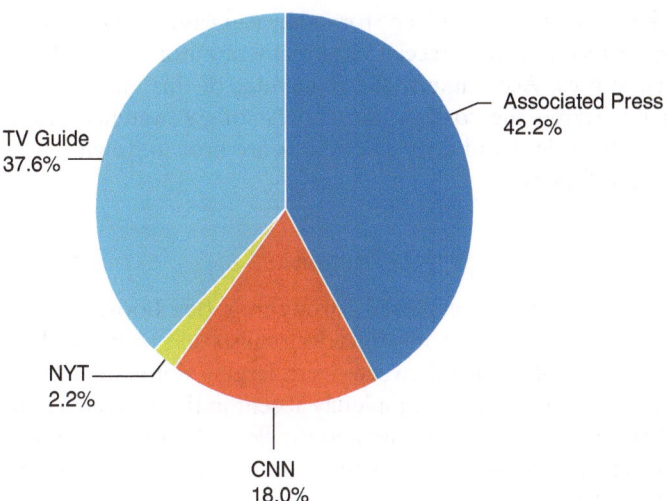

Fig. 7.3 Combined percentage of (re)published stories by influential outlets

dismiss Twitter's journalistic significance based on claims that citizens' acts of journalism are not always original.

Despite the prominence of journalistic conventions designed to bolster independence, networked publics' use of social media platforms can provide a source of influence. In addition to subscribing to a somewhat slower and more measured news cycle driven by the pressure to balance speed with accuracy, legacy publishers pay close attention to users' production and consumption habits on social media, as well as the subsequent metadata it produces. However motivated news institutions are to give the audience what they want, they are increasingly committed to audience feedback and engagement (Lee et al. 2014). In addition to tracking audience metrics (Christin 2014; Petre 2015), some professional newsworkers seek input on audience preferences by creating community journalism projects or by listening intently to what their communities are talking about (Stearns 2015a, b). Such mechanisms, in and of themselves, function as avenues for intermedia agenda-setting. Since networked publics use online platforms such as Twitter to provide evidence of what issues and perspectives matter to them, professional newsworkers are compelled to be *there*, listening intently. While it may be difficult for reporters to read the bulk of responses to a given story, they can easily observe the number of clicks or reactions they receive, and many monitor Twitter for leads on potential stories. Accordingly, the remainder of this chapter focuses on further unpacking the content and context of gatewatchers' tweets as it relates to the #Nerdland case. The results are broken down to discourse, themes, and frames.

Discourse

Like much of the data explored throughout this book, a clear divide stands between posts by professional journalists and those by the twittering public. The #Nerdland tweets were largely dominated by activists, and journalists were almost completely absent in this discourse. However, journalists understandably dominated the flow of information on "news" sites. Notice the difference found between the influencers in the news and #Nerdland datasets. Whereas influencers in the news discourse were primarily split between legacy and online news sites (Fig. 7.4), the network map of #Nerdland influencers is much more evenly distributed and reciprocal (Fig. 7.5). This finding suggests that the role social and symbolic capital (i.e., network ties and status) play is complicated, and is moderated by a variety of other factors including the publisher's field location and the particularities of each post. Based on the data, the only major influencer in the #Nerdland network was Harris-Perry herself, who had over half a million (567,000) Twitter followers at the time of this event. More typical Twitter users comprised the rest of the network, some existed in tightly knit discursive communities and others were only loosely tied to other users. But as with most networked publics, a much broader form of distribution occurred across many relatively distinct network "neighborhoods."

Although the #Nerdland tweets were much more diverse in perspective, the hashtag suffered greatly from context collapse, where users must contend with multiple discourses in a single conversation (Marwick and boyd 2011). Like many trending topics, the popularity of a hashtag attracts others to it in hopes of reaching a larger audience with their (often out of context) comments. Ironically, while spam can disrupt the conversation and context, participation by these users still serve to amplify the core message of a hashtag by helping it "trend" on Twitter. This paradox—that the amplification afforded by social media platforms both dilutes and popularizes a discourse—can affect all kinds of causes, from small chats to

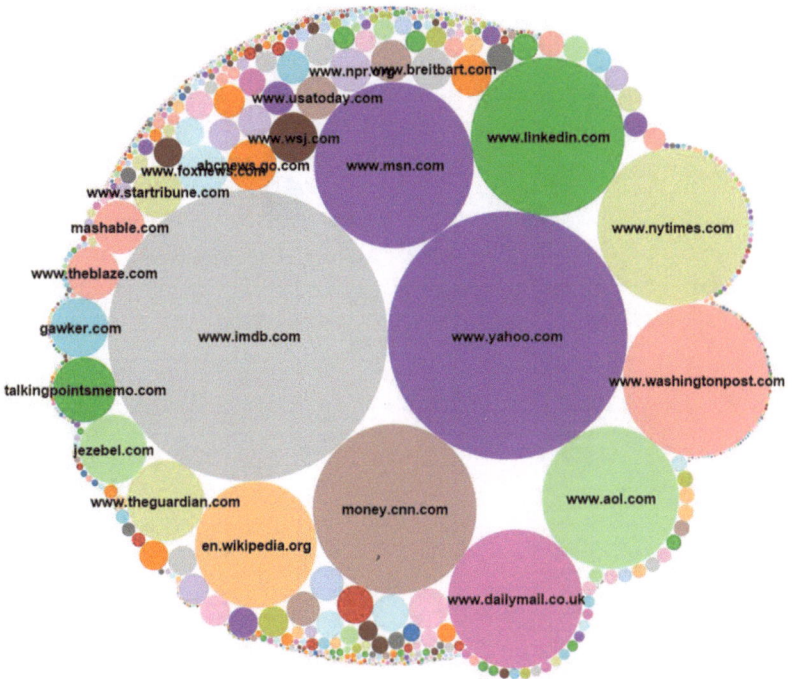

Fig. 7.4   Map of the most influential news sites covering the Harris-Perry story

large social movements (Tufekci 2017). While considering the specific "effects" of communicative acts are beyond the scope of this study, it is useful to acknowledge the difficulty of determining the influence (actual or potential) of #Nerdland tweets, especially given their observed efforts to shape the actions of media organizations.

Themes

In addition to differences in the format (news stories vs. tweets) and discourse (communicative networks), the themes and frames differed significantly between the #Nerdland and news discourses, which were expected across platforms and publishers. On the one hand, traditional journalists were more likely to remain objective in their framing of news stories, fitting their professional norms. On the other hand, journo-activists engaged in affective expression on Twitter, frequently opting to memorialize

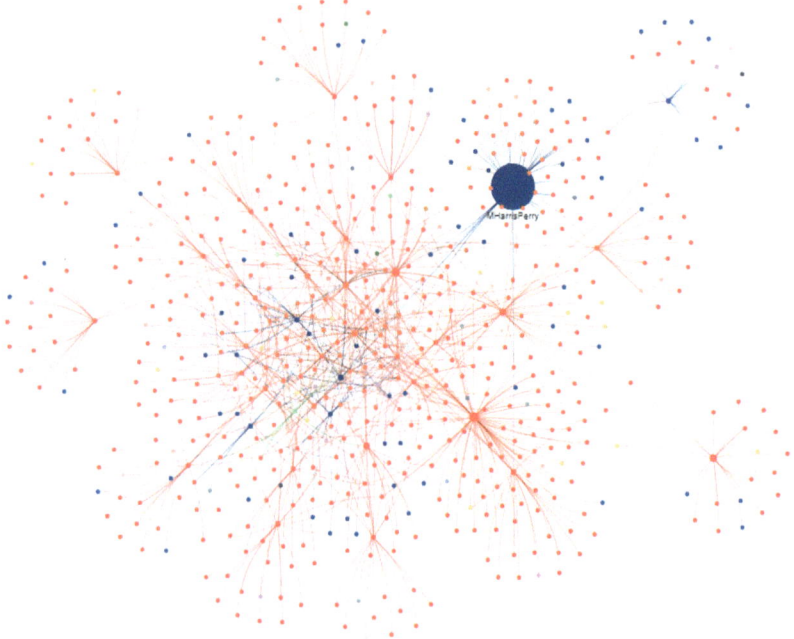

Fig. 7.5   Network map of influencers in #Nerdland tweets

Harris-Perry and her show, as well as to call upon MSNBC to reconsider or respond. Accordingly, this section places particular emphasis on activists' tweets in order to demonstrate their gatewatching functions and discusses them based on two main themes found in the data. Furthermore, particular attention is paid to tweets from the first few days, where the agenda-setting function was higher and the data is much more relevant on average.

Media Criticism
The most visible contribution to the #Nerdland discourse came in the form of media criticism. Whereas many of these criticisms explicitly named "MSNBC" or the "media," others were less explicit, instead relying on the #Nerdland hashtag to define the context. Some of the most direct criticism came in the form of complaints or ultimatums, such as, "I'm a make this perfectly clear to @MSNBC if they are no longer showing the Melissa

Harris-Perry show, I will stop watching MSNBC. #Nerdland." Other prominent activists tweeted about the hashtag's popularity in an attempt to beckon a response from MSNBC. For example, one user tweeted, "#nerdland Trending for three hours. Now #1. Still complete silence from MSNBC," while another tweeted, "Welp! #Nerdland is trending number one and I'm glad. Take notice, @MSNBC. @MHarrisPerry @MHPshow #AskaSista." Still, others chose a less direct approach to media criticism, instead making the case for why Harris-Perry's show was so valuable. Examples include, "People watch the show and use the #nerdland hashtag to connect & discuss with each other issues that are dismissed in other media spaces," and "I hope it doesn't get lost or forgotten that #Nerdland was a vital media platform for stories that wouldn't get any shine anywhere else." Although these tweets were not successful in convincing MSNBC to reconsider its decision to take Harris-Perry off the air, they were certainly significant to journo-activists who sought to draw attention to the issue.

Information Dissemination
Twitter was frequently used as a platform for content distribution—hence, the retweet function—and this case study was no different. Expectedly, a large portion (76%) of #Nerdland tweets were reactions (i.e., retweets and replies), while the remaining 24% were original tweets. Although many of those reactions included additional context or opinion, others used the hashtag to share additional, and often original content. However, most would best be categorized as gatewatching tweets, providing little to no new information about the story, instead using Twitter to react affectively and spread the news of Harris-Perry's exit from MSNBC. The most visible trend was simply to spread the news of Harris-Perry's departure from MSNBC. Still, others offered additional context and insight. For example, one #Nerdland tweeter shared data and analysis about (lack of) diversity in political talk shows, "Check out this 2014 @mmfa graphic about diversity of Sunday talk show guests. https://t.co/vDkfIalbV3 #nerdland."

Frames: Tweets vs. News

As noted, the framing of journalists and journo-activists messages differed drastically. Whereas activists' #Nerdland tweets were more likely to be framed around injustice, often emphasizing issues of exclusion based on race and gender, journalists' stories were more likely to spread MSNBC's official response. Legacy media's reliance on official sources led to coverage that served the status quo of the field. The inclusion of a few, often repeated quotes from Harris-Perry proved to be a notable exception, although in this context, they were used as part of a "he said, she said" frame where truth claims are left unresolved (Rosen 2009). Legacy media had a habit of framing the story as a media spectacle, which scarcely questioned the facts of the matter, and their coverage rarely dug deeper to consider alternative voices or include broader context about MSNBC's recent staffing decisions.

Nevertheless, activists' relative success in amplifying the story through intermedia agenda-setting was demonstrated by legacy news outlets' framing of future news stories around questions of justice. While this limited success is partially attributable to the power of networks and hashtags to serve as "framing devices" (Qin 2015), the #Nerdland community's greatest accomplishment may be the mark they made on the journalistic field itself. Although it is difficult to identify direct, causal linkages between activists' tweets and journalists' news stories, the timeline of events presented above demonstrates a pattern of mutual-shaping and agenda-building from Twitter to the news, and back again. This pattern falls in line with recent studies finding multidirectional agenda-setting influences, where legacy media are used to set the public's agenda, while the public use social media to shape media coverage (Jacobson 2013).

Conclusions

The mediatization of the field, led by a shift in cultural practices and technological affordances, has ushered in new dynamics of agenda-setting, and thus, new roles have opened for nonprofessionals to play at the margins of the journalistic field. Much like their professional counterparts from the political field, citizen activists have long used the instrument of media spectacle to generate attention to their cause (Barnard 2016; Sobieraj 2011). Nevertheless, advancements in networked technologies have led to innovations in (the practices of) networked publics, who now leverage these tools to pursue political goals. To the extent that networked publics succeed in shaping news coverage, they are capable of amassing the kind of influence, or media-meta capital, discussed throughout the book. In the aggregate, these networked individuals provide the webbing for the mediatized superstructure otherwise known as the "fifth estate"—a collection of actors, practices, and platforms that help monitor the workings of public intellectuals, economic elites, government, and mass media (Dutton 2009).

Although this chapter has demonstrated trends in tweets from #Nerdland gatewatchers as well as some similarities and differences with news stories about Harris-Perry's departure from MSNBC, it does not render fully visible the efficacy (or lack thereof) of attempts by networked publics to get and shape news coverage. While direct effects are difficult to operationalize, the process of agenda-building is becoming normalized, given how frequently legacy news outlets treat tweets as a legitimate source of news and markers of public opinion (Bennett 2016; Broersma and Graham 2013; Larsson 2013; Lefky et al. 2015). So, while networked publics may not be able to tell media professionals what to write, they are, at times, successful in shaping what professionals write about (cf. Cohen 1963). Accordingly, #Nerdland activists' use of media criticism served as a form of gatewatching, representing an attempt to hold legacy institutions accountable for perceived errors.

In short, treating social media posts as objects of journalism, whether by politicians, pundits, journalists, or citizens, is an *ipso facto* assertion of their journalistic significance. Although how those tweets are used and responded to may vary greatly, the simple fact they are being included and discussed in legacy and online news stories is a clear demonstration of their journalistic significance. Furthermore, journalists' heavy presence on Twitter suggests that they may be more susceptible to public influence, especially during episodes of media spectacle. Two of these assertions, that tweets are treated as objects of news, and that journalists are open to influence on Twitter, will be examined in greater depth in the next chapter.

References

Altheide, D. L., & Schneider, C. J. (2012). *Qualitative media analysis*. Los Angeles: SAGE.

Bae, H. S. (1999). Product differentiation in cable programming: The case in the cable national all-news networks. *Journal of Media Economics, 12*(4), 265–277.

Barnard, S. R. (2016). Spectacles of self(ie) empowerment? Networked individualism and the logic of the (post)feminist selfie. In L. Robinson, J. Schulz, S. R. Cotten, et al. (Eds.), *Communication and information technologies annual, studies in media and communications* (pp. 63–88). Bingley: Emerald Group. Retrieved November 21, 2017, from http://www.emeraldinsight.com/doi/full/10.1108/S2050-206020160000011014.

Bennett, D. (2016). Sourcing the BBC's live online coverage of terror attacks. *Digital Journalism, 4*(7), 861–874.

Benson, R., & Neveu, E. (Eds.). (2005). *Bourdieu and the journalistic field.* Malden, MA: Polity.

Boynton, G. R., & Richardson, G. W. (2015). Agenda setting in the twenty-first century. *New Media & Society, 18*(9), 1916–1934. https://doi.org/10.1177/1461444815616226.

Brock, A. (2012). From the blackhand side: Twitter as a cultural conversation. *Journal of Broadcasting & Electronic Media, 56*(4), 529–549.

Broersma, M., & Graham, T. (2013). Twitter as a news source. *Journalism Practice, 7*(4), 446–464.

Bruns, A. (2014). Gatekeeping, gatewatching, real-time feedback: New challenges for journalism. *Brazilian Journalism Research, 10*(2 EN), 224–237.

Camaj, L. (2016). Blurring the boundaries between journalism and activism: A transparency agenda-building case study from Bulgaria. *Journalism,* Advanced online publication. https://doi.org/10.1177/1464884916677757.

Carr, J. (2012). No laughing matter: The power of cyberspace to subvert conventional media gatekeepers. *International Journal of Communication, 6,* 2825–2845.

Christin, A. (2014, August 28). When it comes to chasing clicks, journalists say one thing but feel pressure to do another. *Nieman Foundation at Harvard.* Retrieved November 21, 2017, from http://www.niemanlab.org/2014/08/when-it-comes-to-chasing-clicks-journalists-say-one-thing-but-feel-pressure-to-do-another/.

Christopher, T. (2013, March 21). CNN and MSNBC going in different directions on diversity. *Mediaite.* Retrieved November 21, 2017, from http://www.mediaite.com/tv/cnn-and-msnbc-going-in-different-directions-on-diversity/.

Christopher, T. (2014, February 5). Here are all of the black people on CNN, Fox News, and MSNBC. *Mediaite.* Retrieved November 21, 2017, from http://www.mediaite.com/tv/here-are-all-of-the-black-people-on-cnn-fox-news-and-msnbc/#150.

Cohen, B. C. (1963). *The press and foreign policy.* Princeton, NJ: Princeton University Press.

Conway, B. A., Kenski, K., & Wang, D. (2015). The rise of Twitter in the political campaign: Searching for intermedia agenda-setting effects in the presidential primary. *Journal of Computer-Mediated Communication, 20*(4), 363–380.

Couldry, N. (2014). Mediatization and the future of field theory. In K. Lundby (Ed.), *Mediatization of communication* (pp. 227–245). Berlin: Walter de Gruyter GmbH.

Craft, S., Vos, T. P., & David Wolfgang, J. (2016). Reader comments as press criticism: Implications for the journalistic field. *Journalism, 17*(6), 677–693. https://doi.org/10.1177/1464884915579332.

Cushion, S., Kilby, A., Thomas, R., Morani, M., & Sambrook, R. (2018). Newspapers, impartiality and television news. *Journalism Studies, 19*(2), 162–181.

Duggan, M. (2015, August 19). *The demographics of social media users.* Pew Research Center. Retrieved November 22, 2017, from http://www.pewinternet.org/2015/08/19/the-demographics-of-social-media-users/.

Dutton, W. H. (2009). The fifth estate emerging through the network of networks. *Prometheus, 27*(1), 1–15. https://doi.org/10.1080/08109020802657453.

Farhi, P. (2016a, February 28). MSNBC severs ties with Melissa Harris-Perry after host's critical email. *The Washington Post.* Retrieved November 22, 2017, from https://www.washingtonpost.com/lifestyle/style/msnbc-will-cut-ties-with-show-host-who-wrote-critical-email-to-colleagues/2016/02/27/bce30c8e-dd82-11e5-891a-4ed04f4213e8_story.html.

Farhi, P. (2016b, February 29). Is #MSNBCSoWhite? The departure of Melissa Harris-Perry raises the issue. *The Washington Post.* Retrieved November 22, 2017, from https://www.washingtonpost.com/lifestyle/style/is-msnbcsowhite-the-departure-of-melissa-harris-perry-raises-the-issue/2016/02/29/8bc69096-df06-11e5-8d98-4b3d9215ade1_story.html.

Florini, S. (2014). Tweets, tweeps, and signifyin' communication and cultural performance on 'Black Twitter'. *Television & New Media, 15*(3), 223–237.

Florini, S. (2017). This week in blackness, the George Zimmerman acquittal, and the production of a networked collective identity. *New Media & Society, 19*(3), 439–454. https://doi.org/10.1177/1461444815606779.

Gitlin, T. (1980). *The whole world is watching: Mass media in the making and unmaking of the new left.* Berkeley, CA: University of California Press.

Groshek, J., & Groshek, M. C. (2013). Agenda trending: Reciprocity and the predictive capacity of social networking sites in intermedia agenda setting across topics over time. *Media and Communication, 1*(1), 15–27.

Guo, L., & McCombs, M. E. (2016). *The power of information networks: New directions for agenda setting.* New York: Routledge.

Hellmueller, L. (2014). *The Washington, DC media corps in the 21st century: The source-correspondent relationship.* New York, NY: Palgrave Macmillan.

Jacobson, S. (2013). Does audience participation on facebook influence the news agenda? A case study of the Rachel Maddow show. *Journal of Broadcasting & Electronic Media, 57*(3), 338–355. https://doi.org/10.1080/08838151.2013.816706.

Kellner, D. (2009). Media spectacle and media events: Some critical reflections. In N. Couldry, A. Hepp, & F. Krotz (Eds.), *Media events in a global age* (pp. 76–91). New York: Routledge.

Kutz-Flamenbaum, R. V., Staggenborg, S., & Duncan, B. J. (2012). Media framing of the Pittsburgh G-20 protests. In P. G. Coy (Ed.), *Media, movements, and political change (Research in social movements, conflicts and change)* (Vol. 33, pp. 109–135). Bingley: Emerald Group Publishing Limited. Retrieved November 22, 2017, from http://www.emeraldinsight.com/doi/full/10.1108/S0163-786X%282012%290000033008.

Larsson, A. O. (2013). Tweeting the viewer—Use of Twitter in a talk show context. *Journal of Broadcasting & Electronic Media, 57*(2), 135–152.

Lee, A. M., Lewis, S. C., & Powers, M. (2014). Audience clicks and news placement: A study of time-lagged influence in online journalism. *Communication Research, 41*(4), 505–530.

Lefky, T., Brewer, P. R., & Habegger, M. (2015). Tweets on television news: The nature and effects of campaign coverage of Twitter. *Electronic News, 9*(4), 257–269.

Marwick, A. E., & boyd, d. (2011). I tweet honestly, I tweet passionately: Twitter users, context collapse, and the imagined audience. *New Media & Society, 13*(1), 114–133. https://doi.org/10.1177/1461444810365313.

Maza, C. (2016, March 8). The whiteness of the media is a slow-motion train wreck. *Media Matters for America*. Retrieved November 22, 2017, from http://mediamatters.org/shows-and-publications/melissa-harris-perry.

Melissa Harris-Perry exit puts focus on MSNBC's diversity record. (2016, March 3). *Chicago Tribune*. Retrieved November 21, 2017, from http://www.chicagotribune.com/entertainment/tv/ct-melissa-harris-perry-msnbc-diversity-minorities-20160304-story.html.

Meraz, S. (2011). Using time series analysis to measure intermedia agenda-setting influence in traditional media and political blog networks. *Journalism & Mass Communication Quarterly, 88*(1), 176–194.

Meraz, S. (2015). Quantifying partisan selective exposure through network text analysis of elite political blog networks during the U.S. 2012 presidential election. *Journal of Information Technology & Politics, 12*(1), 37–53.

Parmelee, J. H. (2014). The agenda-building function of political tweets. *New Media & Society, 16*(3), 434–450.

Petre, C. (2015, May 7). The traffic factories: Metrics at Chartbeat, Gawker Media, and The New York Times. *Columbia Journalism Review*. Retrieved November 22, 2017, from https://www.cjr.org/tow_center_reports/the_traffic_factories_metrics_at_chartbeat_gawker_media_and_the_new_york_times.php.

Qin, J. (2015). Hero on Twitter, traitor on news: How social media and legacy news frame Snowden. *The International Journal of Press/Politics, 20*(2), 166–184.

Raeymaeckers, K., Deprez, A., De Vuyst, S., & De Dobbelaer, R. (2015). The journalist as a jack of all trades: Safeguarding the gates in a digitized news ecology. In T. Vos & F. Heinderyckx (Eds.), *Gatekeeping in transition* (pp. 104–119). New York: Routledge.

Rosen, J. (2006, June 27). The people formerly known as the audience. *PressThink*. Retrieved November 22, 2017, from http://archive.pressthink.org/2006/06/27/ppl_frmr.html.

Rosen, J. (2009, April 12). He said, she said journalism: Lame formula in the land of the active user. *PressThink*. Retrieved November 22, 2017, from http://archive.pressthink.org/2009/04/12/hesaid:shesaid.html.

Russell, F. M., Hendricks, M. A., Choi, H., & Stephens, E. C. (2015). Who sets the news agenda on Twitter? *Digital Journalism, 3*(6), 925–943.

Stearns, J. (2015a, January 20). Building journalism with community, not for it: Transactional versus transformational, close to the ground. *Medium*. Retrieved November 22, 2017, from https://medium.com/the-local-news-lab/building-journalism-with-community-not-for-it-5c319992aebf#.h2tolizi0.

Stearns, J. (2015b, October 8). In curiosity we trust: A new journalism collaboration is putting people's questions first, Hearken believes. *Medium*. Retrieved November 22, 2017, from https://medium.com/the-local-news-lab/in-curiosity-we-trust-journalism-collaboration-puts-people-s-questions-first-1fb5a8e0d9fe#.1dkj869nn.

Sharma, S. (2013). Black Twitter? Racial hashtags, networks and contagion. *New Formations, 78*, 46–64.

Shoemaker, P. J., & Vos, T. (2009). *Gatekeeping theory*. New York: Routledge.

Smith, A. (2014, January 6). *African Americans and technology use*. Pew Research Center. Retrieved November 22, 2017, from http://www.pewinternet.org/2014/01/06/african-americans-and-technology-use/.

Smith, J. (2016, February 26). Melissa Harris-Perry's email to her #nerdland staff. *Medium*. Retrieved November 22, 2017, from https://medium.com/@JamilSmith/melissa-harris-perry-s-email-to-her-nerdland-staff-11292bdc27cb.

Sobieraj, S. (2011). *Soundbitten: The perils of media-centered political activism*. New York: NYU Press.

Tufekci, Z. (2017). *Twitter and tear gas: The power and fragility of networked protest*. New Haven, CT: Yale University Press.

Vos, T., & Heinderyckx, F. (2015). *Gatekeeping in transition*. New York: Routledge.

Weller, K., Dröge, E., & Puschmann, C. (2011). Citation analysis in Twitter: Approaches for defining and measuring information flows within tweets during scientific conferences. In M. Rowe, M. Stankovic, A. S. Dadzie, & M. Hardey (Eds.), *Making sense of microposts (#MSM2011)* (pp. 1–12). Workshop at the Extended Semantic Web Conference (ESWC 2011). Heraklion, Greece: CEUR Workshop Proceedings Vol. 718. Retrieved November 28, 2017, from http://ceur-ws.org/Vol-718/paper_04.pdf.

Wurff, R. v. d., & Schönbach, K. (2014). Audience expectations of media accountability in the Netherlands. *Journalism Studies, 15*(2), 121–137. https://doi.org/10.1080/1461670X.2013.801679.

Zeldes, G. A., & Fico, F. (2005). Race and gender: An analysis of sources and reporters in the networks' coverage of the 2000 presidential campaign. *Mass Communication and Society, 8*(4), 373–385.

The Spectacle of #TrumpsAmerica: Political Journalism, Networked Publics, and the Battle for Symbolic Power

Shortly after midnight on May 31, 2017, President Donald Trump posted a 43-character tweet that read: "Despite the constant negative press covfefe" [sic]. Within nine hours, the tweet was deleted, but it sparked a fiery and ironic debate on Twitter about whether or not "covfefe" was a word, what it was supposed to mean, and what meaning might be gleaned from the fact that it was posted (and deleted) without explanation (Flegenheimer 2017; Politwoops 2017). Of course, for most who participated, this was more an act of humor or bewilderment than a serious debate. Nevertheless, it illustrates the seriousness with which much of the public regards Trump's Twitter account and the power he exerts through the platform.

Indeed, the following day #covfefe became Twitter's top trending hashtag worldwide (Russell 2017). The hashtag was tailor-made for virality in a mediatized news system. Capitalizing on the trend, Mike Quigley, a congressional representative and member of the opposing party, even created a bill named using COVFEFE as an acronym.[1] Given Trump's infamous use of his personal Twitter account to make official statements as the President of the United States, as well as the platform's prominence as a public forum, the COVFEFE act sought to strengthen the precedent for archiving social media posts by sitting presidents and to limit their ability to "block" users on these platforms (Andrews 2017; Wamsley 2017). But in the age of Twitter, where the news cycle churns rapidly and 500 million 140-character messages are published every day, "covfefe" was a mere blip

© The Author(s) 2018
S. R. Barnard, *Citizens at the Gates*,
https://doi.org/10.1007/978-3-319-90446-7_8

on the radar. After peaking at nearly 2000 stories in each of the two days following the gaffe, news mentions declined drastically and Quigley's legislation, which rarely made headlines, faded away without passing.

While the incident makes for good fodder, this chapter is not about political gaffes, nor about political actors' attempts to take advantage of them to score political points. Rather, the example here offers a vivid illustration of the way messages can spread in the age of Twitter. Beyond the allure of media spectacle, events like #covfefe provide a clear illustration of the manner in which the political and journalistic fields are becoming further intertwined in an age of mediatization (Esser and Strömbäck 2014). While it has long been the case that both fields depend on one another for access and legitimation (Bourdieu 2005), the ongoing revolution in communication cultures and technologies has resulted in significant shifts in the structure and practice of politics (Chadwick 2013; Freelon and Karpf 2015; Kreiss 2014) and journalism (Russell 2016; Vos and Heinderyckx 2015). Given the normalization of Twitter in both journalism and politics, Trump's use of the platform provides a unique opportunity to examine these changing dynamics.

Previous chapters have investigated how practice and power converge at the margins of the journalistic field. Attention now turns to journalism's intersection with the more traditional political field in order to observe the products and practices of journalists and journo-activists in that space, and to compare influence across groups. Thus, this chapter asks: what happens to Twitter's journalistic field in the age of Trump? And what role are citizens playing in this process? After considering Trump's use of Twitter as a form of gatecrashing, spectacle, and symbolic power, the realities of a mediatized field are examined. Next, the form and content of tweets by journalists reporting on @realDonaldTrump are analyzed, which are then compared with those posted by activists. This includes a brief examination of trends in online news coverage. Finally, each group's potential for influence is compared before drawing some conclusions about the hybridizing of journalism and politics in a time of mediatization.

Data for this chapter were drawn from four primary sources. First, tweets from a cohort of 386 political journalists from November 8 to 17, 2016, and May 29 to June 4, 2017, which broadly represent the way reporters tweeted events in the days following the election and during a somewhat typical week in Washington four months into Trump's term in office. Second, tweets including the hashtag #TrumpsAmerica were collected during two time frames: 10 days following the election (November

8–17, 2016) and one week during Trump's presidency (May 29–June 4, 2017). This data represents the role played by networked publics in calls for accountability in politics and journalism. Third, tweets by @realDonaldTrump were collected from June 1, 2016 to June 30, 2017, which was a year spanning the final months of his campaign to his first months in office. Portions of these tweets were briefly assessed for themes, frames, and influence in comparison to other Twitter users. Fourth, two sets of online news stories, including those that mention "covfefe" (May 29 to June 4, 2017) and "@realDonaldTrump" (November 3–17, 2016 and May 29 to June 30, 2017) provide further context for the way Trump's use of Twitter was covered in online news. When considered in concert, the data collected for this chapter offer a diverse array of perspectives that together provide a unique view of the role Twitter and online media play in the battle for symbolic power in the age of Trump.

TRUMP, TWITTER, AND THE NEWS: SYMBOLIC POWER AND MEDIA(TIZED) SPECTACLE

Over 35 years ago, Michael Schudson (1982) published an essay about the role technology played in journalists' coverage of the presidency. At the time, the focus was on the structure and culture of American television and the emergent logics that followed its commercial success (cf. Postman 1985). In light of recent events, the modern equivalent of such an inquiry may well focus on the role Twitter plays in mediating the presidency, due to its social and political (if not commercial) success. Like Schudson, I contend that much of what is seen in modern journalism is less an outcome determined by technological innovation than it is a contingent response to the norms at the heart of the field's foundation. Schudson argued that many of television's emergent norms for covering the presidency had actually long been normalized in other areas of the journalistic field; it just took them a while to take hold in the television environment. Much the same could be said for today's social media environment.

If there was any lingering doubt that contemporary politics and journalism have been mediatized, then the 2016 election cycle should have settled it. The election of Donald Trump might be described as the first "Twitter Presidency." Although presidents before him famously used social media—@BarackObama is still the fourth most-followed account on Twitter—Trump's use of the platform has been groundbreaking.

Trump is a power player on Twitter, between the 42 million followers of his original @realDonaldTrump account and another 21 million followers of the official @POTUS account, he has a growing follower base of over 63 million users. His Twitter audience is a wide mix of supporters, critics, journalists, and political activists from all sides. His audience has also grown significantly over time, more than doubling since he took office. As many pundits have expressed, Trump's use of Twitter demonstrates an unparalleled ability to shape public discourse. His power and position mean that what he says gets covered, even though it is said outside the channels of traditional media and often with a profound contempt for it. Consequently, countless political and economic issues are shaped by the statements Trump makes through Twitter, including (inter)national relations and even the stock value of publicly traded companies (Goldmark 2017).

According to George Lakoff (2017), Trump's tweets accomplish one of four rhetorical objectives: they preemptively frame ideas, divert attention from significant issues, deflect blame by attacking the messenger, or test public reactions to a policy idea. However, as will be argued in this chapter, their overarching function seems to be the creation of media spectacle. While some early studies found Trump's tweets had a nominal effect on shaping the agendas of national newspapers (Conway-Silva et al. 2017), other studies have concluded that "Trump's efforts to court media attention, through staged events, unscheduled interactions, *and* social media activity, were largely successful" (Wells et al. 2016, p. 675; cf. Benkler et al. 2017). A Pew Research Center study of America's top news outlets found that nearly half of the stories analyzed about Trump and his administration were produced "in response to something the president or his staff said or did" and that "roughly one-in-six stories (16%) contained a direct tweet from President Trump" (Mitchell et al. 2017, para. 17). Furthermore, a *New York Times* report concluded that Trump received almost $2 billion worth of free media coverage across all platforms during the 2016 presidential primary race, which was nearly six times that of his closest rival (Confessore and Yourish 2016). While the report did not address the cause of this disparity in "earned media," when seen in light of the campaign's lean spending on advertising during the primaries, it is an indication that Trump's strategy for producing media spectacle—on all platforms, at all times—was largely successful. Thus, although scholarly analyses have yet to determine how successful politicians' social media strategies are in setting the agenda for any given issue, media outlet, or demographic, the sheer volume of media coverage about Trump's tweets provides a clear indication of their success in garnering news attention.

Only weeks into the Trump presidency, The *Washington Post*'s David Fahrenthold spoke about journalists' obsession with Trump's tweets, "The people who are on Twitter are basically political journalists and ten other people. So [Trump] uses Twitter as a way of reaching us, and then we amplify it by getting the message out" (Nilagia 2017, para. 8). Despite the apparent sarcasm about who uses Twitter (and who doesn't), there was a clear acknowledgement of the platform's salience among political journalists (cf. Revers 2017). Thus, according to Fahrenthold, Trump's use of Twitter appears driven, in part, by a desire to *use* the media without having to take questions from them. This is perhaps the primary function of media spectacle, whether by Trump or other influential actors, on social media and beyond.

As discussed in the previous chapter, media spectacle occurs when sensationalism is used to generate attention (Kellner 2009). Trump, both the person and the brand, is the ultimate media spectacle. As a celebrity, marketer, reality TV star, and (unorthodox) politician, his modus operandi is to *attract attention*. According to Kellner (2016, pp. 4–5; cf. Karpf 2016):

> Trump is empowered and enabled to run for the presidency in part because media spectacle has become a major force in US politics, helping to determine elections, government, and, more broadly, the ethos and nature of our culture and political sphere, and Trump is a successful creator and manipulator of the spectacle.

Like his other displays aimed to garner publicity, each of Trump's tweets can be seen as a spectacular pseudo-event: what he says is less important than the fact that he is there *saying it*. But what makes Trump's tweets so newsworthy, and what consequences come from journalists' decisions to report on them? By taking to social media, Trump circumvents traditional gatekeepers to communicate directly with his followers, many of whom are media professionals themselves. In this sense, Trump uses Twitter to engage in his own form of gatecrashing, while at the same time, making an indirect pitch to gatekeepers to cover what he said.

On the one hand, Trump's tweets represent the kind of communiqué gatekeepers are looking for: official statements, which, in his case, are often shocking and disruptive to the status quo. On the other hand, the unparalleled media attention given to Trump demonstrates a kind of fetishism of his Twitter posts, imbuing them with unparalleled symbolic power and helping him amass even more media meta-capital. This dynamic is hardly surprising in the mediatized era, given how easily gatewatchers and gatecrashers amplify Trump's strategic messages even by criticizing them. The use of one platform (Twitter) to communicate directly with members of the networked public also makes it possible for millions of others to follow along. Given journalists' use of Twitter as an "ambient news system" (Chadwick 2013; Hermida 2010), they are frequently *there* to bear witness and spread the word, for better or worse.

As Andrew Chadwick (2013) has argued, the ongoing media revolution has resulted in the formation of a "hybrid media system" that plays an important role in powerful actors' amassing and wielding symbolic power. As was introduced in Chap. 3, this same media environment also makes it possible for social actors to accrue what Nick Couldry (2014, pp. 59–60) called "media meta-capital," which emerges as a super-ordinate form of capital due to its ability to "exercise power over other forms of capital." One's ability to build and wield such power depends, in large part, on their position within the fields of journalism and politics. Overall, the hybrid news environment provides countless opportunities for actors in political and journalistic fields. For example, mediatization affords politicians with a growing array of communication channels. They communicate directly to their social media audiences (gatecrashing), as well as indirectly through sharing by other social media users (gatewatchers) and more traditional journalists (gatekeepers). Though this is the case for most politicians in the twenty-first century, the relationship between Trump and professional journalists is uniquely interesting because his tweets function as both sources and objects of news. When these facts are combined with his public disdain for the media, Trump can also be seen as a major threat to traditional gatekeepers.

With this context in mind, this chapter examined three sets of actors positioned at various locations in the hybrid media system: Trump atop the political and journalistic fields, political journalists at the center of both fields, and journo-activists on the margins of both fields. Given the field dynamics outlined above, the guiding question for the study was: how and to what extent did gatekeepers, gatewatchers, and gatecrashers participate in and respond to the spectacle surrounding the election of Donald Trump? Accordingly, the study explored political journalists' coverage of Trump's use of Twitter, the ways journo-activists used the hashtag

#TrumpsAmerica to respond to the political climate following the election, and finally, the symbolic power of all parties.

Reporting on @realDonaldTrump

The cohort of 386 political journalists were highly engaged on Twitter during the days surrounding the election, peaking at over 14,000 tweets on November 8, 2016. On average, this amounted to 35 tweets per reporter on Election Day, compared to a daily average of roughly 13 tweets overall. While the volume of users' tweets had significant variance, striking patterns were found in their content and tone. Expectedly, political journalists' tweets fell within the typology outlined in Chap. 4: information collection, news dissemination, sourcing, public engagement, brief note-taking, field meta-discourse, other professional (inter)actions, and personal (inter)actions. However, most tweets during this time frame focused on news dissemination, meta-discourse, and other professional (inter)actions.

It is clear that the practices displayed on Twitter differ (often significantly) from those on display in the content of more traditional news products (i.e., online news articles). Indeed, journalists are known to share subtle forms of interpretation on Twitter (Molyneux 2015), and while much of this subjective commentary can be found in the text of their tweets, it is also on display in the supplementary content they share (Lasorsa et al. 2012). For example, although the majority of posts (60%) were original in nature, including tweet-sized bits of insight and news as they occurred in real time, many also used Twitter's retweet and link functions to add commentary or spread additional information.

Linking is common on social media, especially among journalists, largely because it provides an opportunity to drive traffic and share information beyond what is possible in 280 characters. Links are valued in the mediatized journalistic field because they can provide added transparency about the writer's perspective and on what basis they make their claims (De Maeyer and Holton 2016). Of course, journalists' networked habitus share a common logic, which alongside their employers' social media policies, help guide what gets shared and in what context.

Journalists have been found to share (i.e., link and retweet) content from their own news sites with greater frequency than they link to other publishers (Russell et al. 2015). This trend appears to hold true in the data analyzed for this chapter. However, this is difficult to track because

Twitter's retweet function is commonly displayed in metadata as links to a page on Twitter.com. Excluding the large share of (re)tweets with links to Twitter's own website, the remaining majority of links directed users to top news sites such as *New York Times*, *Washington Post*, *Politico*, CNN, Associated Press, *Wall Street Journal*, Buzzfeed, *The Hill*, Bloomberg, and *Huffington Post* (see Table 8.1). Whereas a significant portion of journalists' tweets linking to news sites were posted by several users affiliated with that institution, less prominent digital news sites were linked to primarily by a single but highly vocal user (Political Wire, Axios).

While political reporters were more likely to share content published by their own employer, whether directly from its website or indirectly by retweeting a colleague from the same organization, those users who were more engaged in their professional community on Twitter were also likely to share content from other organizations. Research has shown that journalists working for traditional and digital news organizations are most likely to retweet content from similar organizations, while those working for hybrid news organizations (i.e., those publishing in both print and

Table 8.1 Number of top domain links by political journalists on Twitter[2]

Domain	Count	Percent
twitter.com	18,739	37.27%
nytimes.com	4141	8.23%
washingtonpost.com	3351	6.66%
politico.com	2012	4.00%
cnn.com	1423	2.83%
apnews.com	981	1.95%
wsj.com	832	1.65%
buzzfeed.com	811	1.61%
thehill.com	569	1.13%
bloomberg.com	551	1.09%
huffingtonpost.com	501	0.99%
politicalwire.com	475	0.94%
youtube.com	465	0.92%
snappytv.com	431	0.85%
abcnews.go.com	409	0.81%
time.com	399	0.79%
axios.com	383	0.76%
theatlantic.com	383	0.76%
cbsnews.com	360	0.71%
usatoday.com	331	0.65%

digital formats) are more likely to share content from other sectors of the journalistic field (Barthel et al. 2015). While some might conclude that this suggests a loosening of professional norms and organizational policies about the spreading of content from competing publishers, others might interpret the sharing of information on Twitter across organizations as evidence of a cohesive professional community (i.e., subfield). Given the fast-paced, high-volume Twitter strategy employed by prominent political journalists on Twitter, users who retweet other reporters stand to benefit by curating relevant information for their follower base, which also makes their counterparts more likely to reciprocate (Pabmann et al. 2014).

However, as the popular reporter's disclaimer reads, "retweets are not endorsements." Some iteration of this disclaimer is commonly found in the Twitter bios of countless journalists (Warzel 2014), including 27 of the political reporters examined in this chapter. On the one hand, such an explicit disclaimer may seem unnecessary, given the doxic status of objectivity in the American journalistic field. On the other hand, such proclamations may be increasingly expected of political reporters, given that trust in journalism is at an all-time low (Swift 2016). Indeed, after the 2016 election, when political polarization is on the rise and cries of "fake news" are frequently hurled at those with whom one may disagree, journalists' dissemination of information as purely informational is arguably more important than ever. These disclaimers are especially pertinent, given how the structure and culture of Twitter encourages such simple forms of sharing like retweeting. Nevertheless, journalists offered a surprising amount of commentary on Twitter, especially about statements made by Trump and his team.

The top political journalists examined in this chapter rarely treated Trump's tweets as objects of news. Similarly, journalists rarely retweeted @realDonaldTrump, although when they did, it was often to add commentary, context, or correct the record. Many of these statements can be read as serving multiple audiences. For the public, they were attempts to correct the record. For fellow reporters, they were a reminder about the significance of context and the adversarial press. For example, one prominent political reporter from an influential newspaper tweeted, "It doesn't matter who Trump's flack is (see Sean [Spicer]). WH statements ... are useless. His Tweets should be treated as official policy." Another prominent reporter from the same organization was among the hundreds who retweeted the post, adding, "And calling them 'tweets' minimizes them. They're statements from the president made on Twitter." The latter post was shared over 6000 times, including by six other reporters in the data set.

While less reflexive about how they should be treated by members of the media, other reporters directed attention to Trump's tweets to correct the record. These retweets often began with corrective statements, such as "This is ridiculously out of context;" "This is objectively not [what Trump says it is];" "This shows how Trump simply does not understand governing." These tweets were followed by evidence and context to illustrate the reporter's point. Others opted to hold Trump accountable for statements on Twitter without amplifying them, instead linking to other news organizations' stories for support. One prominent reporter provided this example, "Lest we forget: @potus not a normal president fudging/shading the truth. He says many things that are simply made up https://t.co/EYeUBZfn1F." Thus, if Trump's tweets were primarily media spectacle aimed to garner attention, some reporters appear to have taken the bait. Nevertheless, it is unclear whether the aphorism "all press is good press," applies here, since the vast majority of reporters' tweets that amplified Trump's message appeared to do so primarily to shine a critical light on the statements he made.

Responding to "Covfefe": An Analysis of Journalistic Meta-Discourse

As Chap. 4 demonstrated, journalistic meta-discourse is common across the journalistic field, on Twitter and off. A marker of the profession's "interpretive community" (Carlson 2015), journalistic meta-discourse provides reporters with an opportunity to reflect on the values and practices of gatekeeping. This could be seen as the profession's own version of gatewatching, where reporters offer specific (and often subtle) critiques of journalistic practice. For example, amid the fervor of humor, speculation, and reporting on a trivial event, one reporter tweeted, "Of all the stupid distractions #thistown has obsessed over so far this year, 'covfefe' takes the cake."

As this tweet suggests, political reporters covered the #covfefe "kerfuffle" extensively in the days following the event, using a mixture of humor and straight reporting. Initially, their tweets were mostly driven by humor, which was presumably a reaction to the spectacle that followed the gaffe. Later, many reported on then-Press Secretary Sean Spicer's announcement that "The president and a small group of people know exactly what he meant." The cryptic statement added to the intrigue of the event and further ramped up the spectacle. Once the dust began to settle, many political reporters took the opportunity to inject some humor into the discussion by making jokes about coffee, Russia, and even the passing internet sensation Ken Bone, who rose to pop culture fame after appearing in one of the presidential debates.

Though some might interpret reporters' brief obsession with "covfefe" as a waste of time and energy, others may see at as an opportunity for some light-hearted humor—a rare occurrence for those covering national politics. Professional reporters sharing a beat often form fairly tight-knit communities, and this is particularly true (and visible) on Twitter. Thus, like gathering around a water cooler, it is common to see reporters use Twitter for personal conversations, journalistic meta-discourse and other informalities, as discussed in Chap. 4.

Nevertheless, there is reason to criticize the coverage of the #covfefe kerfuffle. While it is clear that tweets from the executive branch matter in the age of mediatization, the manner in which the #covfefe tweets were covered was undoubtedly spectacular. Besides the basic facts around Trump's initial tweet and deletion, Spicer's (non)response during a press briefing, and the public spectacle that followed, not much about this story needed reporting. Like Hillary Clinton's quip about covfefe being "a hidden message to the Russians," which was shared by 14 political journalists, the story was pure spectacle. The more attention journalists (and the public) paid it, the less attention they were giving to the major events of the week, including Trump's plan to withdraw from the 2015 Paris climate agreement and the scandal about the administration's ties to Russian efforts to influence the election. Again, this realization should raise concerns about the extent to which newsworkers allow the actions of political elites to guide the attention of their reporting, and by consequence, public consciousness.

Examining Digital News on "covfefe" and @realDonaldTrump

While many of the nation's leading political journalists did not tweet about Trump's use of Twitter as extensively as might be expected during this period, there were thousands of news stories dedicated to the topic.[3] Indeed, despite disagreements about fact or policy, journalists have admitted to loving Trump's tweets (Bump 2017). This kind of joyous attitude is on display in an Associated Press story, which showed up 275 separate times[4] in the news stories examined for this chapter:

Covfefe (cuv-fey-fey) noun: A sure sign that President Donald Trump has regained control of his Twitter account. For more than a week, the tweets from @realDonaldTrump were, well, boring. Throughout his first big foreign trip last week, Trump's tweets had the vibe of a garden-variety politician: statements of solidarity with world leaders, retweets of his wife's visits with students and sick children, video clips from arrival statements and formal ceremonies, photos of official dinners. Yawn. Well, Twitterverse, he's back. Starting with a wee-hours tweet that contained the mystifying non-word "covfefe," Trump on Wednesday unleashed a string of tweets that showed the president was holding nothing back, on matters both trivial and consequential. (Benac 2017)

Although this excerpt is hardly representative of the news stories about Trump's use of Twitter, even the "covfefe" gaffe, it represents one dominant theme in coverage of the incident: playfulness. Stories about #covfefe, like journalists' tweets, were far more playful than the bulk of traditional news, and mixed humor with straight reporting. Additionally, many reporters saw the subject as an opportunity to dig deeper into other aspects relating to Trump's use of Twitter. Spanning far beyond the initial incident, such stories covered a variety of related issues, including the legal battles over Trump's blocking of Twitter users, his use of the platform to insult judges, journalists, and other public figures, the typo-riddled tweets of his press secretaries, and even the possibility of Twitter allowing users to edit tweets after they are posted.

Stories about the #covfefe kerfuffle may be remarkable, but they are hardly representative of the way news stories covered Trump's more typical use of Twitter. Of the 22,025 news stories collected that mention "@realDonaldTrump," most contributed in some way to the ongoing media spectacle, whether about the drama of the election, the investigation into Trump campaign officials' alleged ties to Russia, or his public spat with MSNBC hosts Mika Brzezinski and Joe Scarborough. Rather than relying on written quotes or detailed descriptions, these news stories, like the #covfefe stories, regularly embedded tweets from @realDonaldTrump in the body, offset from the text. This tendency is indicative of the manner in which news stories treated Trump's tweets—as newsworthy but tangential comments coming from the president, rather than as statements around which stories should be framed—and is common among news outlets (Moon and Hadley 2014). This practice of embedding, which offers a full textual display of the tweet author's username, also explains why these stories were included in the search results for stories mentioning "@real-DonaldTrump." Consequently, this method of data collection broadened the frame of news to include the critical responses (often in the form of retweets) shared by networked activists. This was a notable contrast from the post-election tweets by political journalists, which mainly raised attention to the comments of actors already deemed influential in the journalistic field.

By June 2017, news stories about @realDonaldTrump had broadened to the variety of issues surrounding presidential politics in the age of Twitter. While reporters continued the practice of embedding Trump's tweets in news stories, they were rarely accompanied by outside (activist) voices. In other words, relatively few stories commented directly on Trump's use of Twitter, and instead, drew on statements he made on the platform to inform stories about a variety of topics in the news at the time. Among the topics were Trump's proposed travel ban, his firing of former FBI Director James Comey, his decision to withdraw from the Paris Climate Agreement, and the terrorist attacks in London. Stories that reflected more directly on Trump's use of Twitter were often critical in nature, mixing objective reporting with affective responses. Some of the headlines included:

- How to Understand Donald Trump's #AmazonWashingtonPost Tweet in 3 Easy Steps
- 'Hide of a rhinoceros' helps NBC's Katy Tur withstand Donald Trump's taunts
- It's Time to Demand Donald Trump's Resignation: Look at the man's tweets—he cannot continue to serve as president
- Trump's long history of calling women 'crazy,' attacking their appearance
- Is chronic sleep deprivation impairing President Trump's brain, performance?

Like the bulk of the news items collected for this chapter, many of the stories in this time frame were published by small newspapers, digital news sites, and local broadcast affiliates. However, some of the most striking headlines, like those listed above, were published by relatively influential outlets, including Yahoo!, *The Washington Post, Rolling Stone*, ABC News, and *USA Today*. The latter two stories were published by ABC News and 20 affiliates, and 81 *USA Today* affiliates, respectively. This finding, although tangential to the analysis at hand, is an indication of the homogenization of media content brought on by a concentrated legacy media industry.

Overall, if Kellner's (2016, p. 3) assertion that regardless of substance, media spectacles produce "popular stories which capture the attention of the media and the public" is accepted, then news coverage of the covfefe kerfuffle largely fits the bill. Although the genre of media spectacle is hardly a new phenomenon, the manner in which it is taken up by journalists, let alone members of the public, may be changing in form and scale. This raises important questions about the extent to which journalistic norms regarding newsworthiness and the gatekeeping process may shift as a result of mediatization. Nevertheless, the stories addressing @realDonaldTrump's use of Twitter more broadly appeared more substantive, though they still contributed (albeit less directly) to the spectacle created by Trump's use of the platform. While this should not be surprising, given the spectacular nature of the news events themselves, it is an interesting contrast to the tweets by political reporters, which were often more nuanced and appeared to devote less attention to Trump's tweets. The contributions of citizens situated at the margins of the political and journalistic fields are explored in the next section in order to complete the comparison.

#TrumpsAmerica: Can Networked Publics Strike Back?

One of the defining characteristics of the age of mediatization is the manner in which media power is increasingly distributed beyond the traditional boundaries of the journalistic field (Kunelius and Reunanen 2016). Similarly, while originated by traditional media organizations and politicians, the means of producing and spreading media spectacle is more broadly distributed than ever (Mihailidis and Viotty 2017). Social media platforms such as Twitter provide networked publics with the ability to create and disseminate spectacular content in a manner that models traditional influence patterns, whether they are driven by a desire for profit or political influence. Thus, while they lack the power and position of more traditional gatekeepers, gatewatchers and gatecrashers have the ability to build and leverage audience influence to their own desired ends.

One site of the contestation of media power can be found in the hashtag discourse from #TrumpsAmerica. Indeed, while Trump successfully fueled the media spectacle, often using Twitter to influence the gatekeeping process (Carlson 2015), citizens—both supporters and critics—followed suit. While the #TrumpsAmerica hashtag emerged after the election to document acts of hate committed against members of marginalized groups, it quickly became a discursive battleground where activists, including both critics and supporters of Trump, engaged in their own brand of spectacle. Perhaps not surprisingly, a majority of the most viewed and shared #TrumpsAmerica tweets were posted by members of the professional journalistic field, although posts by citizen journo-activists were most likely to gain traction for informative, partisan, or pithy remarks. These tweets fell within affective reactions, gatecrashing or gatewatching categories.

Affective Reaction (Political Opining)

A majority of the 36,000+ #TrumpsAmerica tweets collected for this chapter can be read as communicating some form of affective reaction, whether about the results of the election (November 2016) or actions of the president (May/June 2017). Given the diversity of contributors to the hashtag, great variance in the tone and tenor of posts was found, even among those affectively framed. Some reacted positively to the results of the election:

- #TrumpsAmerica ⬛ I'm so glad he won. No more obummer. No more of the lies and deception. A new era is coming. The Awakening.
- Never been more proud to be a deplorable #draintheswamp #TrumpsAmerica #LockHerUp
- finally an end to #Obama's #ProgressiveAmerica, #LiberalAmerica & a new beginning to #TrumpsAmerica; #Capitalism indeed the #NewWorldOrder
- The madman hath overcome endless obstruction and doubt; I'm ready for #TrumpsAmerica and I'm ready to #MakeAmericaGreatAgain!

However, the bulk of early #TrumpsAmerica tweets mixed anger with disappointment or disbelief. For example, some users tweeted, "My heart is so broken. Goodbye clean power plan, goodbye funding for PP, goodbye to trans rights. #TrumpsAmerica" and "#TrumpsAmerica Welcome back, Jim Crow." Beyond mourning the assumed policy changes, many also pointed attention to the emotional labor required of Americans following the election of a candidate who ran on a platform of exclusion, "Today millions of minority Americans got ready for work. Then before they walked out the door, they braced themselves. #TrumpsAmerica." And while some of these tweets were reactions to the political climate in general, many others were a direct result of the reports shared on Twitter.

Gatecrashing (Documenting Hate and Violence)

Sticking with the initial spirit of the #TrumpsAmerica hashtag, numerous contributors shared information, rumors, and commentary about acts of hate and violence that they witnessed or heard about in their communities. Tweets that bear witness were so common that it is not feasible to include or categorize all variants. However, some relatively typical examples illustrate the kind of second-hand accounts being shared: "Someone followed my dad home today to tell him to 'go back to Africa' #TrumpsAmerica #NotMyPresident," "Countless instances, easily, 50+, of women's hijabs being ripped off tweeted on twitter from #Trump supporters since Tuesday #TrumpsAmerica," and "Students at many colleges reporting ethnic or racial harassment since Election Day https://t.co/BdP6zDguS7." The latter posts' inclusion of a linked article summarizing incidents was rare, given how little media attention was paid to the issue.[5] Beyond individual efforts to collect and disseminate information, some users worked to gather evidence of hate-driven acts by posting anonymous surveys and personalized messages with directions, such as "Anytime you hear of anything, tweet the place and if possible a link. Use the hashtag #TrumpsAmerica."

While much less vocal on the hashtag, some Trump supporters sought to debate or dismiss the allegations of hate and violence shared by others. For example, one user tweeted, "Guess What? Liberal Morons can post All the Lies they want about Violence in #TrumpsAmerica Truth Is They R Only Ones Committing Violence!" While there were few confirmed reports of violence targeting Trump supporters following the election, the Southern Poverty Law Center (SPLC) partnered with the nonprofit investigative journalism organization ProPublica to document "bias incidents" following the election. The group identified 1372 such incidents in the three months following the election ("Post-election bias" 2017).

By late May 2017, the partisan rhetoric about journalism and "fake news" had reached new heights, stoked in large part by Trump himself. Accordingly, one user posted a link to a story about broken windows at a Kentucky newspaper office and the "rising anti-press climate" along with the message, "Will Trump tweet about this part of #TrumpsAmerica? He has encouraged acts like this." While there did not appear to be any calls for violence using #TrumpsAmerica, some did point out how Twitter was being used to spread hateful and violent ideologies, "Twitter CEO apologizes for promoting a white supremacist ad on its platform https://t.co/tVgQrjFQ9s #TrumpsAmerica." In doing so, these tweets blurred the lines between calling attention to hate (gatecrashing) while also criticizing media institutions (gatewatching).

Gatewatching (Media Criticism and Amplification)

Many #TrumpsAmerica tweets demonstrate the fuzziness of the gatewatching and gatecrashing categories, since posting information—in this case, about alleged acts of hate—also served the function of amplifying the message. Although a majority of posts to #TrumpsAmerica were primarily about reacting to events in the news or documenting acts of hate, some focused explicitly on gatewatching and media criticism. For example, one user tweeted, "Dear Media: journalism is more than literally just reciting what Trump tweets into an article. FACT CHECK. CONTEXT #TrumpsAmerica." While another tweeted, "Dear media, I hope all the ratings were worth it. #ElectionNight #Trumpocalypse #TrumpsAmerica #TrumpProtest #TrumpRiot." Others criticized media institutions for not adequately covering these incidents, posting messages like, "The media should be ashamed of themselves for normalizing hate speech. Ratings trump human decency. $ trumps human rights #TrumpsAmerica," and "Dear Mainstream Media: when does Trump's refusal to call upon his hate criming thugs to stand down become newsworthy?" [sic].

On the other hand, supporters of Trump engaged in their own form of gatewatching, posting criticisms of the press. For example, one supporter tweeted, "One thing in clear in what is about to be #TrumpsAmerica: our mainstream media needs to get their act together. Epic fail so far. So bad" [sic]. Others went further, apparently aiming to delegitimize the practice and profession of American journalism altogether, "EVERYTHING the media tells you going forward is a LIE. They are wounded and never more dangerous. Its all gunna be desperate lies." While such posts were rare among the data analyzed for this chapter, they illustrate the kind of anti-media sentiment Trump and his supporters displayed since early in the campaign.

Beyond the acts of media criticism, another function of gatewatching is the amplification of media messages. In addition to the basic act of sharing content, one way #TrumpsAmerica contributors amplified messages was through the use of numerous hashtags. Compared to political journalists' tweeting of the events discussed above, journo-activists were far more likely to engage in the practice of hashtagging. As many of the tweets discussed throughout this section illustrate, #TrumpsAmerica contributors included a wide variety of supplementary hashtags. While it is not possible to list each additional hashtag found in the data set, some of the most frequently used were "#trump," "#notmypresident," "#trumpsfirstorder," "#ReportHate" (the official hashtag promoted by the SPLC to document acts of hate), "#Racism," and "#Resist." Many of these examples illustrate the dual significance of hashtags: first, as discursive markers to increase the visibility of a message, and second, as rhetorical devices to convey additional meaning. Such attempts to exercise and amplify symbolic power provide a unique opportunity to assess their potential reach when compared to other discourses examined throughout the chapter.

COMPARING INFLUENCE ACROSS (SUB)FIELDS

In the age of mediatization, those striving for political and journalistic influence can be seen as engaged in a contest for symbolic power and media meta-capital. As discussed in previous chapters, politically motivated actors have long sought to attract and shape media coverage, though the likelihood of their success depends as much on their social position as it does the medium and the message. Thus, a hierarchy of influence can be imagined with opinion leaders from the political and journalistic fields at the top, rank-and-file members below, and everyone else, including marginalized amateurs, toward the bottom. However, the question remains: to what extent does this hierarchy hold for the data examined in this chapter?

The issue of influence, which underlies decades of research into agenda-setting, has been further complicated in the mediatized era. Like the "opinion leaders" from the era of print and broadcast media (Mills 1967), messages shared by traditional gatekeepers with the largest audiences are likely to garner the greatest influence (Yang et al. 2016). Thus, while legacy media have been shown to maintain their "elite hold" over the attention of networked publics, everyday citizens operating on the margins of the journalistic field play an increasingly significant role in the attention economy (Graeff et al. 2014; Meraz 2009). Given the recent growth of political polarization and distrust in the institution of journalism, that elite hold appears to be slipping—at least among the most disaffected members of networked publics. Nevertheless, focusing specifically on Twitter, influence is best measured by considering the size of a user's follower base, their level of engagement with others, as well as the number of clicks, likes, and shares their posts receive.

As shown in Fig. 8.1, the most influential tweeters from the cohort of political journalists come from a variety of legacy (*New York Times, Washington Post, Time,* CNN, NBC, CBS, Fox News, Associated Press, Bloomberg, *McClatchy*) and digital news organizations (Buzzfeed, fivethirtyeight, Axios, Yahoo News). Nevertheless, Trump's use of Twitter clearly wields more influence than any of the political reporters examined in this chapter. Furthermore, given the volume of media coverage that references (and therefore amplifies) Trump's tweets, it is clear that his use of Twitter attracts the biggest audience and is perhaps the largest the platform has ever seen.

By contrast, Fig. 8.2 shows a visualization of influencers from #TrumpsAmerica. A majority of the most influential users were either celebrities (Talib Kweli, Patton Oswalt, Tom Colicchio, China McClain), media organizations (*Raw Story*), or individual media professionals (Joy Ann Reid, Reza Aslan, Alex Gale, Ana Marie Cox). Save for a small number of social movement organizations (UniteBlue), the bulk of contributors to #TrumpsAmerica are rank-and-file members of networked publics. Thus, it is clear that the majority of #TrumpsAmerica contributors who stand out as influential on Twitter possess a kind of media meta-capital befitting of their position and influence in the field beyond Twitter.

Comparing the tweets of both political journalists and #TrumpsAmerica contributors, Fig. 8.3 shows each users' average number of shares for their original tweets.[6] Shares provide one useful mechanism for mapping the flow of influence on social networks such as Twitter (Benkler et al. 2017). As scholars of social networks have long understood, influence on digital platforms often operates according to the "power law" phenomenon, where those in positions of power stand to gain more than those with less

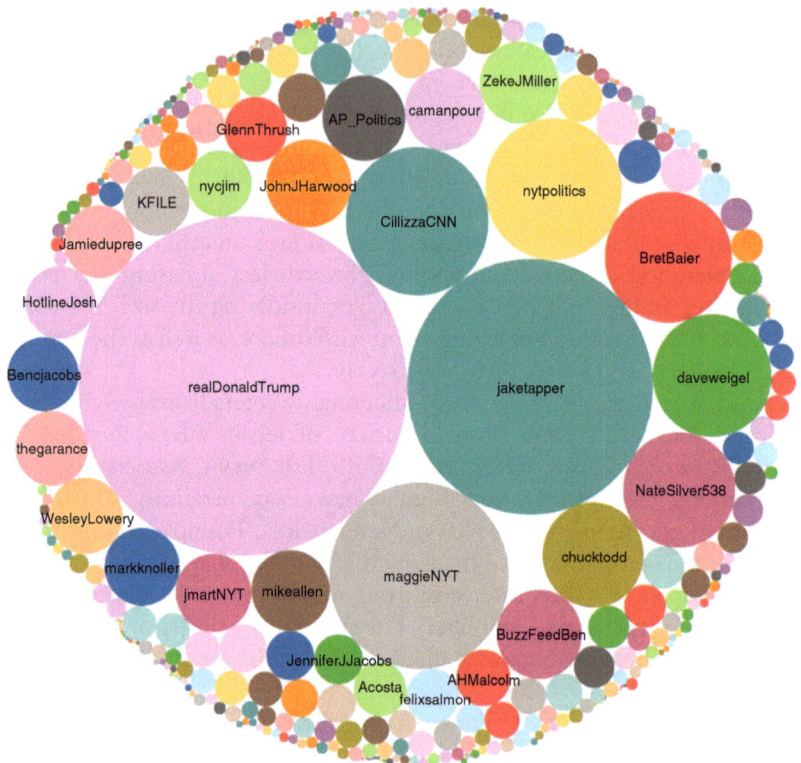

Fig. 8.1 Visual ranking of influencers from cohort of political journalists (Trump included)

status in the field (Meraz 2009). In other words, in the attention economy, the rich get richer, while those from lesser positions strive to attract attention from much smaller, niche audiences. This trend also applies to much of the data analyzed for this chapter, which places Trump atop the influence hierarchy by a wide margin, with professional and citizen reporters falling behind, respectively. Furthermore, despite the occasional instance of virality, professional journalists' position as gatekeepers with access to other channels for disseminating news content makes clear that the gap between their influence over the news compared to gatewatchers and gatecrashers is even wider than is suggested by this analysis. In other words, there is reason to question how accurately this comparison represents

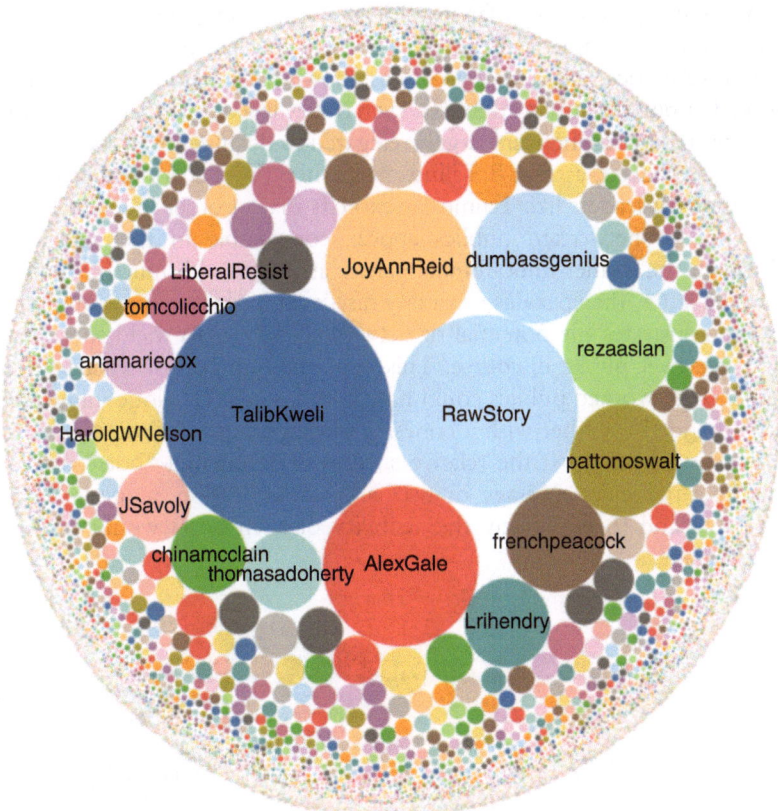

Fig. 8.2 Visual ranking of #TrumpsAmerica influencers

actual influence in the hybrid media system, given that professional journalists and journo-activists are disproportionately represented in the data examined for this chapter (see note above), and also that professionals have greater publishing platforms beyond Twitter.

Overall, the finding that users with position and influence in the traditional journalistic and political fields systematically received more shares, and thus were more influential on Twitter, resonates with other studies about the virality of political posts during the 2016 presidential election (Darwish et al. 2017). Accordingly, the battle for symbolic power, at least as measured by influence on Twitter, appears to have been won by the orthodoxy of the journalistic and political fields. Nevertheless, in the age of mediatization, influence is far from a zero-sum game, and the battle for attention is far from over. Regardless of politics or position, the success of #TrumpsAmerica, albeit marginal, has shown that members of the networked public can attract attention, even if they failed to garner coverage of their desired issues and were largely relegated to the margins of the journalistic field. Indeed, as Fig. 8.3 illustrates, while the media meta-capital of elite thought leaders like Trump far exceeds that of other individuals, the influence of networked publics appear comparable in the aggregate. Although the former undoubtedly garner attention with much less effort than the latter, the episodes of virality discussed in this and previous chapters demonstrates the potential of networked publics to wield substantial influence over public discourse. This begs the question of what level of influence networked publics could have if thousands, let alone millions of users, banded together with a cohesive message and a coordinated communication strategy. If the relative success of automated "bots" used to amplify a particular message or user are any indication, as discussed in Chaps. 2 and 9, it is likely the visibility of such posts would increase substantially.

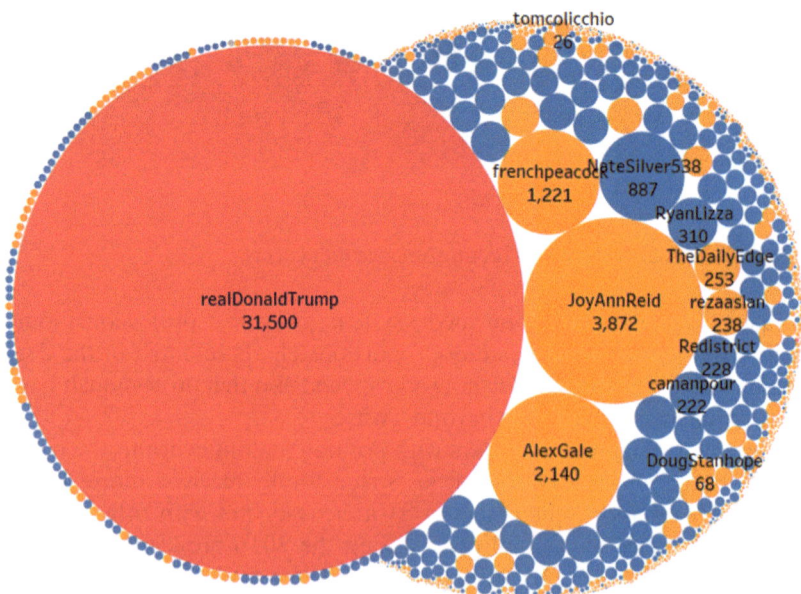

Fig. 8.3 Average shares for original tweets by political journalists (*blue*) and #TrumpsAmerica contributors (*orange*)[7]

CONCLUSION

Through an analysis of news stories, links, tweets, and subsequent metadata related to news events, how political journalists, journo-activists, and even Trump himself, responded to events during two separate time periods were explored. Members of each group contributed to the spectacle discussed throughout the chapter. Traditional gatekeepers maintained attention on Trump's tweets and provided criticism that is (ortho)doxic for the field, though their affective responses are less so. Those (journo-activists) performing gatewatching and gatecrashing roles provided more pointed criticisms, and even took steps to investigate and provide brief reports on an issue (e.g., acts of hate or violence), which they perceived to be under-reported throughout the field. Interestingly, Trump's use of Twitter also served gatewatching and gatecrashing functions by critiquing the products of journalism and disseminating his "alternative facts" directly to the networked public.

Much of this discourse, whether from journalists, politicians, or members of the networked public, has been wrapped in the spectacle surrounding Trump's candidacy and presidency. While it has long been acknowledged that media spectacle plays a central part in politics in a mediatized society (Kellner 2009), this analysis has made clear how central a role Twitter can play in the spread of spectacular news and views. Such a finding should hardly be surprising, given that a core function of media industries is the production and marketing of celebrity (Couldry 2016). Trump's status as a celebrity and media darling was decades in the making, bolstered by his ability to capitalize on publishers' desire for spectacle. Such prolonged, high-profile exposure has helped Trump amass a remarkable measure of media meta-capital, which he has effectively leveraged to promote his business ventures, garner huge ratings for a variety of media companies, and win the office of the presidency. Indeed, whether for the fields of politics or journalism, this spectacle can be used to gain the attention of networked publics, including professional journalists. However, this analysis has also shown that the production and mainstreaming of spectacle can prove challenging for those not already located in positions of influence. That is, there is no guarantee that particular tweets, or even more long-form reporting, will have much of an impact on the workings of the political field. Nevertheless, such uses of social media have, on the whole, already had a significant effect on the structure and practices of the American journalistic field.

Although the data analyzed for this chapter is far from representative of all that American professional journalism has to say about the Trump phenomenon on Twitter and beyond, the content examined should raise serious questions about the growth of media spectacle fueled by the fetishization of tweets by influential actors. To the extent that individual social media posts play a part in shaping traditional news flows, spectacle may be seen as both cause and effect of fetishization, posing yet another challenge to journalistic doxa. These apprehensions are reminiscent of the longstanding concerns raised across the journalistic field regarding press releases and briefings, which provide politicians and other strategic communicators with clear opportunities to set the news agenda. In the end, the advanced mediatization of the political field, at least in the case of Trump, has at the time of this writing proven more powerful for elite political actors than for the bulk of the journalistic field, particularly journo-activists at the margins. Thus, while Twitter may play a significant part in the transformation of American journalism, it is not clear that these changes have resulted in relative gains in the efficacy and autonomy of the journalistic field. In fact, recent events suggest the opposite. Perhaps most strikingly, these developments raise the question of whether journalism's longstanding reliance on the political field (Bennett et al. 2008; Cook 2005) may take on new forms, and may even be susceptible to new channels of state control, in the age of mediatization.

Overall, while Trump is clearly an outlier for both the political and journalistic fields, this case study provides an important illustration of the role Twitter plays in the battle for symbolic power in a time of increasing mediatization. By comparing tweets by journalists, journo-activists, as well as Trump himself, and contextualizing them within the broader landscape of news stories, it is clear that the systemic inequalities existent in analog field contexts persist in the digital realm. Furthermore, the results of this analysis suggest that, at least for Trump, it is possible to attract widespread media attention through the use of Twitter. However, those who possess lesser forms of media meta-capital should expect less impressive results, especially if they lack comparable position among the fields of politics and journalism. Nevertheless, the episodic successes of those with less capital and position make it clear that this hierarchy of influence is not absolute.

Notes

1. The bill is officially named the "Communications Over Various Feeds Electronically for Engagement" (COVFEFE) Act.
2. Percentages are reported as the number of links to the site among all tweets with links.
3. For this chapter, I collected 22,025 stories from 1952 unique news sites mentioning "@realDonaldTrump" and 7721 stories from 1662 unique news sites mentioning "covfefe" during the time frames outlined above.
4. Because the news stories crawled for this chapter comprised a limited sample of English-language news sites hosted in the United States, this AP story was likely published on many more online news sites.
5. The two exceptions were stories from *Inside Higher Ed* (Jaschik 2016), linked above, and the *Huffington Post* (Workneh 2016).
6. It is important to note that while the average number of shares may skew the results, given the varied nature of data collected for this chapter (tweets by political journalists far outpace those by journo-activists), this measure still provides a meaningful metric for assessing influence on Twitter. Thus, it is likely that journo-activists with a high-ranking number of shares would have much lower averages if the analysis was broadened.
7. Retweets were excluded from this analysis due to unreliability of data.

References

Andrews, T. M. (2017, June 7). Trump blocked some people from his Twitter account. Is that unconstitutional? *The Washington Post*. Retrieved November 26, 2017, from https://www.washingtonpost.com/news/morning-mix/wp/2017/06/07/trump-blocked-some-people-from-his-twitter-account-is-that-unconstitutional-as-they-say/.

Barthel, M. L., Moon, R., & Mari, W. (2015). Who retweets whom: How digital and legacy journalists interact on Twitter. *Tow Center for Digital Journalism*. Retrieved November 26, 2017, from http://towcenter.org/research/who-retweets-whom-how-digital-and-legacy-journalists-interact-on-twitter/.

Benac, N. (2017, May 31). Tweet that: #covfefe signals @realDonaldTrump is back. *The Seattle Times*. Retrieved November 26, 2017, from http://www.seattletimes.com/nation-world/tweet-that-covfefe-signals-realdonaldtrump-is-back/.

Benkler, Y., Roberts, H., Faris, R. M., Etling, B., Zuckerman, E., & Bourassa, N. (2017). Partisanship, propaganda, and disinformation: Online media and the 2016 U.S. presidential election. *Berkman Klein Center for Internet & Society at Harvard University*. Retrieved November 26, 2017, from https://dash.harvard.edu/handle/1/33759251.

Bennett, W. L., Lawrence, R. G., & Livingston, S. (2008). *When the press fails: Political power and the news media from Iraq to Katrina*. Chicago: University of Chicago Press.

Bourdieu, P. (2005). The political field, the social science field, and the journalistic field. In R. Benson & E. Neveu (Eds.), *Bourdieu and the journalistic field* (pp. 29–47). Malden, MA: Polity.

Bump, P. (2017, June 6). On behalf of the entire news media, Mr. Trump: Please, tweet away. *The Washington Post*. Retrieved November 26, 2017, from https://www.washingtonpost.com/news/politics/wp/2017/06/06/on-behalf-of-the-entire-news-media-mr-trump-please-tweet-away/.

Carlson, M. (2015). Keeping watch on the gates: Media criticism as advocatory pressure. In T. Vox & F. Heinderyckx (Eds.), *Gatekeeping in transition* (pp. 163–179). New York: Routledge.

Chadwick, A. (2013). *The hybrid media system: Politics and power*. New York: Oxford University Press.

Confessore, N., & Yourish, K. (2016, March 15). $2 billion worth of free media for Donald Trump. *The New York Times*. Retrieved November 26, 2017, from https://www.nytimes.com/2016/03/16/upshot/measuring-donald-trumps-mammoth-advantage-in-free-media.html.

Conway-Silva, B. A., Filer, C. R., Kenski, K., & Tsetsi, E. (2017). Reassessing Twitter's agenda-building power: An analysis of intermedia agenda-setting effects during the 2016 presidential primary season. *Social Science Computer Review*, Advanced online publication. https://doi.org/10.1177/0894439317715430.

Cook, T. E. (2005). *Governing with the news: The news media as a political institution* (2nd ed.). Chicago: University Of Chicago Press.

Couldry, N. (2014). When mediatization hits the ground. In A. Hepp & F. Krotz (Eds.), *Mediatized worlds: Culture and society in a media age* (pp. 54–71). New York: Palgrave Macmillan.

Couldry, N. (2016). Celebrity, convergence, and the fate of media institutions. In P. D. Marshall & S. Redmond (Eds.), *A companion to celebrity* (pp. 98–113). Malden, MA: John Wiley & Sons, Inc. https://doi.org/10.1002/9781118475089.ch6.

Darwish, K., Magdy, W., & Zanouda, T. (2017). Trump vs. Hillary: What went viral during the 2016 US presidential election. In G. L. Ciampaglia, A. Mashhadi, & T. Yasseri (Eds.), *Social informatics* (pp. 143–161). Cham, CH: Springer. Retrieved November 26, 2017, from https://doi.org/10.1007/978-3-319-67217-5_10.

De Maeyer, J., & Holton, A. E. (2016). Why linking matters: A metajournalistic discourse analysis. *Journalism, 17*(6), 776–794. https://doi.org/10.1177/1464884915579330.

Esser, F., & Strömbäck, J. (Eds.). (2014). *Mediatization of politics: Understanding the transformation of western democracies*. New York: Palgrave Macmillan.

Flegenheimer, M. (2017, May 31). What's a 'Covfefe'? Trump tweet unites a bewildered nation. *The New York Times*. Retrieved November 26, 2017, from https://www.nytimes.com/2017/05/31/us/politics/covfefe-trump-twitter.html.

Freelon, D., & Karpf, D. (2015). Of big birds and bayonets: Hybrid Twitter interactivity in the 2012 presidential debates. *Information, Communication & Society, 18*(4), 390–406. https://doi.org/10.1080/1369118X.2014.952659.

Goldmark, A. (2017, April 7). Episode 763: BOTUS. *National Public Radio*. Retrieved November 26, 2017, from http://www.npr.org/sections/money/2017/04/07/522897876/meet-botus-planet-money-s-stock-trading-twitter-bot.

Graeff, E., Stempeck, M., & Zuckerman, E. (2014). The battle for "Trayvon Martin": Mapping a media controversy online and off-line. *First Monday, 19*(2). Retrieved from http://firstmonday.org/ojs/index.php/fm/article/view/4947.

Hermida, A. (2010). Twittering the news: The emergence of ambient journalism. *Journalism Practice, 4*(3), 297–308.

Jaschik, S. (2016, November 11). The incidents since election day. *Inside Higher Ed*. Retrieved November 26, 2017, from https://www.insidehighered.com/news/2016/11/11/students-many-colleges-reporting-ethnic-or-racial-harassment-election-day.

Karpf, D. (2016, June 19). The clickbait candidate. *The Chronicle of Higher Education*. Retrieved November 26, 2017, from http://www.chronicle.com/article/The-Clickbait-Candidate/236815.

Kellner, D. (2009). Media spectacle and media events: Some critical reflections. In N. Couldry, A. Hepp, & F. Krotz (Eds.), *Media events in a global age* (pp. 76–91). New York: Routledge.

Kellner, D. (2016). *American nightmare: Donald Trump, media spectacle, and authoritarian populism*. Rotterdam: Sense.

Kreiss, D. (2014). Seizing the moment: The presidential campaigns' use of Twitter during the 2012 electoral cycle. *New Media & Society, 8*(8), 1473–1490.

Kunelius, R., & Reunanen, E. (2016). Changing power of journalism: The two phases of mediatization. *Communication Theory, 26*(4), 369–388. https://doi.org/10.1111/comt.12098.

Lakoff, G. (2017, March 8). Trump's Twitter distraction. *George Lakoff*. Retrieved November 26, 2017, from https://georgelakoff.com/2017/03/07/trumps-twitter-distraction/.

Lasorsa, D. L., Lewis, S. C., & Holton, A. E. (2012). Normalizing Twitter. *Journalism Studies, 13*(1), 19–36. https://doi.org/10.1080/1461670X.2011.571825.

Meraz, S. (2009). Is there an elite hold? Traditional media to social media agenda setting influence in blog networks. *Journal of Computer-Mediated Communication, 14*(3), 682–707. https://doi.org/10.1111/j.1083-6101.2009.01458.x.

Mihailidis, P., & Viotty, S. (2017). Spreadable spectacle in digital culture: Civic expression, fake news, and the role of media literacies in "post-fact" society. *American Behavioral Scientist, 61*(4), 441–454. https://doi.org/10.1177/0002764217701217.

Mills, C. W. (1967). *Power, politics, and people: The collected essays of C. Wright Mills.* New York: Oxford University Press.

Mitchell, A., Gottfried, J., Stocking, G., Matsa, K. E., & Grieco, E. (2017, October 2). *Covering President Trump in a polarized media environment.* Pew Research Center. Retrieved November 26, 2017, from http://www.journalism.org/2017/10/02/covering-president-trump-in-a-polarized-media-environment/.

Molyneux, L. (2015). What journalists retweet: Opinion, humor, and brand development on Twitter. *Journalism, 16*(7), 920–935. https://doi.org/10.1177/1464884914550135.

Moon, S. J., & Hadley, P. (2014). Routinizing a new technology in the newsroom: Twitter as a news source in mainstream media. *Journal of Broadcasting & Electronic Media, 58*(2), 289–305. https://doi.org/10.1080/08838151.2014.906435.

Nilagia, M. (2017, February 8). David Fahrenthold on transparency, sourcing, B.S. and other advice for covering President Trump. *The Poynter Institute.* Retrieved November 26, 2017, from http://www.poynter.org/2017/david-fahrenthold-on-transparency-sourcing-b-s-and-other-advice-for-covering-president-trump/448312/.

Pabmann, J., Boeschoten, T., & Schafer, M. T. (2014). The gift of gab: Retweet cartels and gift economies on Twitter. In K. Weller, A. Bruns, J. Burgess, M. Mahrt, & C. Puschmann (Eds.), *Twitter and society* (pp. 331–344). New York: Peter Lang.

Politwoops: Deleted Tweet from Donald J. Trump, R. (2017). *ProPublica.* Retrieved November 26, 2017, from https://projects.propublica.org/politwoops/tweet/869766994899468288.

Post-election bias incidents up to 1372; New collaboration with ProPublica. (2017, February 10). *Southern Poverty Law Center.* Retrieved November 26, 2017, from https://www.splcenter.org/hatewatch/2017/02/10/post-election-bias-incidents-1372-new-collaboration-propublica.

Postman, N. (1985). *Amusing ourselves to death: Public discourse in the age of show business.* New York: Penguin Books.

Revers, M. (2017). *Contemporary journalism in the US and Germany: Agents of accountability.* New York: Palgrave Macmillan.

Russell, A. (2016). *Journalism as activism: Recoding media power.* Malden, MA: Polity.

Russell, F. M., Hendricks, M. A., Choi, H., & Stephens, E. C. (2015). Who sets the news agenda on Twitter? *Digital Journalism, 3*(6), 925–943. https://doi.org/10.1080/21670811.2014.995918.

Russell, J. (2017, May 30). With one misspelled word, President Trump gifts Twitter the #covfefe meme. *TechCrunch*. Retrieved November 26, 2017, from http://social.techcrunch.com/2017/05/30/covfefe/.

Schudson, M. (1982). The politics of narrative form: The emergence of news conventions in print and television. *Daedalus, 111*(4), 97–112.

Swift, A. (2016, September 14). Americans' trust in mass media sinks to new low. *Gallup News*. Retrieved November 26, 2017, from http://www.gallup.com/poll/195542/americans-trust-mass-media-sinks-new-low.aspx.

Vos, T., & Heinderyckx, F. (2015). *Gatekeeping in transition*. New York: Routledge.

Wamsley, L. (2017, June 12). The Covfefe Act has a silly name – but it addresses a real quandary. *National Public Radio*. Retrieved November 26, 2017, from http://www.npr.org/sections/thetwo-way/2017/06/12/532651827/the-covfefe-act-has-a-silly-name-but-it-addresses-a-real-quandary.

Warzel, C. (2014, April 15). Meet the man behind Twitter's most infamous phrase. *Buzzfeed*. Retrieved November 26, 2017, from https://www.buzzfeed.com/charliewarzel/meet-the-man-behind-twitters-most-infamous-phrase.

Wells, C., Shah, D. V., Pevehouse, J. C., Yang, J., Pelled, A., Boehm, F., Lukito, J., Ghosh, S., & Schmidt, J. L. (2016). How trump drove coverage to the nomination: Hybrid media campaigning. *Political Communication, 33*(4), 669–676. https://doi.org/10.1080/10584609.2016.1224416.

Workneh, L. (2016, November 11). Countless acts of hate have been carried out since Trump's win. *Huffington Post*. Retrieved November 26, 2017, from http://www.huffingtonpost.com/entry/countless-acts-of-hate-have-been-carried-out-since-trumps-win_us_5825ee38e4b02d21bbc86211.

Yang, S., Quan-Haase, A., & Rannenberg, K. (2016). The changing public sphere on Twitter: Network structure, elites and topics of the #righttobeforgotten. *New Media & Society*, Advanced online publication. https://doi.org/10.1177/1461444816651409.

CHAPTER 9

Twitter and Beyond: Journalistic Practice, Platforms, and the Future of Media Power

Having witnessed the evolution of Twitter and its growth in the media ecosystem since early 2009, I have long been convinced of the platform's significance for the fields of journalism, politics, and beyond. This book is a testament to what I have learned as a result of that process. The examples from the previous chapters are only a few of the many cases where Twitter plays a central role in the interactions of these fields. Although this list is far from comprehensive, the analysis conducted throughout this book has focused on the products and processes of networked journalism as seen on Twitter. As such, the research presented here speaks to the mezzo-level transformations occurring in the journalistic field.

This book has illustrated that Twitter is far more than a platform for political debate, celebrity gossip, and breaking news. While the parts of the platform examined in this book often appeared to be full of professional journalists talking among themselves, other portions of the research made clear that Twitter's journalistic field included a wider range of actors. For every media professional discussing and distributing their work on the platform, there are countless more nonprofessionals willing to help identify sources, spread news, or offer feedback on what they think is missing from a story. It is *because* of the diversity of its uses and users that Twitter has etched out its place in, and as a point of influence for, American journalism.

This concluding chapter synthesizes what has been learned from the previous chapters. Accordingly, it begins with a brief overview of what I have argued throughout the book regarding the hybridity of journalistic

© The Author(s) 2018   177
S. R. Barnard, *Citizens at the Gates*,
https://doi.org/10.1007/978-3-319-90446-7_9

practice on Twitter. Next, it considers how the case studies examined throughout the book illustrate the enduring structural transformation of the journalistic field, before considering the role played by "citizen journalists." Finally, the chapter reflects on some key battlegrounds in the enduring fight for media power.

TWITTER AND THE ELEMENTS OF JOURNALISTIC PRACTICE

The case studies presented in previous chapters examined the content and context of journalistic production on Twitter. Each case is representative of an event where journalistic actors operate in the boundary spaces of the field. The content, and the labor that went into producing it, helps reveal the elements of practice displayed by journalists on Twitter, whether professional or not. This analysis, and the inferences it has gleaned, is made possible by the media(ted) artifacts preserved on digital platforms. In turn, these are made possible by the (meta-)discursive reflections journalists willingly share in and about their practice.

If it is true, as I have argued, that the mediatization of the journalistic field has resulted in a hybridizing of traditional journalistic structures and institutions, then it stands to reason this shift would also be reflected in journalistic practice. Journalists use Twitter to follow the latest news, connect with sources, share news, engage with members of the public, reflect on recent events, and maintain their reputation as networked professionals. As hybridized supplements to more traditional methods of reporting, these Twitter practices provide networked journalists with alternative means of amassing journalistic capital, and each of these acts further shapes journalists' networked habitus. Through added opportunities for access and visibility, this work, much like the Twitter practices of networked politicians and citizens, provides journalists with a means of wielding power in and beyond the journalistic field. In other words, media work produces far more than content; on the macro-level, these practices constitute the structure of the field itself. Indeed, with every Twitter (inter)action, journalists are (re)constructing their field's elements of practice, which includes contributing to the formation of new iterations of mediatized capital.

As a largely professional practice, the production of journalism is interminably bound by the institutionalized norms, or doxa, of the field. The position of news agents and organizations within this field is shaped, in large part, by their ability to build and maintain various forms of capital, including social ties (social), knowledge and educational credential(cultural), monetary (economic), and status (symbolic). Journalistic actors dialectically draw upon their position and disposition (habitus) to guide their actions in the field. Within this framework, news workers generally adhere to the taken-for-granted norms and values (doxa) that govern their work in the field. This includes following the professional doxic norms of objectivity, truthfulness, verification, attribution, independence, and public service, which structure the form and content of news (Craft et al. 2016; Kovach and Rosenstiel 2014). But in the digital age, many have also adapted new, hybrid practices shaped by transformations in technology, politics, and popular culture (Chadwick 2013).

As is clear from the Twitter-journalism practices examined throughout this book, the platform has played an increasingly significant role in the work of many networked journalists.

Recall what *Denver Post* reporter Daniel Petty said of Twitter's journalistic significance, as discussed in Chap. 2, "We in mainstream media have a bias toward Twitter…it's where we're spending most of our time" ("Hashtag: #Journalism" 2013). This sentiment was reiterated by Petty's fellow panelists, and also in the journalistic meta-discourse analyzed in Chap. 4. Such admissions provide a window into reporters' habitus, which is becoming increasingly hybrid and networked in this time of mediatization. Whether or not contemporary journalists are beholden to Twitter, they work in a field whose practice has been shaped by the platform.

Twitter's rise within the journalistic field is accompanied by a transformation in journalistic capital. Indeed, the reporting practices deployed on Twitter, along with the hybrid habitus that develop and deploy them, have recursively helped (re)formulate the field's capital. Whether professional or not, journalists are evaluated, in part, on the facility with which they navigate the emergent power dynamics of the mediatized field, where Twitter plays a noteworthy role. Journalists' repertoire of capital is made up of their ability to cultivate ties, access knowledge communities, drive web traffic, and accumulate status, which they continue to build and draw upon in future (inter)actions—on Twitter and beyond. The sum of this capital, which remains tied to traditional media structures yet embedded in the broader environment of mediatization, produces an emergent, synthetic form of capital referred to as media meta-capital.

As Nick Couldry (2014, pp. 59–60) has theorized, media meta-capital is the capacity of media to "exercise power over other forms of capital" as a result of its immense symbolic power in an age of mediatization. Each of the actor groups represented in this book have the capacity to amass and wield media meta-capital, albeit to varying degrees. Professional journalists' media meta-capital hinges primarily on two related factors: their authority to explain and capacity to disseminate accurate information. Both of these capacities are enabled by journalists' access to (mass) media, of which Twitter is both an intermediary and end in itself.

While they generally lack access to mass media channels, citizen journalists and journo-activists rely primarily on platforms like Twitter to spread information and as a consequence, build and wield meta-capital. As shown throughout the book, this capacity depends, in large part, on the collaborative capacity of networked publics to amplify messages and draw attention to causes. Their success is measured, in part, by their (in)ability to attract and shape legacy media attention on the issues they care about. Despite what the network affords actors on the margins of a given field, those who have already amassed more traditional forms of capital are still most likely to wield influence in the new media ecosystem as well. This was most certainly true for the traditional opinion leaders dominating much of the discourse in #Ferguson, #Nerdland, and #TrumpsAmerica. Nevertheless, those possessing elite-level status in traditional field contexts are especially well-disposed to wield media meta-capital, as demonstrated in Chap. 8 discussion of Donald Trump and his unparalleled symbolic power. Recall, however, that this symbolic power was hardly attributable to any individual, but rather, to the network—including professional and citizen journalists—whose actions, critical or not, added to the spectacle by helping amplify Trump's messages far beyond their initial reach. Despite the persistence of such a power imbalance, social actors from a variety of field locations have demonstrated a capacity to wield media meta-capital, and by extension, are taking part in (re)shaping the structure of the journalistic field.

(Re)Working the Gates: On Twitter and Beyond

In 2006, prominent progressive bloggers Jerome Armstrong and Markos Moulitsas Zúniga published a book about the state of American politics and what role political blogs and crowd-funding campaigns—then the newest and most popular platforms for citizen media—could play in its transformation (Armstrong and Zúniga 2006). While their outlook was a bit optimistic, Armstrong and Zúniga were among the first to understand just how significantly a communication revolution could transform the field of politics. Their core argument, summed up by the book's title,

Crashing the Gate, was that a new cohort of networked publics had entered the field, crying out for change. The work these bloggers were doing could destabilize traditional power structures maintained by political parties, they argued, because elites no longer had sole control of the media system. More than a decade later, it is clear that the advancement of mediatization poses a comparable, perhaps even a greater, challenge to journalism than it does to politics.

One site of this challenge is the journalism profession's traditional authority to serve as gatekeepers. The literature on news gatekeeping is focused on the process of selecting and editing information so that the news and views that end up getting published are actually fit to print (Shoemaker and Vos 2009). In other words, gatekeeping is the necessary work required for (raw) information to become (polished) news—that is its manifest function. From this perspective, control of the gates is seen less as a professional priority, a privilege that must be protected, than it is a matter of fact that comes with the territory of being (or working for) a publisher.

But in a time when anyone with access to the web could theoretically become a publisher, gatekeeping also has a latent function: it separates the news and views of those deemed legitimate from those that are not. Legacy news organizations may have lost some authority in recent decades (Swift 2016), but they are still the primary arbiters of what civil society deems to be true, regardless of delivery platform. Such authority to perform acts of legitimation and differentiation are part and parcel of professional fields, which, as discussed in Chap. 3, are known to have a long history of building and maintaining boundaries. Journalism is no exception. It is, however, an exceptional illustration of how a profession's traditional dichotomies—like author vs. audience, reporter vs. citizen, and fact vs. opinion—can break down in the digital age.

In the contemporary hybrid media system (Chadwick 2013), the work of professional journalism and citizen journo-activism overlap and intersect in various ways. Occasionally, this hybridity is visible on the page (or screen), as demonstrated in Chap. 4 when professional meta-discourse revealed reporters' adaptation to digital journalism practices developed by citizens and professionals on Twitter and beyond. Or, when citizen reporting is adopted and broadcast by legacy institutions, as illustrated in Chap. 5 examination of the aftermath of the 2013 Boston Marathon Bombing. Field hybridity also occurs when typically distinct groups converge in the same physical and discursive space, as was the case in 2014 and 2015, when professional journalists and journo-activists from Ferguson, Missouri responded to the killing of Michael Brown. Each of these cases produced myriad accounts that were not of a distinct (professional) journalistic or political (activist) tradition, but rather, hybrids that served to further blur the boundaries between form and field.

Another aspect of hybridity is the changing dynamics of media work. This includes a blurring of boundaries between work and leisure, brought about by the combined techno-cultural phenomenon of mediatization as well as the political-economic reality of late capitalism (Comor and Compton 2015; Paulussen 2012). While benefiting from the hybrid practices and labor conditions following this shift, many legacy news organizations have failed to smoothly adapt their norms and values to align with this era. For example, in October 2017, the *New York Times* and the *Wall Street Journal* tightened restrictions on their reporters' social media use, purportedly to strengthen the veneer of objectivity during a time of increased political polarization (Perlberg 2017; "The Times" 2017). While ostensibly sticking to the core value of objectivity could be seen as virtuous, such restrictive policies may lead to decreases in journalistic productivity on the platform, as one study found that "journalists who work for organizations that place restrictions on Twitter and Facebook use were less likely overall to use the platforms to engage in activities related to both source and research-based activities" (Santana and Hopp 2016, p. 400). Although these changes raise questions about how and to what extent policy will shape journalistic practice, and vice versa, they are indicative of news organizations' ongoing acclimation. Indeed, as the case studies discussed throughout this book have illustrated, the age of mediatization is characterized in part by a new media environment where the dynamics of media work and participation are more fluid (Deuze 2007). Such fluidity is illustrated by three characteristics of networked news: producers, processes, and products.

First, the individuals and institutions that produce the news are an increasingly hybrid bunch. While it is obvious that citizen journalists are situated at the intersection of multiple fields, media professionals are themselves adapting to the changing environment, working in a field where the lines between hard news, feature stories, and sponsored content are increasingly blurry. Second, these hybrid positions result in hybrid reporting processes. As shown in Chaps. 4, 5, and 6, professional journalists have adapted reporting and networking techniques from citizen bloggers, made social media monitoring a serious part of their daily newsgathering routines, and sought ways to supplement those experiences by following up with on-the-ground reporting. Third, the products resulting from this work invariably take hybrid forms. Not only does this include reports created and shared in a multitude of converged media environments, but also, the content of these reports can often blur the boundaries between objective and affective style. This is not only true of citizen journo-activists, but increasingly of many professionals as well, as illustrated in Chaps. 6 and 8.

While the liquidity of labor conditions (Deuze 2007; Paulussen 2012) throughout the media fields pose challenges for the functioning of journalism as a public service and professional field, a latent function is the inclusion of networked publics who are steadily broaching journalism's gates. Indeed, the rapid dissemination of networked technologies across much of American society has resulted in a similar shift in techno-cultural practices. Whether intently political, artistic, journalistic, or otherwise, citizens' contribution to media fields has opened up the field to influence from those not traditionally granted access beyond journalism's gates. This, in turn, demonstrates how networked publics, through their use of digital media, are helping to transform the (power) structures and practices of the journalistic field.

On Twitter and beyond, participation in the journalistic field takes on a variety of hybrid forms. Whereas professionals often use the platform to share content, identify sources, sort out facts, discuss their work with fellow professionals, and engage members of the public, citizen journalists take to Twitter to collect, post, and share original content (gatecrashing), as well as to curate and critique legacy news products (gatewatching). Just as journalism professionals' use of social media is said to add transparency to the news process (Lasorsa et al. 2012), so too is gatewatchers' constant monitoring of the flow of information. Furthermore, this hybridization also provides a means of evaluating the structures and processes of cultural production, whether through the selection of techniques and technologies, the creation of accountability mechanisms, or the policing of moral boundaries.

Altogether, this assortment of journalistic actors and practices across the political, journalistic, and cultural fields has resulted in the emergence of what was defined in Chap. 3 as a *mediatized superstructure*, which is an assemblage of networked individuals, techniques, and technologies that, once populated by a critical mass, provides a relatively stable and persistent mechanism for the vetting and spreading of information. The concept provides a means of theorizing the restructuring of journalism as publics are increasingly networked with(in) the field. As seen on Twitter, this assemblage of actors and practices allows for and can even encourage the creation, sharing, vetting, and criticism of journalism, including both its form and function as well as individual pieces of content (Davis and Chouinard 2017).

The vitality of this mediatized superstructure depends largely on the "space of flows," whereby networked publics produce and disseminate information, and by consequence, alter the power dynamics within and across fields (Castells 2015). Journo-activists have utilized Twitter to exercise what Matt Carlson (2015) has termed "advocatory gatekeeping pressure," often targeting legacy media coverage of political issues. To the extent such pressure is empirically grounded and inclusive of underrepresented groups, two important interventions in contemporary journalism, this pressure has the potential to add to the vitality and diversity of the journalistic field. This kind of citizen oversight is precisely what Bill Dutton (2009) had in mind when he theorized the emergence of a "fifth estate."

Whatever we call it, the existence of this mediatized superstructure is visible in each of the cases examined in this book. For example, considering news flows from Boston to Yemen, Chap. 5 described how Twitter is often implicated in hybrid forms of pro-am journalism, while Chaps. 6, 7, and 8 examined how networked publics participate in the spreading and (re)shaping of news. However intentional, such collaboration is enabled by the existence of a mediatized superstructure made up of journalists and networked publics driven to further the understanding of news events as they occur. At the same time, these actors vie for position and influence, at times adding to, but also challenging, the capital and legitimacy of the journalistic field (Craft et al. 2016). This begs numerous questions about the consequences of citizen action in the mediatized journalistic field.

COLLABORATION, COMPETITION, AND CONTESTATION: GATEWATCHING AND GATECRASHING AS CITIZEN JOURNALISM

While the power to publish may be more widely distributed than ever, and even as networked publics' agenda-setting abilities are growing, the ability to consistently reach the masses still remains largely in the hands of the elites (Meraz 2009; Yang et al. 2016). This conclusion resonates strongly with much of the findings presented throughout this book, which illustrate how elite actors are most likely to garner influence on Twitter. Although citizen actors do sometimes generate enough media spectacle to reach this critical mass, they fail to go viral far more often than they likely desire. Nevertheless, when working in concert, networked publics have the power to gain greater attention, thus affecting the structures and practices that make up the journalistic field. This occurs through citizens' contributions to professional reporting (i.e., participatory journalism), their public criticism of journalistic products and processes (i.e., journo-activism), as well as through the more independently produced alternatives (i.e., citizen journalism) they offer.

Despite their persistent relevance, the reader will notice that the book rarely uses the terms "citizen journalism" or "alternative journalism." Indeed, because of the aforementioned fluidity of journalistic forms, this study has maintained a relatively broad interpretation of these practices, highlighting distinctions where relevant but otherwise opting not to reify the boundaries of a practice and profession undergoing significant transformation. Instead, the book has examined how networked publics engage in practices like gatewatching and gatecrashing. These terms are not used as euphemisms, although they may at times be read as synonymous. I have opted, instead, to focus primarily on accountability practices that networked publics use to spread, critique, and ultimately, advance the products and practices of journalism. This is largely because the term "citizen journalism" has been used to describe acts ranging from original reporting to the sharing and commenting on news (Goode 2009), and also because it is often difficult to decipher the origins of knowledge production in digital spaces.

Whether or not it is characterized as "citizen" or "alternative journalism," members of the public have long played a complex role in the creation, dissemination, evaluation, and response to professional reporting (Atton 2008). Although the latter three practices may best be characterized as gatewatching, the reporting bearing the label "citizen journalism"— or as it has been discussed throughout the book, "gatecrashing"—must be produced and disseminated by members of the public without the assistance of professional news organizations. Whatever we call them, gatecrashers provide alternative brands of news that skew, often far, from the profession's traditional doxa. At the same time, those on the margins of the field have also been found to uphold many of journalism's core values and practices (Craft et al. 2016). Moving beyond mere mimicry and collaboration, gatecrashers produce and disseminate their own original content, often aiming to provide legitimate alternatives to traditional sources of news.

While it may be considered amateurish by many seasoned professionals, much of what has been labeled citizen journalism has been produced by, or with the help of, individuals who were previously employed as professional journalists (Lindner et al. 2015). However puzzling, this is a fitting reality of the age of digital journalism, where the people formerly known as the professionals are adapting to life and work in a hybrid news system whose market structures do not have the carrying capacity to sustain the work of many news organizations, both new and old (Lindner and Larson 2017). To the extent that this hybrid journalism is disseminated on platforms flooded with a variety of publishers, as is the case with Facebook and Twitter, professional and citizen journalists may be in competition for audience attention. Accordingly, those working in the margins of the journalistic field may be driven to contest the legitimacy of legacy news and vice versa. Recent studies suggest that legacy media are particularly vulnerable to these criticisms today (Swift 2016; Shearer and Gottfried 2017). As Mary Chayko (2016, p. 110) put it, "A decline in news organization's reputation for fairness and accuracy can benefit the independent journalist or citizen journalist, who can then appear to the general public as just as, if not more, trustworthy."

Although the work of gatewatchers may at times challenge the legitimacy of journalistic products at the individual level, few have engaged in a systematic critique of the practice and institution of journalism as a whole. While this is generally true of progressive alternative media, many on the political Right have worked hard to delegitimize journalism. Pioneered by Fox News, reporting that aims to sow doubt and offer "alternative facts" has been mirrored by popular outlets like Breitbart, Alex Jones' Info Wars, and even Donald Trump himself. However, when read in aggregate, it is easy to see how such a panoply of critiques can serve to call into question the legitimacy of a profession. As the case studies presented throughout this book make clear, the work of networked publics is rarely coherent or coordinated enough to wage such an attack. Citizens are indeed broaching journalism's gates, but they do so on their own terms, and mostly in reactive, issue-specific fits and episodic spurts, which are likely to be lost among the cacophony of voices and the constant churn of the news cycle. We have not (yet) seen the emergence of a media reform movement on par with those of previous decades, although the battle for internet freedom provides one site of potential resistance. Thus, gatewatchers' calls for change may (or may not) be heeded in the political realm, where most are ultimately aimed. But the work of networked publics is, at least in the aggregate, proving to be consequential for the journalistic field.

By focusing on what happens at journalism's gates—what kinds of information are allowed through, according to what standards, and from which sources—gatewatchers are serving the role of a fifth estate. They are "watching the watchers." Holding legacy media accountable to public standards is not an insignificant civic act. At the same time, many of these acts have a secondary meaning of holding public officials accountable. That is, by critiquing, publishing, and publicizing critical information, journo-activists are simultaneously accomplishing two goals. Their gate-watching, which first appears to be aimed at media institutions, is largely done with the express goal of holding public officials accountable. This is exactly why acts of journalism must be seen simultaneously as political. Journalism is a form of activism, even when it is not.

In summary, as I have argued throughout this book, the boundaries, norms, and practices of the journalistic field are undergoing notable transformation due to the growing significance of citizen journalists using digital media. While new entrants play an increasingly significant role in the journalistic and political fields by wielding affective, symbolic power, their actions do not supersede the traditional, institutionalized forces that have defined the profession for over a century. Beyond contributing to a changing journalistic field, citizens' foray into journalism within this time of mediatization is also transforming the political field, which may ultimately lead to a redefinition of what it means to be a "good citizen" (Kligler-Vilenchik 2017). However intentional, this contestation, among many others, has implications for the dynamics of media power.

The Future of Media Power

It goes without saying that the analysis presented here is far from comprehensive. Nor have the power dynamics it has examined been settled. Far from it. To be sure, there are many cases from the past, present and future that, if examined thoroughly, would complicate the conclusions reached here. This is to be expected, for this book has not aimed to make a definitive statement on the matters of media power and practice. It has only sought to add to the conversation about the role networked publics and platforms are playing in the transformation of American journalism by drawing on my own research on Twitter. Nevertheless, this research has uncovered a number of factors that will likely prove significant for the future of media power. These concerns can be divided into three broad, overlapping categories: labor, logics, and literacies.

The relations of labor(ers) play an important role in structuring the flow of capital, both within and beyond the journalistic field. Furthermore, as users of social media platforms, networked individuals not only contribute to their fields of interest—for example, citizen journalists and journo-activists adding value to the journalistic field—but also to the profit of the media companies that own the platforms. On Twitter, users are doubly valuable: their attention is sold to advertisers, and the content they create is sold to researchers, including marketers, as data. Networked publics are also valuable to legacy and digital news publishers, given how frequently reporters incorporate users' social media posts in their stories (Broersma and Graham 2013).

According to Christian Fuchs (2014), the era of mediatization has brought about a set of relations where citizen "prosumers" are coerced into volunteering their labor on the basis of ideology. Fuchs' contention that networked individuals' unremunerated labor amounts to exploitation is contingent on their ideological commitment to prosumption, including the opportunities for interaction and identity construction it enables. This point is instructive in that it calls attention to the economic value added by some work performed by networked publics. Nevertheless, it overlooks the fact that much of the work performed by networked individuals, especially those gatewatchers and gatecrashers discussed throughout this book, is motivated by social and political ends—and indeed, that social relations are not solely defined by economic relations. As David Hesmondhalgh (2015) argues, prosumption does not amount to exploitation, in large part because, unlike more traditional labor relations, the conditions of prosumer labor do not include the kind of threats (force, starvation, etc.) typically associated with exploitative labor relations. Nevertheless, the voluntary labor performed by networked publics does help media companies—including traditional publishers and social media platforms—amass capital while also contributing to the oversupply of media work, which together can be said to devalue the work of professionals.

On top of the potential for competition with citizen journalists, the new media ecosystem is increasingly flooded by an array of publishers vying for the public's attention. The field's culture of competitiveness, along with the technologies that enable detailed tracking of web traffic, have driven many media organizations to create and distribute content based on its ability to drive traffic, and therefore, revenue. As Caitlin Petre (2015, para. 22) has shown, the most popular news analytics provider, Chartbeat, is now used by "80 percent of the most-trafficked publishers in the United States, as well as media outlets in 35 other countries." No matter which provider publishers subscribe to, analytics are used to help editors select which stories to prioritize, as well as to deselect those that are not attracting the attention expected of them (Carlson 2017; Tandoc 2014). And given how the rise of algorithmically driven analytics platforms shape institutional practices over time (Christin 2017), this is just the tip of the iceberg.

Despite the significance of increased competition from below, the labor conditions prominent across American journalism are shaped, in large part, by the field's core logics. As Bourdieu (2005) has long noted, news organizations' drive to turn ever-increasing profits challenges the profession's autonomy to produce news in the public interest. Critical, investigative journalism is time-consuming and expensive, and is often reported in long-form. Both factors, cost and length, pose challenges for news production in the age of mediatization, given that online platforms provide less profit per reader than traditional media. Also, the competition for audience attention, driven largely by social media platforms, makes it difficult to get, let alone keep, readers' attention. In fact, these two factors—getting readers' attention (i.e., clicks) and keeping it (i.e., time spent on a webpage)—are basic metrics for news sites, and are now key factors in some platforms' compensation of authors (Williams 2017). These pay-per-click strategies are yet another step in the deprofessionalization of news work. Although freelance journalism has some benefits, including added mobility and flexibility (Massey and Elmore 2011), freelancers are seeing a decline in pay, benefits, and autonomy compared to their salaried counterparts, which means increasing workloads and instability (Cohen 2016).

Cost minimization strategies have also led many news organizations to automate and outsource their reporting. Nicole Cohen (2015) told the story of Journatic, since rebranded as LocalLabs, a media company that provided automated "hyperlocal" news to a number of large-market legacy newspapers, including the *Chicago Tribune*, *San Francisco Chronicle*, and *Houston Chronicle*. While many newspapers stepped away from Journatic after learning of its methods, which included using fake bylines on automated stories, many other prominent publishers have since been experimenting with automated reporting. This "(ro)bot journalism" entails the use of computer algorithms to write news stories (Cohen 2015), engage with audiences (Phelps 2017), boost content across multiple platforms (Keohane 2017; Lokot and Diakopoulos 2016), promote native advertising (Moses 2017), predict performance of every published story (Marburger 2017), and consequently, shape editorial judgements (Carlson 2017). Many of these strategies are, in part, an adaptation to social media platforms' recent monopolization of user attention.

Social media platforms have been credited with an agenda-setting power, in large part because of their ability to attract and channel users' attention. Indeed, Facebook and Twitter are among the most popular social media platforms, and a growing majority of their users get news on the sites (Shearer and Gottfried 2017). This power grows as the trend of ownership concentration, which has defined mass media for decades, makes its way onto the web (Bagdikian 2014; Wu 2011).

Despite these notable concerns about ownership, the future of networked fields rests largely on how closely (or not) platforms adhere to principles of neutrality. Although many prominent web companies, including Twitter, Facebook, and Google publicly support net neutrality—the policy that aims to ensure online content flows equally, regardless of its source—they still play an outsized role in channeling web traffic. As scholars of technology have long argued, there is no such thing as a neutral platform. Choices are made, both programmatic and editorial, which shape what is allowed or promoted on a particular platform, what it requests, demands, allows, encourages, discourages, and even refuses of its users (Davis and Chouinard 2017). Through the use of black-box algorithms that determine what content users see, the logics of which vary, depending on a host of undisclosed factors, these platforms are emerging as the age of mediatization's new gatekeepers.[1]

While social networks like Twitter and Facebook are quick to pat themselves on the back when they contribute to the functioning of liberal democracy, they have a relatively poor record of addressing the latent affordances of their platforms, as evidenced by their feet dragging following revelations that they were used to spread hatred and fake news. Although the companies' hesitation is in part a reality of the current techno-political moment, where hyper-partisanship and the complex assemblages of human-machine interfaces make it difficult to determine what information is legitimate, the desire to maintain the dominance of their platforms also discourages them from taking responsibility or changing how they filter content. Despite the challenges, which also include monitoring abuse, hate speech, and terrorist propaganda, Twitter is inclined to uphold their policy on anonymity and maintain the presence of automated bots because their affordances are unique to their platform and are seen as integral to the innovation and free speech they aim to foster.

To the extent that these logics continue to shape the flow of attention and information, they will have profound effects on the future of media power. As such, their (in)visibility is of central importance as networked publics strive to accumulate the literacies necessary to maintain position and autonomy in the age of mediatization.

From algorithms, automation, and fake news to privacy threats, profit models, and stealthily promoted content, the new media landscape poses significant challenges for citizens using the networks for matters of public importance, all of which will likely only increase in the future. These challenges justify a renewed attention on the struggle for media literacy, and indeed, competence, in a time of profound change (Russell 2016). However, creating a media literate public in this landscape is something of a Catch-22. On the one hand, critical media literacy cannot be (fully) accomplished through the kinds of privatized platforms that have gained popularity today, due in large part to the tensions driven by the profit incentives discussed above. This concern is exacerbated by the prominence of apps and interfaces obscuring the programmatic properties that structure user experiences. On the other hand, it appears that large-scale media literacy cannot be accomplished without social media platforms. For they already play far too prominent a role in citizens' information habits—a trend that is likely to grow, given the American public's already noted declining confidence in legacy news providers (Swift 2016; Shearer and Gottfried 2017).

If the profession of journalism is to uphold the promise of the fourth estate, then it must continue to adapt to the age of mediatization, while striving to regain autonomy from the political and economic forces that have long stood in its way. To the extent they remain in control of the gates to legitimation—whether for information, practices, or producers—journalism professionals must still focus on producing important, actionable journalism in the public interest. The production of spectacle and the wielding of influence for its own sake, while alluring and profitable, will only threaten the authority of journalism whose publics are literate in matters of media power. Likewise, if networked publics are to fulfill their fifth-estate potential, they must not only continue the accountability practices discussed throughout the book, but also help spread the logic and practice of twenty-first century media literacy, which is necessarily participatory. Just as scholars must retool and reorient their analytic lenses to clearly see the changes occurring in the age of mediatization, journalism professionals, along with their citizen counterparts, must rebuild the structures and practices required to support a vital public sphere. After all, the future of the field, and by extension, the republic, is at stake.

NOTE

1. Google is less a platform than an intermediary, but its prominence means that it has a comparable amount of influence in shaping the flow of web traffic.

REFERENCES

Armstrong, J., & Zúniga, M. M. (2006). *Crashing the gate: Netroots, grassroots, and the rise of people-powered politics.* White River Junction, VT: Chelsea Green Publishing.

Atton, C. (2008). Alternative and citizen journalism. In K. Wahl-Jorgensen & T. Hanitzsch (Eds.), *The handbook of journalism studies* (pp. 265–278). New York: Routledge.

Bagdikian, B. H. (2014). *The new media monopoly: A completely revised and updated edition with seven new chapters.* Boston, MA: Beacon Press.

Bourdieu, P. (2005). The political field, the social science field, and the journalistic field. In R. Benson & E. Neveu (Eds.), *Bourdieu and the journalistic field* (pp. 29–47). Malden, MA: Polity.

Broersma, M., & Graham, T. (2013). Twitter as a news source. *Journalism Practice, 7*(4), 446–464. https://doi.org/10.1080/17512786.2013.802481.

Carlson, M. (2015). Keeping watch on the gates: Media criticism as advocatory pressure. In T. Vox & F. Heinderyckx (Eds.), *Gatekeeping in transition* (pp. 163–179). New York: Routledge.

Carlson, M. (2017). Automating judgment? Algorithmic judgment, news knowledge, and journalistic professionalism. *New Media & Society*, Advanced online publication. https://doi.org/10.1177/1461444817706684.

Castells, M. (2015). *Networks of outrage and hope: Social movements in the internet age* (2nd ed.). Malden, MA: Polity.

Chadwick, A. (2013). *The hybrid media system: Politics and power.* New York: Oxford University Press.

Chayko, M. (2016). *Superconnected: The internet, digital media, and techno-social life*. Los Angeles: SAGE.

Christin, A. (2017). Algorithms in practice: Comparing web journalism and criminal justice. *Big Data & Society, 4*(2), Advanced online publication. https://doi.org/10.1177/2053951717718855.

Cohen, N. S. (2015). From pink slips to pink slime: Transforming media labor in a digital age. *The Communication Review, 18*(2), 98–122. https://doi.org/10.1080/10714421.2015.1031996.

Cohen, N. S. (2016). *Writers' rights: Freelance journalism in a digital age.* Chicago: McGill-Queen's University Press.

Comor, E., & Compton, J. (2015). Journalistic labour and technological fetishism. *The Political Economy of Communication, 3*(2). Retrieved from http://www.polecom.org/index.php/polecom/article/view/59.

Couldry, N. (2014). When mediatization hits the ground. In A. Hepp & F. Krotz (Eds.), *Mediatized worlds: Culture and society in a media age* (pp. 54–71). New York: Palgrave Macmillan.

Craft, S., Vos, T. P., & Wolfgang, D. J. (2016). Reader comments as press criticism: Implications for the journalistic field. *Journalism, 17*(6), 677–693. https://doi.org/10.1177/1464884915579332.

Davis, J. L., & Chouinard, J. B. (2017). Theorizing affordances: From request to refuse. *Bulletin of Science, Technology & Society, 36*(4), 241–248. https://doi.org/10.1177/0270467617714944.

Deuze, M. (2007). *Media work*. Malden, MA: Polity.

Dutton, W. H. (2009). The fifth estate emerging through the network of networks. *Prometheus, 27*(1), 1–15. https://doi.org/10.1080/08109020802657453.

Fuchs, C. (2014). *Digital labour and Karl Marx*. New York: Routledge.

Goode, L. (2009). Social news, citizen journalism and democracy. *New Media & Society, 11*(8), 1287–1305. https://doi.org/10.1177/1461444809341393.

Hashtag: #Journalism redefined [Session 1] [VideoCast]. (2013, September 20). *University of Denver Videocast*. Retrieved November 19, 2017, from http://videocast.du.edu/video/hashtag-journalism-redefined---session-1.

Hesmondhalgh, D. J. (2015). Exploitation and media labor. In R. Maxwell (Ed.), *Routledge companion to labor and media* (pp. 30–39). New York: Routledge.

Keohane, J. (2017, February 16). What news writing bots mean for the future of journalism. *Wired*. Retrieved November 26, 2017, from https://www.wired.com/2017/02/robots-wrote-this-story/.

Kligler-Vilenchik, N. (2017). Alternative citizenship models: Contextualizing new media and the new "good citizen". *New Media & Society, 19*(11), 1887–1903. https://doi.org/10.1177/1461444817713742.

Kovach, B., & Rosenstiel, T. (2014). *The elements of journalism: What newspeople should know and the public should expect* (3rd ed.). New York: Three Rivers Press.

Lasorsa, D. L., Lewis, S. C., & Holton, A. E. (2012). Normalizing twitter. *Journalism Studies, 13*(1), 19–36. https://doi.org/10.1080/14616 70X.2011.571825.

Lindner, A. M., Connell, E., & Meyer, E. (2015). Professional journalists in "citizen" journalism. *Information, Communication & Society, 18*(5), 553–568. https://doi.org/10.1080/1369118X.2015.1012530.

Lindner, A. M., & Larson, R. P. (2017). The expansion and contraction of the journalistic field and American online citizen journalism, 2000–2012. *Poetics, 64*, 40–52. https://doi.org/10.1016/j.poetic.2017.08.001.

Lokot, T., & Diakopoulos, N. (2016). News bots. *Digital Journalism, 4*(6), 682–699. https://doi.org/10.1080/21670811.2015.1081822.

Marburger, J. (2017, April 26). These are the bots powering Jeff Bezos' Washington Post efforts to build a modern digital newspaper. *Neiman Foundation at Harvard*. Retrieved November 26, 2017, from http://www.niemanlab.org/2017/04/these-are-the-bots-powering-jeff-bezos-washington-post-efforts-to-build-a-modern-digital-newspaper/.

Massey, B. L., & Elmore, C. J. (2011). Happier working for themselves? *Journalism Practice, 5*(6), 672–686. https://doi.org/10.1080/17512786.2011.579780.

Meraz, S. (2009). Is there an elite hold? Traditional media to social media agenda setting influence in blog networks. *Journal of Computer-Mediated Communication, 14*(3), 682–707. https://doi.org/10.1111/j.1083-6101.2009.01458.x.

Moses, L. (2017, August 23). The Washington Post brings artificial intelligence to its native ads. *Digiday*. Retrieved November 26, 2017, from https://digiday.com/media/washington-post-brings-artificial-intelligence-native-ads/.

Paulussen, S. (2012). Technology and the transformation of news work: Are labor conditions in (online) journalism changing? In E. Siapera & A. Veglis (Eds.), *The handbook of global online journalism* (pp. 192–208). Malden, MA: Wiley-Blackwell. https://doi.org/10.1002/9781118313978.ch11.

Perlberg, S. (2017, October 10). Here's the memo that just went out to WSJ staffers regarding social media usepic.twitter.com/CJimkfQtfW [Tweet]. Twitter. Retrieved November 27, 2017, from https://twitter.com/perlberg/status/921020199318511616.

Petre, C. (2015, May 7). The traffic factories: Metrics at Chartbeat, Gawker Media, and The New York Times. *Tow Center for Digital Journalism*. Retrieved November 26, 2017, from https://www.cjr.org/tow_center_reports/the_traffic_factories_metrics_at_chartbeat_gawker_media_and_the_new_york_times.php.

Phelps, A. (2017, April 26). This is how The New York Times is using bots to create more one-to-one experiences with readers. *Neiman Foundation at Harvard*. Retrieved November 26, 2017, from http://www.niemanlab.org/2017/04/this-is-how-the-new-york-times-is-using-bots-to-create-more-one-to-one-experiences-with-readers/.

Russell, A. (2016). *Journalism as activism: Recoding media power.* Malden, MA: Polity.

Santana, A. D., & Hopp, T. (2016). Tapping into a new stream of (personal) data: Assessing journalists' different use of social media. *Journalism & Mass Communication Quarterly, 93*(2), 383–408. https://doi.org/10.1177/1077699016637105.

Shearer, E., & Gottfried, J. (2017, September 7). *News use across social media platforms 2017.* Pew Research Center. Retrieved November 26, 2017, from http://www.journalism.org/2017/09/07/news-use-across-social-media-platforms-2017/.

Shoemaker, P. J., & Vos, T. (2009). *Gatekeeping theory.* New York: Routledge.

Swift, A. (2016, September 14). Americans' trust in mass media sinks to new low. *Gallup News.* Retrieved November 26, 2017, from http://www.gallup.com/poll/195542/americans-trust-mass-media-sinks-new-low.aspx.

Tandoc, E. C. (2014). Journalism is twerking? How web analytics is changing the process of gatekeeping. *New Media & Society, 16*(4), 559–575. https://doi.org/10.1177/1461444814530541.

The Times Issues Social Media Guidelines for the Newsroom. (2017, October 13). *The New York Times.* Retrieved December 7, 2017, from https://www.nytimes.com/2017/10/13/reader-center/social-media-guidelines.html.

Williams, E. (2017, August 27). Hi, Rob. *Medium.* Retrieved November 27, 2017, from https://medium.com/@ev/hi-rob-1a37f0fa0706.

Wu, T. (2011). *The master switch: The rise and fall of information empires.* New York: Vintage.

Yang, S., Quan-Haase, A., & Rannenberg, K. (2016). The changing public sphere on Twitter: Network structure, elites and topics of the #righttobeforgotten. *New Media & Society,* Advanced online publication. https://doi.org/10.1177/1461444816651409.

Appendix: Methodology

This book approached studying the changing journalistic field through a close examination of Twitter data. This data is supplemented with content from digital news stories, which allows for comparisons between the content and practices visible on Twitter and those made available on publishers' own platforms. Although this approach does little to expose the journalists and journalistic practices not reflected on these platforms, what is represented is ripe for analysis, given the variety of textual and meta-data that digital platforms like Twitter make available. Overall, the combined consideration of journalistic practices and meta-discourse provides a revealing window into how professional and citizen journalists use Twitter, as well as how they talk about that use.

The empirical Chaps. 4, 5, 6, 7, and 8 feature case studies, each chosen for exhibiting unique facets of Twitter's journalistic field. While these chapters are intended to stand on their own, together the case studies create a mosaic of the field's ongoing transformation at a time of mediatization. One of the strengths of case studies is that they provide an opportunity to examine an issue in detail while bracketing off most other points of intersection that might otherwise be of interest. However, selection bias is always a problem. Whatever is left out of the sample is difficult to bring into view, and the final picture can easily be left incomplete. Accordingly, the case studies are not meant to be read as a definitive or holistic examination of journalism, whether on Twitter or beyond. Rather, they offer detailed snapshots of facets of the field's structure and practice occurring over the span of seven years.

© The Author(s) 2018
S. R. Barnard, *Citizens at the Gates*,
https://doi.org/10.1007/978-3-319-90446-7

Mixed-methods analysis is applied to each of these case studies, consisting of digital ethnography, content analysis, hyperlink analysis, and social network analysis. The digital ethnographic component of this research utilized online participant-observation methods (Coleman 2010; Jensen 2010; Kozinets 2009). Observations of Twitter's journalistic field began in 2009 and continued through 2017. In early years, these observations were broad-ranging, seeking to understand the norms and practices of journalists, which were displayed on Twitter as well as in a variety of links to personal blogs and news sites. Accordingly, these textual exchanges were initially documented using the internet archiving tool, Zotero. They were often accompanied by field notes, which aimed to explain or interpret the significance of the observed practices and draw connections to other observed patterns in the practice and literature on contemporary journalism. Furthermore, in order to provide a richer and more systematic analysis, the research incorporated insights from observations into examinations of textual data using digital ethnographic content analysis (DECA).

DECA is a method that utilizes online participant-observation to inform data collection, coding, and analysis of emergent themes in online content (Barnard 2016, 2017; Altheide and Schneider 2012). This included analysis of the *form* of the Twitter platform (i.e., its structure and affordances) as well as the *content* of discursive (inter)actions surrounding Twitter's journalistic subfield. After exploring patterns in the data for each empirical chapter, DECA was performed on a subsample of theoretically relevant tweets. The coding procedure, which was invariably guided by contextual insights gathered through digital ethnography, followed Altheide and Schneider's (2012) "double loop of analysis," as the initial open coding led to more refined, selective codes based on emergent patterns and theoretically grounded questions (Strauss and Corbin 1998). Coding addressed the tweets' *format* (text, link, image, retweet, and/or reply), *frames* (what is being discussed, and how), *themes* (patterns in the text), and *discourse* (fields of meaning, relevance, and audience) (Altheide and Schneider 2012, pp. 51–53). Rather than treated as distinct phenomena, results from the analysis of frames are primarily reported in other sections as relevant.

The bulk of the DECA was completed using the computer-assisted qualitative data analysis software (CAQDAS) program, Pulsar, which also made it possible to systematically collect tweets and digital news stories. While this is true of Chaps. 6, 7, and 8, Chap. 4 relied on The Archivist for data collection and DiscoverText for coding and analysis. Given Pulsar's use of metadata to automatically code for format and provide an approximation of discourse (through social network and influence metrics), the qualitative coding procedure focused primarily on identifying frames and themes in the text of the tweets. On occasion, additional analyses and visualizations were completed using the software Tableau.

Furthermore, link analysis (LA) and social network analysis (SNA), which entail the plotting and examination of hyperlink patterns and network ties using metadata derived from Twitter-based communication, were used. Given the interest in the themes of journalistic practice, and in particular, the polarization and hybridity apparent in these mediatized fields, this study combined DECA with LA and SNA to examine Twitter content from each of the cases examined in the book. LA and SNA performed in this study examined (dis)connections between users' field position and the discursive ties created by their posts. The network ties presented in Chaps. 6 and 7 are based on Pulsar's "engagement" metric that includes both mentions and retweets. Furthermore, the size and centrality of the nodes are determined by Pulsar's "influence" metric, which combines the volume of a user's mentions with their number of followers and engagement with other users.

Additional details on the methodological approach to collecting and analyzing data for each chapter is presented below.

CHAPTER 4: "TWEET OR BE SACKED"

Chapter 4 examines the patterns emerging from journalists' practices and meta-discourse; the methods applied included a mixture of digital ethnography and content analysis. As previously noted, data from Chap. 4 is unique compared to other chapters in that it was collected in 2011 using the now-defunct program The Archivist. Although the program relied on Twitter's "garden hose," which is rate-limited to no more than 1% of all traffic on the platform (Gaffney and Puschmann 2014), the searches yielded such small results that we can reasonably assume they constitute most, if not all, the available content at the time of the search (see Fig. A.1).

These tweets were coded and analyzed according to the DECA process described above. Themes of practice emerged according to the observed patterns in journalistic (inter)action and also in accordance with the *elements of practice* (see Fig. 3.1) pertaining to Bourdieusian expressions of journalistic capital, habitus, and doxa. Furthermore, frame-based codes focused on the interests, values, and field positions exhibited through

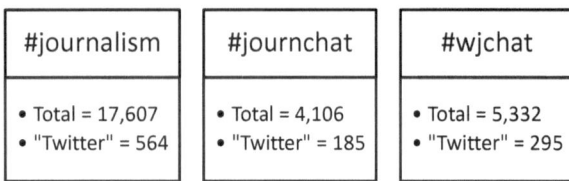

Fig. A.1 Sample of tweets from Chap. 4

speech acts on Twitter. Thus, coding for themes helped reveal trends in journalistic practice on Twitter, while frames revealed the accordant values and position-takings exhibited by actors' practice in the field. For example, the tweet "My social media discussions are largely an outlet for my work. Real reporting can be done via #Twitter. But not all of it #wjchat" was coded as fitting the news dissemination theme and heterodoxy frame due to its restrained approval of Twitter for journalism, while its expression of the actor's practices and dispositions demonstrated its added relevance to the habitus theme. A similar strategy was used in the coding of data for other chapters.

Chapter 5: The Pros and Cons of Pro-Am Journalism

Unlike the other case studies included in this book, the analysis in Chap. 5 is not based on a systematic examination of a collected set of Twitter data pertaining to the event. This is due, in large part, to the difficulty of systematically collecting and analyzing relevant journalistic tweets and digital news content from the time. This challenge was exacerbated by the thousands of stories and millions of tweets posted in response to the Boston Marathon bombing. Instead, the chapter's analysis and argument is based on participant-observation as well as detailed readings of pertinent Twitter posts and news stories. Beginning on the day of the bombing, detailed field notes were taken that included observations from Twitter as well as news stories from television and the web. These notes were later used to guide online searches for news, information, and journalistic meta-discourse pertaining to media professionals' and citizens' collaborative coverage of the bombing.

Chapter 6: Tweeting #Ferguson

Like the remaining chapters, data for Chap. 6 was collected and analyzed using Pulsar, a platform with access to Twitter's GNIP "power stream," which allowed full access to all tweets published on the platform (Gaffney and Puschmann 2014). After months spent conducting regular observations of #Ferguson, which began on August 10, 2014, relevant Twitter "lists" featuring journalists and activists tweeting about #Ferguson were identified.[1] With deduplication, this amounted to 81 Twitter users. Eleven users were added, and a small portion reclassified as either journalist or activist, according to their Twitter bio and observed participation in #Ferguson. This yielded a sample of 92 users, 45 of which were professional reporters, while 47 were activists at the time the events in Ferguson occurred (see Table A.1). Four peaks in the #Ferguson Twitter discourse

Table A.1   List of Twitter users from Chap. 6 in alphabetical order

Activists	Activists (cont.)	Journalists	Journalists (cont.)
anoncopwatch	melodythemellow	akjohnson1922	michaelhayes
antoniofrench	missjupiter1957	alanblinder	neilmunshi
atchley_sr	mollyrosestl	alicesperi	noblejonesontv
bassem_masri	montaguesimmons	baltospectator	paullewis
bdoulaoblongata	mspackyetti	bkesling	pdpj
beastlibrarian	nettaaaaaaaa	bmoreconetta	phampel
beautybind	obs_stl	brianstelter	raydowns
blklivesmatter	only1alexis	byjoelanderson	rebeccarivas
britrican	opalayo	chriskingstl	rembert
brownblaze	osope	chrislhayes	robcrilly
deray	revolutionbksb	craigmelvin	robertdedwards
dhorubashakur	revsekou	donlemon	robertklemko
edie_howe	seanjjordan	elonjames	ryanjreilly
egoetschius	search4swag	emarvelous	sarasidnercnn
erincounihan	sirosenbaum	geedee215	shimonpro
fergusonaction	sophialamar1	greta	stephaniediffin
haikuunsung	stackizshort	iamsakuma	timcast
handsupunited_	susankitchens	jelani9	trymainelee
hollablackgirl	tefpoe	jimdalrympleii	wesleylowery
hownowbrowndowd	the4th_duck	johnkellyksdk	yamiche
innov8ion	trillaryklinton	jonswaine	zackroth
jcos24	unrulyrev	laurakhettiger	
kwrose	wesknuckle	mattdpearce	
mcshanerachel		megynkelly	

Table A.2   Sample and timeline of Ferguson events

Begin	End	Data plot	Total tweets	Peak
Aug. 9, 2014 (Michael Brown shot)	**Aug. 21, 2014** (calm returns; grand jury begins)		21,475	2878 (Aug. 18)
Sept. 25, 2014 (police chief Dotson apologizes to Brown family)	**Sept. 30, 2014** (police officer shot on Sept. 27 in unrelated event; sporadic actions)		7876	1328 (Sept. 29)
Oct. 14, 2014 (police arrest dozens of protesters)	**Oct. 23, 2014** (leaked autopsy report on Oct. 22)		5738	769 (Oct. 23)
Nov. 17, 2014 (state of emergency declared)	**Nov. 27, 2014** (Grand Jury announcement Nov. 24)		13,145	2978 (Nov. 25)
			48,234	

Dark blue = all posts
Light blue = reactions (RT & @reply)

were identified, which ranged from six to thirteen (average ten) days (See Table A.2). These peaks, which occurred once a month for four months—the time when mentions of "Ferguson" and "#Ferguson" were greatest—correspond with major actions taking place in Ferguson, Missouri. Although the number of journalists' tweets were nearly equal to activists' tweets in the first few weeks following the event, activists' tweets made up a majority of the dataset (70%) overall (see Table A.2). While searching explicit mentions of "#Ferguson" or "Ferguson" by specific users allowed for a targeted sampling, it missed similar tweets from all other relevant users as well as those that did not include the search terms. Furthermore, the reliance on Twitter data rendered invisible professional journalists' primary reporting on more mainstream media platforms, which likely differed in tone and tenor from their tweets.

CHAPTER 7: WE STAND WITH #NERDLAND

Chapter 7 examines Twitter users' attempts to attract news media attention to the departure of Melissa Harris-Perry, and is the first of two chapters that incorporate online news articles. To assess gatewatchers' use of Twitter, all tweets containing either "Nerdland" or "#Nerdland" were collected beginning February 26, 2016, the day before Harris-Perry's exit from MSNBC was made public, until April 1, 2016, long after public attention to the issue had subsided. This data was compared and contrasted with digital news stories collected using Pulsar's news website crawler. Pulsar defines a "News" site as an independent publisher of original news stories that are not aggregated and are accessible without a fee. However, as this analysis shows, "original" is misleading, given how many of the stories collected were republished on numerous news websites. Stories published between February 26 and March 4, 2016, the last date news outlets devoted significant attention to the issue, were included in the dataset.

While an examination of the news story content was beyond the scope of this study, the form and frequency of this content was analyzed in the aggregate and compared with similar trends in public tweets. Gatewatchers' tweets were coded according to a narrow set of themes and frames pertaining to the chapter's research questions, which are discussed at greater length in the chapter. SNA methods were also applied to the users' tweets to examine the flow of information and influence on Twitter. The colors in the network map (Fig. 7.5) represent the Twitter users' self-defined country of origin, which included Australia, Brazil, Canada, Central African Republic, Colombia China, Ecuador, Egypt, France, Germany, Greece, India, Iran, Ireland, Italy, Ivory Coast, Japan, Mexico, Netherlands, New Zealand, Philippines, Poland, Spain, South Africa, United Kingdom, Uruguay, United States, and the United Arab Emirates. These colors are not to be confused with the randomly chosen colors on the influence map (Fig. 7.4), which was created in Tableau using Pulsar's "influence" metric that combines the volume of a user's mentions with their number of followers and engagement with other users in the data set (also described above).

Chapter 8: The Spectacle of #TrumpsAmerica

Chapter 8 compared and contrasted tweets and digital news stories, which were both collected and analyzed using Pulsar. This data is drawn primarily from two distinct time periods. First, November 3–17 represents the two weeks surrounding the 2016 election—the time the #TrumpsAmerica hashtag emerged and when Twitter-based discussion reached a peak. Second, May 29–June 4, 2017 was the week of the "covfefe" gaffe and an otherwise typical week in Trump's presidency. As described in the chapter, data was collected from four distinct categories: #TrumpsAmerica contributors, tweets by @realDonaldTrump, tweets from a cohort of 386 prominent political journalists (see Table A.3), and digital news stories about Trump's use of Twitter.

Beyond using Pulsar to code tweets according to emergent themes and frames, the chapter includes visual maps of influence (Figs. 8.1, 8.2, and 8.3) using Tableau.

Due to the need to compare influence across three user cohorts (Trump, political journalists, and journo-activists), Fig. 8.3 was constructed using an approximated metric of users' average shares rather than use Pulsar's influence metric, which has limited external validity. As noted in that chapter, this approach is not without limitations, since it may inflate the results for users who had only a few, highly shared tweets in the dataset.

Table A.3 List of political journalists from Chap. 8 in alphabetical order

1bobcohn	devindwyer	joshgerstein	OKnox
1PatriciaMurphy	Dharapak	joshhafner	palafo
AaronBlake	DHBerman	joshledermanAP	PaulLewis
abbydphillip	dickstevenson	JoshuaGreen	pdicarlocnn
abettel	DLeonhardt	JournoMaggie	Peggynoonannyc
Acosta	DomenicoNPR	jpaceDC	pemalevy
adambeam	DonovanSlack	JudyKurtz	perrybaconjr
AdamBKushner	DrewHampshire	juliebosman	peterbakernyt
adamsmithtimes	DylanByers	juliehdavis	PeterHamby
AdamWollner	EamonJavers	juliemason	petermaer
AHMalcolm	edatpost	justinsink	Philip_Elliott
ajjaffe	edhenry	jwpetersNYT	PhilipRucker
Alex_Roarty	edhornick	karentravers	pkcapitol
alexanderbolton	ElaheIzadi	kasie	pmdfoster
AlexBrownNJ	eliotnelson	KateNocera	politicalwire
alexburnsNYT	ElizaRules	katiesmithallen	POLITICO_Steve
AlexNBCNews	elizthompsn	katiezez	PoliticoCharlie
AlexPappas	emilyaheil	KellyO	PoliticoKevin
AlexParkerDC	emilykpierce	kendratypes	politicoroger
AliABCNews	emilyrs	kenvogel	PoliticoScott
aliciacohn	Emma_Dumain	KevinBohnCNN	PoliticsReid
amanbatheja	EmmaVAngerer	KFILE	PostRoz
amieparnes	ErinMcPike	khennessey	PostScottWilson
AmyAHarder	ethanklapper	kkondik	PrestonCNN
amychozick	feliciasonmez	KObradovich	pwgavin
AmyEGardner	felixsalmon	kseelye	rachelrhartman
amyewalter	FoxReports	KThomasDC	RalstonReports
AndrewNBCNews	frankthorp	ktummarello	rdmurphy
anitakumar01	freedlander	ktumulty	realDonaldTrump
AnjeanetteDamon	gabrielsherman	l_whittington	rebeccagberg
AnnGerhart	gbennettpost	LarrySabato	RebeccaRKaplan
anniekarni	gdebenedetti	lauraelizdavis	RebeccaShabad
AP_Politics	georgecondon	laurenonthehill	Redistrict
apalmerdc	GingerGibson	learyreports	reidcherlin
ArletteSaenz	GlennThrush	leslielarson	reidepstein
asheinin	GrahamDavidA	LisaDNews	ReutersZengerle
AshleyRParker	GreenwireJeremy	llerer	rickdunham
ASimendinger	Hadas_Gold	lucytimes	rickklein
asymmetricinfo	henrycjjackson	LukeRussert	robyoon
badler	hillhulse	Maddie_Marshall	ron_fournier
Bencjacobs	hollybdc	MaeveReston	ronlieber
BenLeubsdorf	HotlineJosh	maggieNYT	russellberman
bennyjohnson	howardfineman	MajorCBS	ryanbeckwith

(continued)

Table A.3   (continued)

bethreinhard	HowardKurtz	MarcACaputo	RyanLizza
BFischerMartin	hramer	marcambinder	sallyjenx
bfouhy	IsaacDovere	MarcNBCBoston	SarahBakerNBC
billkeller2014	its_amt	marincogan	SarahHuisenga
BobCusack	j_strong	MarkHalperin	SarahMMimms
bobschieffer	jackhealyNYT	markknoller	SaraMurray
BresPolitico	jacksonjk	MarkLeibovich	SavannahGuthrie
BretBaier	jaconi	markzbarabak	scontorno
brikeilarcnn	JakeSherman	MatthewDalyWDC	ScottFConroy
brookebrower	jaketapper	mattklewis	scottwongDC
burgessev	jameshohmann	MattVas	SeanGHiggins
BuzzFeedBen	JamesPindell	Max_Fisher	ShanTravisNews
ByronTau	jamiedupree	mckaycoppins	Shawna
cam_joseph	JamieGrayTweets	megancarpentier	shearm
camanpour	JanCBS	MelindaKCMO	shiracenter
CarlCannon	jasondhorowitz	MEPFuller	shushwalshe
CarolCNN	jbendery	meredithshiner	singernews
carolelee	JBennet	MichaelCBender	sppeoples
CarrieNBCNews	jdelreal	michaelcrowley	standupkid
ChadPergram	JeffreyGoldberg	michaelpfalcone	steinhauserNH1
ChrisLicht	JeffYoung	michaelphirsh	StephanieEbbert
ChrisStirewalt	jeffzeleny	michaelroston	stevebenen
christinawilkie	jeneps	michaelscherer	stevebousquet
chucktodd	Jennasakwa	mikeallen	steveholland1
CHueyBurns	jennifereduffy	mikebarnicle	stevenjay
CillizzaCNN	JenniferJJacobs	mikememoli	stevenportnoy
CNHorn	JesseRodriguez	mikeviqueira	StevenTDennis
CNNValencia	JessicaTaylor	mikiebarb	SteveSebelius
ColleenMNelson	JessicaYellin	Milbank	stiles
CookPolitical	JFKucinich	mkady	StuPolitics
costareports	JillAbramson	mkraju	suellentrop
DanaBashCNN	JillDLawrence	mmcauliff	susanferrechio
danbalz	jimgeraghty	mmurraypolitics	SusanPage
DanEggenWPost	jimrutenberg	mollyesque	Taylor_West
DanH_TIME	jkirchick	moody	tbridis
DanielStrauss4	jmartNYT	mpoindc	TCurry_Himself
DanLothianTV	jmsummers	MrWalterShapiro	terencesamuel
danmericaCNN	JNSmall	mviser	TerryMoran
dannowicki	jodikantor	mweinger	TexasTribAbby
davecatanese	joehagansays	NateSilver538	thegarance
davelevinthal	JohnBerman	nathanlgonzales	TheLloydGrove
daveweigel	johndickerson	nationaljournal	TheOnlyArcher
DavidChalian	johngizzi	nbj914	TimAlberta

(*continued*)

Table A.3   (continued)

davidjoachim	JohnJHarwood	Neda_Semnani	timgrieve
DavidMarkDC	johnroconnor	ngjennings	toddzwillich
DavidMDrucker	jolingkent	nickconfessore	TomBevanRCP
DavidMuir	jonallendc	nielslesniewski	tomdiemer
DavidNakamura	jonathanweisman	NikolenDC	TroyKinsey
davidshepardson	JonEasley	NKingofDC	Tyrangiel
DavidWastell	jonkarl	NPRmelissablock	vplus
DaviSusan	jonresnickDJI	nycjim	WaPoSean
deirdrewalshcnn	Jordanfabian	NYTnickc	WesleyLowery
deucecrew	jordanjfrasier	nytpolitics	wuerker
			ZekeJMiller

REFERENCES

Altheide, D. L., & Schneider, C. J. (2012). *Qualitative media analysis* (2nd ed.). Los Angeles, CA: SAGE.

Barnard, S. R. (2016). "Tweet or be sacked": Twitter and the new elements of journalistic practice. *Journalism, 17*(2), 190–207. https://doi.org/10.1177/1464884914553079.

Barnard, S. R. (2017). Tweeting #Ferguson: Mediatized fields and the new activist journalist. *New Media & Society*. Advanced online publication. https://doi.org/10.1177/1461444817712723.

Coleman, E. G. (2010). Ethnographic approaches to digital media. *Annual Review of Anthropology, 39*(1), 487–505. https://doi.org/10.1146/annurev.anthro.012809.104945.

Gaffney, D., & Puschmann, C. (2014). Data collection on Twitter. In K. Weller, A. Bruns, J. Burgess, M. Mahrt, & C. Puschmann (Eds.), *Twitter and society* (pp. 55–67). New York: Peter Lang.

Jensen, K. B. (2010). *Media convergence: The three degrees of network, mass and interpersonal communication*. New York: Routledge.

Kozinets, R. (2009). *Netnography: Doing ethnographic research online*. Thousand Oaks, CA: SAGE.

Strauss, A., & Corbin, J. M. (1998). *Basics of qualitative research: Techniques and procedures for developing grounded theory*. Thousand Oaks, CA: SAGE.

NOTE

1. Both Twitter lists were created by members of the journalistic field: https://twitter.com/chriskingstl/lists/ferguson/members; https://twitter.com/voxdotcom/lists/ferguson-news/members.

Index[1]

---

[1] Note: Page numbers followed by 'n' refer to notes.

© The Author(s) 2018
S. R. Barnard, *Citizens at the Gates*,
https://doi.org/10.1007/978-3-319-90446-7